Revelation: For a New Age

An Interpretation of
The Book of Revelation

by

Dorothy Elder

DeVorss & Company
P.O. Box 550
Marina del Rey, California 90294-0550

ISBN: 0-87516-446-3

Library of Congress Card Catalog Number: 81-65477

Printed in the United States of America

Revelation: For a New Age

Dedicated to
My Spiritual Teachers
on This Side and
The Other
who have helped
in this endeavor.

Foreword

Dorothy Elder is a dear and valuable friend and I am honored to be asked to write a Foreword to her book, "Revelation: For a New Age."

Mrs. Elder is an educator with degrees from New Mexico Highlands University and the University of Colorado. She studied Oriental religions and culture in Kyoto, Japan, with New York University. Her interest and study of New Thought religions has been deeply personal. The study of Jungian psychology and philosophy has been over many years.

In general, the Apocalyptic literature has been neglected because of so much misunderstanding as to its meaning. In recent years, however, there has been increased interest in spiritual unfoldment rather than in material gain, and this has resulted in increased interest in the book of Revelation. Mrs. Elder has been guided and urged from within to write this book. She has received higher wisdom and intuitional awakening to explain its many symbols and references. The book helps to open doors as to the meaning of this great last book of our Bible. Thus the author's book is timely, as well as scholarly, spiritual, clear and inspiring.

In the study of her volume, one gains a deeper faith to confront the political, social, educational, religious, and economic chaos of today. One realizes anew that "The Lord God Omnipotent reigneth." (Revelation 19:6). Properly understood in metaphysical language, the teachings in the book of Revelation can lead one to Cosmic Consciousness. And this is what her book is about.

To quote John the Revelator:

> Behold I make all things new,
> a new heaven and a new earth,
> a new Jerusalem,
> No more death, neither sorrow nor crying,
> the healing of the nations.
> behold, I make all things new.

Dr. Grace L. Faus
Bailey, Colorado
September 30, 1980

Contents

Foreword by Dr. Grace Faus........................... vii

Preface... 1

Chapter 1 ..... THE MESSENGER 10

For all people; Kundalini; the Messenger and the Message;
Jesus Christ the Teacher; Our Inner Christ; Seven candlesticks
and churches relating to the seven chakras; keys to Heaven

Chapters 2 & 3 . THE MESSAGES 25

Churches as Chakra centers; awakening of the Kundalini;
First chakra, Faith; Second chakra, Creative energy or Sex
energy; Third chakra, Intellect; Fourth chakra, Love; Fifth
chakra, Seeking God through Worship (hearing, desire, commitment, will, meditation, living exemplary life); Sixth
chakra, Wisdom or Intuition; Seventh chakra, Enlightenment

Chapter 4 ..... A VIEW OF THE THRONE................. 75

The throne; the Mandala as a symbol of wholeness; seven
spirits of God as opened chakras; four living creatures as
mind, body, emotions, spirit; twenty-four elders as 12 Powers
of man, both physically and spiritually perfect

Chapter 5 ..... THE SCROLL........................... 84

The Scroll as our personal record of life; the opening of the
Scroll; the Lamb of God as pure life and substance of Being;
Holy Spirit as life force; a New Song

Chapter 6 ..... OPENING OF SIX SEALS 90

Individuation through balance; opening of the seals; Four
Horsemen as spirit, emotions, intellect and body; balance
needed for enlightenment; the ego as a block; results of misuse
of Kundalini; Dark Night of the Soul; rising again through
Self-knowledge

Chapter 7 . . . . . THOSE AROUND THE THRONE 99

Third Eye as Christ Consciousness; Twelve tribes as Twelve Powers; 144,000 symbolic of infinite number reaching completion; angels (divine thoughts) worshipping; description of the kingdom of Heaven

Chapter 8 . . . . . SEVENTH ANGEL, BURNING DROSS 108

Silence the great Teacher; Fire, cleansing; man's use and misuse of fire; first angel, burning out conscious dross; second angel, cleansing unconscious; third angel, divine intervention, Wormwood; fourth angel, depression; a warning that predicts good

Chapter 9 . . . . . BURNING OF DROSS (continued) 116

Fifth angel, star cleanses the unconscious of negatives; locusts, negative conditions; Karma; Reincarnation; turning negative thoughts to positive; Sixth angel, the spine as the River Euphrates; mythology; animal instincts

Chapter 10 . . . . THE INNER CHRIST 130

Entrance of the Cosmic Man or the Inner Christ; the unopened scroll; eating of the sweet that becomes bitter

Chapter 11 . . . . TWO WITNESSES 136

Two olive trees as Ida and Pingala; Shiva and Shakti; Yoga brings enlightenment; danger of Kundalini raising; Centeredness in God prerequisite to positive experience; the Seventh angel, reveals the kingdom of Heaven

Chapter 12 . . . . THE REVELATION 145

Inner male and female gives birth; the Divine Child is born; the Dragon (negativity); intercession of Divine Grace saves the Child; the Wilderness experience after New Birth; Good and evil; female consciousness attacked by the Dragon; the Earth (love) rescues her

Chapter 13 . . . . THE BEAST 157

Beast from sea (unconscious); recognizing our negative traits and forgiving ourself; the beast out of earth (conscious mind); 666 as a mark of incompletion; faith can overcome opposites

Chapter 14 .... WARNINGS AND HARVESTING.............. 165

Mt. Zion, the kingdom of Heaven; 144,000 who are chaste;
the angelic messages; judgment as Karma; materialism must
fall; worship of the beast brings torment; the white cloud and
the Son of man (you and me) reaps; changing interpretations
of God

Chapter 15 .... SEVEN PLAGUES FOR OUR CLEANSING 176

Seven angels bring cleansing; worship, chanting a mantra; the
wrath of God as our projection; the blessings of the plagues

Chapter 16 .... MISUSE OF OUR POWERS 181

Seven plagues: first, illness of body; second, illness of emotions (unconscious both personal and collective); third, war;
fourth, heart attacks or lack of love; fifth, sensuality; sixth,
change of physical to spiritual; Armageddon, a battle within
man's consciousness; seventh, chaos based on past

Chapter 17 .... JUDGMENT OF MATERIALISM 197

Jezebel; earthly desires that separate us from our Good; earthly institutions that represent Jezebel: government, church,
education, family, society; Jezebel as lust

Chapter 18 .... BABYLON FALLS 207

Rejoicing over the end of materialism; the merchants of today
and the military (sailors) weep; our earthly consciousness
(Babylon) falls

Chapter 19 .... REJOICING FOR ONENESS 212

Rejoicing and praise; the meaning of Amen and Hallelujah;
the marriage of opposites; Shiva and Shakti or God and Holy
Spirit; the meaning of Jesus Christ as prophet; the testimony
of Jesus; Christmas as the birth of Christ Consciousness in
each one; Jesus as brother and teacher; the rider of the White
Horse as Faith and Truth; another battle between material and
spiritual; birds of prey (spiritualization) feast on negative and
destroy it

Chapter 20 .... THE BOOK OF LIFE 224

Dragon symbolism; those who have reached perfection; first
resurrection; second resurrection; the final battle of Gog,

negative emotions; dealing with guilt; the Book of Life, our
record; books of world religions; second death, life on earth

Chapter 21 .... ENLIGHTENMENT 238

New Heaven (here and now) and New Earth (no suffering or
tears); New Jerusalem (a new consciousness); Enlightenment
described: Hindu, Buddhist, Sufi, Taoist, Christian Mystic;
the Bride and the Marriage; the New Age, God centered;
death; active imagination; Omega Point; living water; 12
gates, 12 foundation stones; Voidness, the temple of God;
Essence of Light; Transformation of physical to Pure Light

Chapter 22 .... LOVE, FREEDOM, JOY FOREVER!! 263

Water of life as Kundalini; tree of life as spine and chakra
centers; man's evolution through the great Patriarchs; Jesus
our Wayshower, epilogue; seven last statements of John; I
Jesus, the Christ within speaks; the invitation "Come"; Joy at
last

References 278

Appendix,
    Part I: ... THE KUNDALINI POWER 287

Appendix,
    Part II: ... WORLD RELIGIONS ON THE KUNDALINI
                    POWER 292

Preface

The title of this book is the most important statement that can be made in this preface. The whole theme of the book will be one of the New Age. What New Age? A good question, especially if you have not been aware of what is happening in our world in the religious, moral, ethical, political and psychological areas. Those who are watching with seriousness and wonder are beginning to realize that we *are* in a New Age.

Now the Book of Revelation from the New Testament has been an enigma to many ministers and theologians, experts in the field of religion, who do not claim to understand it well enough to take a stand. Thousands of books have been written on it. Most of these have the theme of "hellfire and damnation" that will come down upon the world unless people repent and turn to Jesus Christ to be saved—classic Christian theme since the time of the apostles of Jesus and Paul. The great holocaust is coming—so the declarers of doom are preaching. The world must turn around, be saved by Christian creeds or it will be burned in an unholy fire and all mankind, who are not saved by the gospel of Jesus Christ, will be lost.

This is the fundamentalist view. However, many other Christians interpret Revelation from a more liberal stand. For the person who has risen in consciousness to the intellectual level and somewhat to the love level, this may be good enough. But I find it difficult to believe that a loving God would bring to mankind this kind of devastation. So I approach the task from an alternate position.

My position will unfold gradually throughout the book, but briefly it is that Jesus Christ brought us great teaching from the mind of God, and if we follow the teaching we will reach the ultimate of Oneness in consciousness with the Source of all Being. Jesus Christ taught the followers in his lifetime on earth and is inspiring us as we go on our Journey. His teachings were in veiled language and for 2000 years we have been interpreting them in light of our own consciousness of all that is Good. Because he was such a great teacher and example, I believe his way is for all of mankind and indeed much of his teaching was very similar to other great religious leaders. And our Eastern brothers in our world have much to offer us as we go on our Path. Thus, the Eastern and Western may become One and the world will reach the Ultimate in consciousness.

A few scholars and mystics have seen beyond the fundamentalist interpretation of Revelation in our Western world. Charles Filmore, with his wife, Myrtle, co-founders of the Unity School of Christianity, saw Jesus Christ's teaching as meant for the New Age for mankind. Revelation was, to him, a directory of procedures that would take men and women to a higher consciousness. His teachings were pretty much based on the teaching of Jesus Christ and Paul to some extent, although he went beyond Paul's teachings. He mixed his interpretation of Jesus Christ with Eastern philosophy and religions. Another was Paramahansa Yogananda, an Indian pandit and guru, who saw the need to combine the Christian and Hindu viewpoints in order to bring the East and the West together to strengthen each of them and establish one World. His organization is the Self Realization Fellowship in Los Angeles. He saw Revelation as a directive to each person to develop his consciousness and the use of the kundalini power to reach perfection in body and spirit.

Elizabeth Turner, a member of Charles Fillmore's team, has written an interpretation for individual development of spiritual understanding based on Revelation. Sig Paulson and Ric Dickerson, also a part of the Unity movement have taken up the same theme. There are others who have undertaken the task of re-interpreting Revelation for the New Age.

In addition to these mentioned, I have turned to the great Swiss psychologist, Carl Jung. He had great forethought and understanding of the spiritual needs of mankind. Since Revelation is mainly symbological, his writings have been of great assistance in interpreting the mythological and symbolical meanings. He broke with Freud because he believed that the deepest need of each person was to develop a contact with his/her Self, or spiritual center. He was a psychologist, a philosopher, a religionist, and a lover of humanity, and devoted his life to healing as well as revealing many truths as he saw them. His deep studies of alchemy have brought much clearer understanding to those who study the Bible. He wrote many books, the full understanding of which has not been thoroughly achieved. His teaching center is in Zurich, Switzerland.

So who am I to undertake such a powerful task? I ask myself that many times but the answer always comes loud and clear, "You are the one." So here is the basis of my journey of interpretation. If anything that is written in this book strikes a chord of truth in the consciousness of your being, then perhaps you may learn something that will be of help to you on your Journey.

As a form of introduction I will give you a brief resumé of my life. My rearing was undertaken by a man of high moral principles and a woman deeply religious, who lived rather than spoke of her beliefs. My father was a self-proclaimed agnostic. He had had a strict Christian, moral upbringing but had rejected the Bible as God's word, decried the teaching of the Protestant and especially the Catholic church, and believed in his own mind or ego. He had a lonely journey. My mother was a sweet, loving woman who understood others but was unable to shake free from the shackles of her husband's strength and dominance. She was not very happy as she was not always able to express her true Self. Such was life for women in the early Twentieth Century. They are both part of this book.

I grew up on a farm, finished high school, and had two years of college. At marrying age I chose to marry a man who was a composite of my two parents. He was deeply religious (fundamentalist Christian) and a highly moral man. I thought I had found the person who would encourage me and help me grow in religious and spiritual ways, for I longed for that since my family had not been very religious. Three fine children were born to this marriage and our life was comparatively happy until I was required to go to a fundamentalist Christian church and rear my children there. I knew this was not the way for me and felt I owed to my children another option. I moved to a more liberal congregation and there was opened up a new vista to my Spiritual search. Spiritual matters, religious institutions, learning about life, serving, avoiding pain, doing my duty as wife and mother had not fulfilled me. All of this was part of my search but there was more.

I will not bore you with other details, but in time I was divorced, received two degrees, and counseled teenagers for twenty years. But I am getting ahead of my story.

At about age thirty I had a spiritual experience that changed my life and beliefs. Up until then I had "believed" in the God that the church taught about, but had no personal experience. After this vision, I KNEW for myself that God was a part of my being. I went beyond faith. I KNEW. How grateful I am for that awakening!

After my divorce, at age 50, I started a quest for my spiritual answers by attending or belonging to many different denominations: Unitarian, Methodist, Presbyterian, Congregational, Baptist, Christian, Church of Christ, Unity, Spiritualist, Religious Science, all of which added to my knowledge and understanding but none of which satisfied my longing. I was looking for my answers through men and women of the cloth, Sunday School teachers, those who seemed to have a working knowledge of God and his teachings. Some of these I found to have "feet of clay" and their religiosity was only a *facade*. The theology courses I had taken showed me the confusion and disagreements of theologians and philosophers. The intellect was their main tool and the intellect needs to be bypassed if we are to really KNOW. For KNOWING God is of the heart and emotions also. And to KNOW God is just the beginning.

Finally a greater catastrophe came to me than the divorce which had been very painful in that day's society. My son was killed in Vietnam! Previous to hearing of his death I had a precognitive dream which I knew had come from God since it gave me so much strength and support during this trying period. It was then that I knew I must make a deep search and come to some conclusion about my spiritual belief. I started on the Path. I did not know then that, once started, there is no getting off. Once the commitment has been made one has to continue. And so, I found meditation, or it found me, and that made all the difference!

I have told you all of this so that you will know me as a person just like you, who came into this world with strengths and weaknesses, who made mistakes, and overcame many of them, who loved and lost, who found her way out of the "morass" of human consciousness, and who has been given the task of teaching what I have learned, not only from the intellect but also from my creative Center.

So here I am in the year 1979 on the front deck of a mountain cabin in the Rocky Mountains. My life is happier and more fulfilled than ever. I have retired from counseling teenagers and am devoting my life to consciousness building and teaching others as they find what I have to teach helpful to them. My credentials are shaky according to the theological world. My credentials are shaky according to my own human consciousness, but my credentials are excellent when it comes to what I really KNOW: GOD IS and His desire for you and me is bliss, peace, and awareness of Him forever.

When I realized that I needed to find my own Path, I began reading. I read many books. For several years I read incessantly everything that came my way that spoke Truth to me. Some of the most impressive were: *The Religions of Man* by Huston Smith; *Our Oriental Heritage* by Will Durant; *The Sermon on the Mount* by Emmet Fox; *Varieties of Religious Experience* by William James. All gave me much food for thought and awakened my consciousness to the long history of the Christian religion and its beginnings in Eastern thought and the Jewish religion. I knew that my way lay through many religious understandings and away from the traditional Christian concept.

As I was a student of psychology, and had rejected Freud's

theories because he did not treat the spiritual need in man, I turned to Carl Jung. How exciting to find a psychologist who understood the real yearning of man and the incompleteness in his being which he tries to fill with everything but knowledge of his spiritual being. Reading Jung was not easy; perseverance brought understanding. Finally, books were incomplete too. Men and women who had been inspired to share their experience and knowledge were gratefully loved, but my own path required my own contact with the Creative Principle, with Divine Being, with the Ultimate Source of all, with God. I hope that reading this book will help you come to the conclusion that only through individual search and development can you find the ultimate answer for your own spiritual needs.

I was a part of some groups that also added to my understanding and growth. Some were in churches, some were in the educational world. But ultimately, meditation seemed the route I must take.

And so I started to meditate!

I found out about it through a Spiritualist church. I had never heard of meditation in a Christian church. Prayer, yes, and I knew how to pray, to talk to God, to praise Him, to ask Him for help, and all of this is still important. Prayer is not to be abandoned when we meditate. But meditation is in some ways opposite to prayer in that one LISTENS in the SILENCE and turns off words and thoughts. The Christian church, based on their interpretation of the Bible and Jesus' teaching, found very little in the New Testament about meditation as such, although Jesus went apart from the multitude many times and advised his apostles to do likewise, but the word meditation was either lost in translation, or prayer was used in the broad sense of meditation.

Meditation is the stopping of the thoughts that race through our head. It may be a total silence, it may take the form of a monolog, or a dialog. It is defined differently by different teachers and groups. It is experiencing the spirit, bliss, peace. It brings us close to our Inner Being, our Soul, our Self, our Spirit within. We learn about the true source of Life, Love and Light, the Ultimate Source of the world. My method was developed through some reading, some lectures, Yogananda's teachings, although I was never initiated into Kriya Yoga, and through my own experimenting. If for you this is too difficult, then find a group, a teacher, a guru, a method. Each one, if he really desires to meditate, will be led to his rightful way.

Out of meditation came so much grace and love and direction for my life which has led me toward the throne of grace. I hope it will bring you that and more.

Now to the thesis on which this book is written.

If you have been reading any of the literature coming out of the New Thought movement in the last 50 years, you are aware of the New Age theme. There are books that go into this subject in detail, so I will discuss it only briefly. A book by Walter Starcke, *The Ultimate Revolution,* was helpful to opening my eyes.

One, by Marilyn Ferguson, *The Aquarian Conspiracy,* is excellent. There are many others that have been written on this subject.

The astrologists have also been predicting for a long time that a new phase of life is beginning for planet Earth. There are Christian writers who are moving with the change in our times brought on by scientific discoveries and ethical understandings.

After the atomic age was ushered in, many thinkers and religionists were aware of the change in mankind in all areas of endeavor. Music and art became more abstract and less "hung up" on rules of the past. Modern poetry seemed to be saying something that not even the poet understood. Communication systems took advantage of the breakthrough in scientific knowledge and our world became One through instant communication. A devastating war was fought and won by allied forces due to the possession of certain powerful knowledge about making bombs that could blow up the entire world. We landed on the moon. We explored space. I could go on and on, but the Bomb had a major spinoff.

As human beings we realized that our life was very tenuous, to say the least, and many became more serious about "What follows death?" "How can we avoid being demolished by nuclear power?" "Why am I here?" "How can I have happiness for my short life on earth?'' All of these are basic questions and they are either conscious or unconscious. Many knew that a New Age was here. So they looked to the old institutions and were not satisfied. They threw up their hands in despair and decided to go on a search themselves, the youth of the world, particularly. In searching they turned to other religions besides Christianity, Judaism, their parents' religions. Many older people were also searching. The youth may have turned to drugs, to pacifism, ecology, interest in the environment, cults of various descriptions, and many found their answers. There are many older people doing the same. The search still goes on.

Basically the theme of this book will be a New Age in Spiritual Understanding going beyond much that has been taught in Western organized religion. We have had the Christian teaching around for 2000 years. It is basic to our way of thinking, but when we let the light of Eastern teaching in, we find a New Dimension. The Eastern teaching, per se, may not fit the Western man and woman but with the teachings of Jesus Christ and the Eastern understanding, we may be able to develop our own personal direction that leads us to that which we yearn for. Jesus taught of this New Age. In Matthew 24 and 25 there are, according to some biblical scholars, words that describe the New Age. Jesus, in his last hours on earth told his followers that he had to leave them so that they would not depend on Him. He assured them that he would send them the Comforter, the Paraclete, who would dwell within them and through whom great things would be done.

The Book of Acts tells about the visitation of this Paraclete, or Holy Spirit, and what a change it made in the lives of Jesus' apostles who, like me, were uncertain they were equal to the task set before them. But after the visitation of the Holy Spirit— read it for yourself. Let us too, have the visitation of the Holy Spirit and let it change our life so that we may participate fully in the New Age!

Just a word or two to those who have been reared in the traditional interpretation of Jesus' teachings and Paul's work of establishing the Church. The Bible account of Jesus' teachings was written by those who many times did not know him and went on the report of those who did. It was also written many years after his Death and Resurrection. However, I have accepted as a true account these writings. I have used the Revised Standard Version of the Bible as my reference point. There are books that give a different account of Jesus' life and teachings. One is *The Aquarian Gospel of Jesus the Christ* by Levi. This gives an account of His life from age 12 to 33 and teaches that he was taught by the great Masters of Greece, Egypt, and Hindu mystics. His teachings are Universal and include all men. Let us open our ears and eyes to the Truth as revealed by Him and as it comes from our Inner Being Who knows All.

It is a beautiful Journey being in Tao with our Inner Being. Welcome and enjoy. It is an INSIDE JOB.

You might like to keep a Bible near as you read this book, as I have not quoted all of Revelation. The Bible used for most of the quotations is the Revised Standard Version published by Thomas Nelson Inc., New York (1972).

My deepest gratitude goes to Dr. Grace Faus, who edited the manuscript; to Dr. Jeff Raff who taught me much about Jungian psychology; and to all those friends who encouraged me.

CHAPTER 1

The Messenger

As I approach this great Book, humility and centeredness on my inner Christ are uppermost. The work has been given to me and through His Grace and direction I will attempt to be a clear interpreter, an intermediary between the Divine and man, as we all are to one degree or another. The value of His word has been lost on many. Perhaps something that is recorded by me will "Ring a bell" in the reader's mind and new insights, new directions, new ecstasy and peace can be experienced. This is my prayer.

The usual interpretation of this Book has been clouded by the ancient past, the mythological symbols it contains, the vested interests of the church fathers and the limitation of consciousness of the interpreter. This Age is now passing, the Age of Christian doctrine of "hellfire and damnation," the doctrine of fear and guilt, the doctrine of outer authority for man's spiritual growth, the age of interpretation based on past history and primitive ways of expressing worship of the Divine. For the New Age, we must look to the Inner Spirit for guidance, each of us, and thus form our own hierarchy of authority.

For too long our individual soul has been lost in the consciousness of the race and we have failed to express that Self indicated in the tried and true phrase, "Know Thyself," for to know thyself is predicated on knowing "Thy Self."

We have gone, as mankind, far out to outer space. We have experienced the holocaust of Hitler and the destruction of millions of lives; we have within our hands power enough to demolish everything on God's earth. Now He is saying "Stop! You must! Listen to My Voice! Become quiet and hear me! Then inherit the Holy City, the Kingdom of God, right here and now," for He said "The dwelling of God is with man," (Rev. 21:3) and Jesus said "The kingdom of Heaven is within you." (Luke 17:21) So our approach is from the inner to the outer and is for the teaching of each individual. Revelation is for the enlightenment of each because we are "in light" and only need to recognize it.

The setting for the Book and the author's identity are important, as John, the seer, wrote from the level of his own consciousness and authorities say it was written about 70 A.D. Who wrote it has not been finally decided by authorities that I researched, but if it was John, the disciple, we would expect his frame of reference to be strongly Christian. The church was being formulated and organized. The Christians were being persecuted by the Roman government. The need for secrecy, for anonymity in writing such a book was necessary. Whoever wrote it, I believe, had achieved a state of enlightenment and was given the task of recording, for each of us, a map, a guide, a directory for our own achievement of total Oneness with the Creative Force we call God. He was in the fourth dimension and believed Jesus Christ was the Messiah and that he was coming again to save the redeemed.

This historical setting, both theological and practical, directs the choice of words, of symbolism, of mythological content. However, because I believe that Jesus Christ came for all men, for all religions, for all nations, I shall approach the interpretation on a more universal basis and will include many of the commonalities between Christianity and other great religions. The teachings of this Book are, I am convinced, for every man and woman. "Go ye into all the world and preach the gospel to the whole creation." (Mark 16:15)

I have introduced another factor into the interpretation that has been an esoteric truth for thousands of years, but because the authorities were afraid it would be misused and bring harm to the common man, we in the West have not been taught about it. In the East it has been common knowledge from ancient India, Egypt, to modern day Japan and China. That of which I speak is the kundalini power. This power lies at the base of the spine, coiled and without movement unless the individual awakens it.

This is many times done by a guru or by meditation. I shall not go into detail here, but the appendix on kundalini power gives some insights from those who have experienced it and are willing to talk about it. As our race grows in consciousness of the Good, we will learn more and more about it. For to me, the great energy lying dormant at the base of the spine of the human being is our energy source and is pure Spirit, the Holy Spirit, the Christ.

The book of Revelation can be interpreted from at least two directions: first, as a consolation to people of that time who were in despair and being persecuted. It was no doubt a great comfort to them. They understood the symbols and words better than we do, and thus the writing fortified Christians who were being persecuted. John wanted them to know that "God is all powerful to save those who trust him," according to Elizabeth Turner.[1] The same interpretation is used by many fundamentalist Christians of today.

Second, it can be interpreted as hidden truths to be uncovered for our teaching for today and the New Age. This is the interpretation that I am undertaking and is for the aspirant who wants to reach Oneness with his inner Christ or God. By Christ I mean the Divine spark of God within each of us. If the reader will clear his mind of the usual interpretation given Revelation he will be well on his way to understanding and hopefully accepting the second interpretation idea. However, that will take a conscious desire to KNOW and an act of personal will to overcome the past teachings. It will be an adventure and one that may change his life. But the rewards are great.

In order to work slowly into this interpretation, I will take it one verse at a time. It will take extensive explanation to help you get the setting from which it is written. So the first chapter will be long. As you read, meditate and Center and try to listen with the "Third Ear." Hearing is the key. All through the Book of Revelation we are reminded to listen. Jesus said: "He who has ears let him hear," (Matt. 11:15) and "He who is of God hears the words of God; the reason why you do not hear them is that you are not of God." (John 8:47) What I have written is only the beginning, a beginning for your own listening and for your own healing.

We shall start by reading Verse 1 carefully. "The Revelation of Jesus Christ, which God gave him to show his servants what must soon take place; and he made it known by sending his angel to his servant John," is the beginning. Angel means or is symbolic of a spiritual thought or a messenger of God.The angel, the spiritual thought, introduces into consciousness a spiritual idea direct from Jehovah or the I AM presence. The angel that appeared to him was no doubt a vision, an apparition seen by his physical eyes, but many say that a vision is really the projection from the inner to the outer. So I would suggest that the angel of the Lord refers to John's own inner Christ. This Christ is the same in Jesus Christ, John, and ourselves. It is also called the Holy Spirit. And so the Holy Spirit is revealing these Truths to him for the Holy Spirit is "the executive power of both Father (God) and Son (the idea in man) carrying out the creative plan."[2]

John was listening to his inner wisdom and that Spirit revealed to him the way of salvation, the way to higher consciousness, the way to enlightenment. John, of course, did "see" a figure, a numinous figure that he classified as an angel of Jesus Christ and it spoke to him, whether from the heart or audibly is uncertain. It does not matter, but usually the perceiver of a vision hears telepathically.

Verse 2 is describing John, "who bore witness to the word of God and to the testimony of Jesus Christ, even to all that he saw." With this John establishes who he is, and to whom he is loyal.

Verse 3 seems strange: "Blessed is he who reads aloud the words of the prophecy, and blessed are those who hear, and who keep what is written therein; for the time is near." Our question is why it should be read aloud. The King James translation reads, "Blessed is he that readeth" and perhaps the sound of the words of this great prophecy carries energy that is valuable for raising the vibration of our body, mind and spirit just as the mantra is used by some devotees. In any case we are admonished to listen, right from the beginning.

"Blessed is he" needs to be explained. Throughout the Bible the pronoun "he" is used to designate both male and female. I shall often use only the pronoun "he" as I write, but bear in mind I certainly do not mean only the male. "Male and female created he them" is said of the creation of humanity, and even though in most religious writings the pronoun "he" may be used exclusively, we know that women, or the "shes," are included in the male pronoun. Some students wonder if one must incarnate as a male to reach enlightenment! Women are usually so much more interested in spiritual matters that I am sure the promise is meant for them also. So far as I know, however, there are few accounts of illumined women. Some are: Saint Teresa, Saint Joan of Arc, Saint Hildegarde, and Saint Catherine of Genoa. And what a difference they made in the world! However, we must remember that man and woman, the masculine and the feminine are expressed in each of us. Whether our physical body is male or female does not make that much difference. In any case I shall use the masculine pronoun in the generic sense.

Verse 4 gives John's address to the seven churches in Asia and the usual salutation from God "who is and who was and who is to come," the Timeless One. Time is a man-made concept but God is timeless. He then says, "Grace to you and peace from the. . . . seven spirits who are before this throne." Seven refers to the divine law of perfection for the divine-natural man. In Revelation 4:5 there is a reference to "before the throne burn seven torches of fire, which are the seven spirits of God." So I would interpret the seven spirits to be the seven centers, or chakras, which have been raised to perfection by the Holy Spirit within John. He is setting the stage. He is saying that he is in a state of enlightenment and that what he has to say is coming from the throne of grace.

The seven spirits before the throne of God has been interpreted by Edyth Hoyt in her *Studies of the Apocalypse of John of Patmos*. She says, "The seven spirits indicate seven thoughts of

God: Love, Light, Wisdom, Truth, Power, Beauty, and Life. These are the qualities attributed to His Presence from Persian background and all minister to man's needs."[3] (Edyth Hoyt wrote extensively on Bible interpretation and based her interpretations on a Bible interpreted by Dr. Richard Moulton.)

And then in Verse 5-6, John acknowledges his guru, Jesus Christ. Now in the Eastern religions a guru, a master, a teacher is necessary if one is to grow in consciousness. For the Westerner, this is a difficult concept to accept as one is expected to be totally obedient to his guru. However, we need some teacher and John is suggesting that Jesus Christ should be or is our teacher. And Jesus Christ is representative of our inner Christ. So we are again admonished to listen to our inner Christ. We do need someone, however, as we go on our Journey, to talk with about our development and so we need a mentor, a listener, and perhaps we will find someone who is further along the path with whom we can share our own wanderings and wonderings. How fortunate if we are directed to a true Master. In any case we will find our own and at all times will listen with our Inner ear.

In relation to the above, God speaks through books, through teachers, through ministers, through priests, and through nature. They are all fine sources. We listen to them also, but unless the little "click" occurs within our own consciousness, what they are teaching may not be truth for us. The youth of America have made journeys to India to find a guru and have been disappointed. Others have found their Teacher. There are numerous gurus who have come to America and established ashrams and have teaching centers and retreats for the development of consciousness. All are not genuine, unfortunately. Be aware of your Inner Guide. If your desire is genuine and sincere, you will find the right Teacher.

So for John, in the Book of Revelation, it was Jesus Christ and will be for us. Jesus Christ, man and God as One, who overcame death and taught us how to overcome it; Jesus Christ, the embodiment of all the characteristics of all the great religious leaders; Jesus Christ, was resurrected and appeared to many after his resurrection, or translation. There are accounts in the Bible of saints who were translated as, for instance, Enoch (Heb. 11:5), Moses, Elijah, John the Beloved. (Annalee Skarin, in her book *Ye Are Gods,* goes into this subject more deeply.) Jesus Christ was resurrected and gave his apostles the teaching that would help them overcome death, and he teaches us also.

How the body is resurrected after death or does not see death is called translation, and has been the subject of discussion for centuries. The rishis explain resurrection from the dead as follows: As the chakra centers in the ethereal or subtle or spiritual body are energized and opened, the effect is felt in the physical body and it also becomes energized. The physical body eventually vibrates with the energy of light and there is no death after that. In his *Autobiography of a Yogi,* Yogananda explains it thusly:

> KRIYA YOGA is a simple, psychophysiological method by which human blood is decarbonized and recharged with oxygen. The atoms of this extra oxygen are transmuted into life current to rejuvenate the brain and spinal centers. By stopping the accumulation of venous blood, the yogi is able to lessen or prevent the decay of tissues. The advance yogi transmutes his cells into energy. Elijah, Jesus, Kabir, and other prophets were past masters in the use of Kriya or a similar technique, by which they caused their bodies to materialize and dematerialize at will.[4] (Kriya Yoga is the name of a particular type of yoga that Yogananda taught.)

In a series of books, *Life and Teachings of the Masters of the Far East,* by Baird T. Spalding,[5] this is gone into with much greater depth, if you are interested.

And the end of Verse 5 reads: "and from Jesus Christ the faithful witness, the first-born of the dead, and the ruler of kings on earth." Kings, a word symbolic of our earthly consciousness, is used often.

Verses 5 and 6 also bring up a point on which I want to spend considerable space. "To him who loves us and has freed us from our sins by his blood and made us a kingdom, priests to his God and Father, to him be glory and dominion forever and ever. Amen."

Jesus Christ, our Wayshower, is expressing his love for us right now as I write and you read these words. For we are free through his example. The phrase "gave his blood for us" is the expression which Christians have interpreted to mean that Jesus being crucified has given us forgiveness for sins. It is true that Jesus incarnated on earth as a human being, had the blood of a human being coursing through his veins, and died on the cross as a sacrifice but not for the forgiveness of our sins. The lesson we were supposed to learn was in the resurrection. He was crucified, as that was the common method of punishing criminals and dissidents. But he arose from death and proved that we too can do the same, for he told us we could. And so he shed his blood in order for us to learn about the overcoming of death and thus change our own negative attitude toward death, toward guilt, toward the old concept of sacrificing an animal or a human being for the sins of the many. We must do it ourselves. God came to earth in Jesus in order to teach this Truth and he is in us teaching us now.

He has been misunderstood, or should I say his teachings have been misunderstood for 2000 years, because his teaching was so complex for the human understanding of that day, and indeed now. He shed his blood, or he was born into a human state of existence in order to teach us and to exemplify what we are capable of, for his teaching about the raising of the consciousness of Love, of the Christ within us, has brought us a new dimension. He was of the Piscean Age and introduced us to the Aquarian Age of balance between the human and the Divine.

Jesus Christ, in his resurrection and ascension, makes us aware of the activation of the Paraclete, the Holy Spirit, which resides in each of us. We have the Spirit of knowing how to overcome the physical earthly thoughts and actions that bring us suffering. All great religions of our world teach about the spirit within man. He demonstrated it. Our task is to do likewise. He frees us from our sins through his teaching and "made us a kingdom, priests to his God and Father."

Our Buddhist, Islam and Hindu brothers do not, of course, look to Jesus for their savior. But they honor him as a great teacher. Each people and race has been sent gods or saviors who have spoken to them in their language where they are. We who follow Jesus were blessed by his presence. I expect we have all lived other lives in other climes and knew other religions. Jesus Christ appears to speak more directly to us because of our background, our Judeo/Christian background.

Jesus' example is, among other teachings, his spiritual commitment to his Inner Voice, the Father. We are where we need to be for our religious or spiritual development and our karmic debt. So Jesus came to teach us how we could reach enlightenment and has much to teach others of other religious persuasion. He is for all of mankind.

Verse 7 is the one that fundamentalist Christians quote as proving that Jesus is coming to earth again: "Behold he is coming with the clouds, and every eye will see him, everyone who pierced him, and all tribes of the earth will wail on account of him." Let us look at this metaphysically. Metaphysical is defined as beyond physical senses.

Clouds sometimes obscure our vision. The cloud might refer to John's vision of the holiness of Jesus Christ as his vision was surrounded by a numinous light. Clouds also symbolize the presence of the Mind of God in spiritual visibility, a sign of high consciousness. Everyone will see him for as we grow in consciousness of our inner Christ, we too may have a vision, a numinous experience of seeing into another dimension.

Mankind has taken this passage at face value and has interpreted it as a reappearance of Jesus in the clouds, as the Jews expected the Messiah to appear, but I feel the metaphysical interpretation is Truth. He comes to each of us as we invite him and wipe away the clouds of *maya* from our vision. And Universal realization of the Christ will bring Universal blessing.

The wailing spoken of is, of course, human reaction to high experience. Bliss brings tears, plaintive cries, and these are cries of joy and not of sorrow.

Verse 9: "I, John (means Jehovah has been gracious) your brother who shares with you in Jesus the tribulation and the kingdom and the patient endurance, was on the island called

Patmos on account of the word of God and the testimony of Jesus." In this verse he is addressing the Christians in veiled but familiar language. Patmos is a real geographic island, a stony island, and could symbolize our emotional and mental state when we start our search, our Journey.

He says in Verse 10 that he was "in the Spirit on the Lord's Day." Being in the Spirit is a very important state of being, for it indicates a Oneness with God and this comes to us through deep meditation or prayer. We must be entirely alone, aware of our need and in deep silence to have the vision of truth for ourself. John was in another dimension due to his deep state of awareness of the Spirit within. I know of no other route to take to the kingdom of Heaven. When we go deeply enough into the inner we experience visions, voices, conversations with our Inner Self, physical changes, deep rapture, and out-of-this-world experiences. And the Lord's Day, in my understanding, is any day when we are in the Spirit, which could be every day.

I hope that you are beginning to realize the great symbology of Revelation. For instance, "I heard behind me a loud voice like a trumpet." The raising of the kundalini power makes the aspirant aware of great sounds within his own body. More about that later from Yogananda.

Since our basic premise is that this is a "Revelation of symbolic exposition of a yogic science which allows man to escape his bodily prison and resume his true identity with God,"[6] we shall treat the seven churches as the seven chakra centers in the etheric body that need activation in order to become filled with light so that the aspirant may be enlightened.

The "book" mentioned refers to the instruction that we are to receive about it, the Holy Spirit, that is to be sent to each of the power centers. It might be interesting to observe, in an aside, that science does not accept these power centers yet in the physical, but Kirlian photography may eventually pinpoint them.

An account of the photographing of the chakra energy is given by Elmer Green in "Beyond Biofeedback." Swami Rama, mentioned in the account, is the founder of the Himalayan Institute in Honesdale, Pennsylvania. Quote from page 209: "One day after returning from Chicago, where Swami Rama had given public lectures, he showed me a Polaroid picture in which most of his chest was obscured by a disk of pale pink light. I asked for an explanation, and he said that he had mentioned during a lecture that it was possible to turn on the subtle energy in a chakra so intensely that it would become visible to the naked eye. On hearing that, a skeptical physician in the audience had demanded that the Swami demonstrate it so he could take a picture with a Polaroid camera. The Swami said several pictures were taken and that I could keep one.[7]

All of the churches are named (in verse 11) and these messages must have been important to the members of those churches at that time. However, the messages are for us now.

Now we come to a description of the messenger in John's vision. Verses 12-15: "Then I turned to see the voice that was speaking to me, and on turning I saw seven golden lampstands, and in the midst of the lampstands one like a son of man, clothed with a long robe and with a golden girdle around his breast; his head and his hair were white wool, white as snow; his eyes were like a flame of fire, his feet were like burnished bronze, refined as in a furnace, and his voice was like the sound of many waters;" As suggested earlier this can be taken as a description of Jesus Christ's angel, of the Holy Spirit, of some enlightened being, any of whom were representatives from God. The description is in man's terms, but I suspect that the Revealor was so overcome that his description was given in the grandest terms possible in his vocabulary. He was well versed in the Old Testament and we find something of the same description in books of the Old Testament, Exodus 28:4 and Daniel 7:13,9 and Daniel 10:5 being two of them. For me this figure is the Holy Spirit, the Spirit within Jesus and the Spirit within John that was speaking to him.

The expression "son of man" is a term used by Ezekiel when referring to himself. Some have interpreted it as "Spirit of God." Others use "Mind of man." It seems to be a mystery according to Edyth Hoyt in her *Studies in the Apocolypse*.[8] She suggests that "Spiritual man" is what Jesus meant in referring to himself for Son is capitalized and therefore indicates Spirit and man. Man is always written in the lower case. Jesus stressed time after time that he was a man but at the same time God was his Father. (Oddly enough, "Son" is not capitalized in Verse 13).

Verse 16 reads, "in his right hand he held seven stars," and connected with that is verse 12, "and on turning I saw seven golden lampstands." As for the symbolism of the passage I should like to quote Yogananda from his "Autobiography of a Yogi": "Awakening of the occult cerebrospinal centers (chakras) is the sacred goal of the yogi. Western men have not understood that the New Testament Book of Revelation contains the symbolic exposition of yogic science, taught to John and other close disciples by Lord Jesus. John mentions (Rev. 1:20) the 'mystery of the seven stars' and the 'seven churches:' these symbols refer to the seven lotuses of light described in yoga treatises as the seven 'trap doors' in the cerebrospinal axis. Through these divinely planned 'exits' the yogi, by scientific meditation, escapes from the bodily prison and resumes his true identity as Spirit."[9]

Fillmore, in his *The Revealing Word* calls the candlesticks "receptacles of spiritual light." They are the spiritual aspect of the seven churches, the spiritual wisdom and understanding side of the churches. Churches are an aggregation of spiritual ideas in individual consciousness. Thus I have reached the conclusion that the seven candlesticks refer to the seven branches from the spine that end in the seven chakras, the etheric body. I have assigned to each of these a spiritual idea which must be developed in order for us to reach the final state, the seventh chakra. I should like to make it clear that reaching the state of enlightenment may not be complete for many, many lives although we may experience it occasionally.

The beautiful description of the speaker is "one like a son of man" and the spirit, the angel of Jesus Christ, would take this form in John's mind. The long robe with the golden girdle will be seen again and again as we come to the description of the throne and those who are around it, those who have reached the enlightened state. The whiteness of the head and hair is reminiscent of the description of Moses when he came down from the mountain (a high state of consciousness), "and the people of Israel saw the face of Moses, that the skin of Moses' face shone." (Exod. 34:35) Also Jesus on the mountain of transfiguration is described: "his face shone like the sun and his garments became white as light." (Matt. 17:2) White is a symbol of purity and perfection.

The "feet of burnished bronze refined in a furnace" symbolizes fire and the burning out of the dross of materiality. Feet symbolize understanding and the enlightened being, the man filled with the Holy Spirit, has undestroyable understanding. It is said by the alchemists that fire, the serpent fire perhaps, symbolizes Christ, the Holy One within. This fire will cleanse us of all impurities and our feet will be as burnished bronze.

"And his voice was like the sound of many waters" symbolizes the Aum, the vibration of the Holy Spirit. This will be explained in a later chapter, but again is related to the opening of the chakras. Yogananda says in his *Autobiography*, "Aum is the cosmic vibratory power and sound behind all atomic energies. The Aum that reverberates throughout the universe (the "Word" or "voice of many waters" of the Bible) has three manifestations or *gunas*, those of creation, preservation and destruction."[10]

"And from his mouth issued a sharp two-edged sword" reminds us of the "sword which turned everyway" and protected the garden of Eden and the Tree of Life. We will find as we go along that there is more connection between Genesis and Revelation than we ever imagined. A sword is symbolic of many ideas. One from *Interpretation of Fairy Tales* by von Franz, a Jungian analyst and writer, who suggests that in the apocalypse it is the Logos functioning as God's decisive Word, judging the world.[11] Also, "Sword means the transformation of the vital spirit of man into the Divine."[12] So says Jung. In another place, in his book *Psychology and Religion,* Jung says the sword is Christ, the Holy Spirit. I take the position that sword is symbolic of Truth and Truth cuts both ways; it is a defense and a protection if needed. If ignored it is a punishment; a negative reaction accrues. The flaming sword mentioned in Genesis may have the same connotation but from a different angle.

John, like all of us, when we have a vision, recognized it as being of high import and fell down to worship. In chapter 22 we will read that he did the same thing but was admonished to rise up, to not fear, to accept the angel as one like himself. The angel then describes himself as "the first and the last," as the Alpha and Omega, as the Living One, as the Holy Spirit.

"I died, and behold I am alive forevermore" is again referring to our human state and our divine state through the Holy Spirit and our human body.

The Holy Spirit, our inner spirit, is alive forevermore. Within each of us is a spirit that will not die, which lives on life after life and becomes more closely vibrating with the Godhead and when it reaches Perfection or Totality will never go through the human death again. For we are reaching for immortality. We are reaching for the Tree of Life and the angel is saying "I have made it. Let me show you how to do the same."

Each of us, through our Holy Spirit, has the keys to Hades and Death. For the Holy Spirit is our life. We also have the keys to Heaven, as well. It lies within the mind, the consciousness of each of us. We can be of a high estate or we can continue living one earth life after another, experiencing the negative (Hades) and death of the body, death of the psyche, death in all its aspects. He is going to tell us how we can avoid using the keys to Death and Hades and will take us step by step through the seven churches or stages and the teaching each has to offer: the keys to Heaven.

According to Buddha, if we live on earth we are all subject to suffering through desire and attachment. But there is a way to avoid the pain of living on this earth. Meditation and living the Eightfold Path, which is very much like Jesus' Beatitudes, is the answer.

So our beliefs, our desires, our thoughts, our actions all conduct us to a higher state of consciousness. Jesus in the Sermon on the Mount has given the Christian these directions. Lao Tzu in the Tao te Ching does the same. The Upanishads, the Bible of the Hindus, and the Koran for Islams, all contain great noble truths for our direction. The Book of Analects of Confucius, also. They all teach us how to achieve a high estate. Revelation has it all in one book of our Bible, and if we will read it as a symbolic journey we will understand it better, at least at our level of evolution. There will be many ups and downs but our sure guide will be there. Sometimes we will have flashes of a small Samadhi but then we will come down and go through more cleansing. Even these small flashes of ecstasy are worth our efforts. Eventually, if we persevere, we will reach and stay in the final state of enlightenment.

God is in our midst and wants us to be joyous, fulfilled, without need, and One with Him. In His Grace he has shown the Way and it is for all nations, all men, all nationalities of the Earth. We are all one people. He is in all of us.

The Messages

Both of these chapters deal with the seven churches and since they relate to the changing of the body, mind, and spirit and I do not discuss them in sequence, I shall discuss both chapters together.

The raising of consciousness requires a change in the body, mind and spirit. All are irrevocably connected so we can expect directives as to how to bring them to perfection in our development as Revelation continues.

Several authorities, Charles Fillmore and Yogananda among them, in the Western world have taught that the message to the seven churches were directives to the aspirant on the Path, the seven churches being symbolic of the seven chakra centers in the body. According to yogis that write on this subject, the chakras are centers of whirls of energy at certain locations in the ethereal body or spirit body or aura of the physical body. They are connected to the physical body at certain endocrine gland centers. Mystics have connected the raising of the energy in these centers with perfecting of personal characteristics, raising the vibrations of the physical body, and perfecting the consciousness of the Spirit. Thus body, soul and spirit are all affected. Soul in this case is defined as mind.

Before continuing on this interpretation I should like to discuss briefly the symbolism of the number seven. Later I will deal with other numbers that are important in this study.

Seven has been considered throughout the ages as a symbol of individual perfection or completeness. According to Jung in his book *Psychology and Alchemy,* seven indicates the highest state of illumination.[1] Seven is used prolifically throughout the literature, the history, and the religions of the world. For instance:

seven gods of the planets; seven days of creation; the seven lamps on the golden candlestick that was made expressly for use in the tabernacle in the wilderness; the candlestick of gold with its lamps, which was used later in the temple that Solomon built at Jerusalem. Seven is considered a lucky number; the "age of reason" is considered to be at age seven. The cells of our body are said to renew themselves every seven years; there are seven notes in an octave of music; there are seven days in the week; there are any number of things and cycles in our world that are multiples of seven.

We could go on and on with additional examples. Books on numerology are a good source of information on number symbology. Suffice it to say, seven has some kind of mystical place in our earthly life and the seven stages of development through the chakras bring us to completion of our spiritual Journey.

The Hindus and Buddhists teach that enlightenment occurs when the kundalini power or *Shakti* is raised up the spine through the seven centers and comes together with the spiritual power or *Shiva* residing in the cranial area. When this happens total enlightenment occurs. Few people reach this complete state of enlightenment, but the ideal is always calling man on. Many meditators experience what are called little samadhis or ecstasy, but they last only a brief moment. True enlightenment is for eternity. Most authorities seem to be on safe ground when they point to Buddha and Jesus as having this high state. Others teach that the Bodhisattvas of the Buddhists have arrived at this state but have chosen to remain on earth in spirit form, rather than become a Buddha, in order to help mankind progress. There are those living now who claim to have reached this perfect state. In any case something IS calling us to perfection and *when* we arrive there is up to each of us and our choices.

Methods of raising the kundalini power from the lowest chakra at the base of the spine to the seventh chakra, above the head, are many. The various yogis teach their method. All, or almost all, agree that centering on the Supreme Energy within the consciousness, or meditating, is necessary. The reason for wanting to raise this great love and power must be centered in God or negative results will accrue, they say.

In the Christian teaching there is mentioned the baptism by the Holy Spirit and the reaching of enlightenment by the apostles gathered in the upper room (high state of consciousness) after Jesus' Ascension. The Book of Acts gives this account. The Hindu and Buddhist masters can baptize their disciples by touching them and they may still contact the essence of the master when he is absent by concentrating on his picture or a thought of him. (Many accounts of this are given in *Autobiography of a Yogi.*) You may remember that Jesus told his disciples that "lo, I am with you always, to the close of the age." (Matt. 28:20)

The raising of the consciousness through meditation, letting go of the negative and centering on the Divine, will change the physical body, open the chakras, and thus bring into balance the mind, soul, and body. What do the churches (chakras) represent?

Charles Fillmore, in the *Metaphysical Bible Dictionary,* under the metaphysical meaning of seven, has this to say: "We know that the tabernacle and the Temple represent the body of man, and the seven lamps were symbols of seven centers in the organism, through which intelligence is expressed."[2] He goes on to say that the seven centers are seeing, hearing, tasting, smelling, feeling, intuition and telepathy.

Ram Dass, who was Dr. Richard Alpert, an American who became a mystic, teaches in the United States and has written several books. Among them is *Be Here Now,*[3] in which he has written at length on the chakras and the kundalini. There is no complete concensus among mystics as to what personal characteristics each chakra represents, so I have chosen, with the help of several of them and this book by Ram Dass, the following.

First chakra at the base of the spine, faith; Smyrna

Second chakra in the area of the sex organs, creative power; Pergamum

Third chakra in the vicinity of the solar plexus, intellect; Ephesus

Fourth chakra at a location near the heart, love; Philadelphia

Fifth chakra at the throat center, seeking God or worship; Thyatira

Sixth chakra at the Third Eye between the eye brows, wisdom; Sardis

Seventh at or above the crown of the head, Union with the Divine; Laodecia

I shall discuss each of these in terms of reaching enlightenment.

FAITH

Begining with the first chakra which I have designated Faith, we start with a given, for we all have faith in some degree. If you are sitting on a chair, and have no physical disability, you have faith that you can arise from that chair. Most of our life actions are built around faith in something or someone. Now what is faith? I like the definition given in the Bible: "Now faith is the assurance of things hoped for, the conviction of things not seen." (Heb. 11:1) Faith that we all have fits that definition. However, I wish to discuss the faith in a Power greater than we are.

There are those who say they have no faith in a Supreme Power and have never needed to believe in it. Usually they are talking about faith in the God that the church has taught and preached about, and since they have rejected the church they feel they have rejected God. They, however, do believe in something and it may be the same as a Supreme Power but called by another name. Maybe it is personal power, wisdom, their own intellect, another human being, etc. This is still faith. And some day, the Infinite will be sought when "all the chips are down" and their spontaneous prayer will be "Oh God." God is within all in the Universe. This has been a mainstay of belief by mankind down through the ages. This may be called by the scientists, energy. And energy, they agree, pervades everything. It is not understood but its existence is accepted. And so must we.

Faith, in my way of thinking, is a given although perhaps not in God. It is a part of us. Faith may be described on a continuum from thinking, to believing, to knowing, to being One and then that is Oneness that we seek. It is said in the Bible that "Faith comes by hearing and hearing by the word of God." The hearing may not be related to what others are saying but to what we may hear coming from our Inner Being. And we are listening although unaware of it.

Faith in our own ability to handle anything in life is commendable but strengthens our self ego, the personality, and separates us from God or Oneness with Him. The ego is the observer and a part of our being that we should never lose, according to the Taoist and Carl Jung. The Zen Buddhist might not agree. But faith in the small self is bound to come to naught and then it is that we often turn to God.

There are many chapters in the Bible that teach about faith. Hebrews 11 is excellent. The book of Matthew is replete with teachings from Jesus on faith. Charles Fillmore has devoted a great deal of his teaching to faith.

For those who wish to develop their faith faculty to a higher level, I should like to quote him: "It is an error to think that God gives anybody anything that has not been earned. The Holy Spirit comes upon those who pray in the 'upper room.' The upper room is the high place in consciousness where man realizes the presence of Divine Mind. When there has been an aspiration and a reaching out for the spiritual life, the *faith faculty* becomes active in consciousness."[4] And from the same book: "Faith words should be expressed both silently and audibly."[5] In other words, what we say and think, centered in faith, will bring results. Affirmations, both silent and spoken, help activate faith.

The Bhagavad Gita, the scriptures of the Hindu, gives us this assurance: "He who has faith has wisdom, who lives in self-harmony, whose faith is his life and he who finds wisdom, soon finds peace supreme." And verse 40: "He who has no faith and no wisdom and whose soul is in doubt, is lost. For neither this world or the world to come nor joy is ever for the man who doubts."[6]

It would seem then, that Faith is a given, but only you can activate it in order to start on your Path to supreme Oneness as described in Revelation. Faith in our ego may stop the flow at the first chakra or center and the kundalini may never be awakened to course through the rest of the centers.

The kundalini power at the base of the spine in the first chakra is the basic energy that feeds our body and which rises along the spine and affects each chakra center and our whole being. It is often called the serpent energy and is symbolized by a serpent with his tail in his mouth. The serpent energy is awakened by attention, meditation, baptism by a guru, or development of our spiritual awareness. It may be used for the Good or the negative in a person's life. It, like faith, exists but will become active only when we give it thought and attention.

Throughout Revelation we will find attention drawn to our listening to what the "Spirit says to the churches." And also a reminder of the reward that we will receive when we have conquered. If the Spirit speaks to you through anything in this interpretation, listen to It. Your life will be enriched and beginning with Faith, taking the leap into the Void, will be the start of your Journey.

In the message addressed to the church at Smyrna, we read: "I know your tribulation and your poverty (but you are rich) and the slander of those who say that they are Jews and are not, but are a synagogue of Satan. Do not fear what you are about to suffer." When we start on our Journey we have many misgivings. We feel we are poor, we have tribulation, we are slandered by society, we listen to those who say they have the Truth but are of Satan which Fillmore translates as the great Universal negative. We may be in prison; we may be tested. But the scripture says: "Be faithful unto death, and I will give you the crown of life."

So we must be faithful in the face of all of our tribulations because we believe the promise of Him who is on the throne,

"the words of the first and the last, who died and came to life."
Yes, trouble is often the experience that brings us to our knees
and turns us to our Faith, no matter how weak, and will in the
long run be a blessing. "And he who conquers shall not be hurt
by the second death." The second death, according to Fillmore,
occurs at the dissolving of our physical organism, a cessation of
vital force and action in the body.[7] So we are being promised that
we will never die but will have eternal life. And it all starts with
one small step, Faith. And the paradox is that it is the greatest
step.

Arousing the Holy Spirit by Faith is our first responsibility
and symbolically this is allowing the kundalini power to awaken
and begin its coursing into the other centers. In this manner the
physical is changed into the spiritual and Oneness with God is
achieved. The Holy Spirit is always waiting for our listening and
acting.

You may wonder what all of this has to do with Jesus Christ's
teaching or the teaching of the Christian church. As I have
suggested, this is esoteric knowledge that has been protected by
the interpreters of the Bible through symbology and by the church
fathers who understood it. Revelation is teaching this truth and
the words used are symbological because the time for understanding the great truth had not come. There are many in the world
now who believe that the time has come to reveal this Truth and
I shall give you references in Appendix—Part II if you wish to
pursue further knowledge about it. In the meantime, I only ask
that you come to this interpretation with an open mind. I believe
the meaning of Revelation will become clearer if you do.

And so the first center, Faith, is activated and we shall go on
to the second, the Creative Power.

CREATIVE POWER

The second chakra I have designated creative power. Most
Hindus place the second chakra in the vicinity of the sexual organs
which lie very close to the base of the spine and the first chakra.
This creative power may be used for sexual energy or it may be

conserved and sent on its way to open the other chakra centers. Those who "misuse" it may never get very high in consciousness raising. Fillmore writes on this center in his *The Twelve Powers of Man*. He says about the holy stream of life: "Only those who come into consciousness of the spiritual body can feel this holy stream of life. It is the servant of the ego, the I which man is, and through his failure to recognize the divine intelligence, which should show him how to use it in the right way, he blunders ahead in his ignorance and the lamb of God is slain from the foundation of the world. *The greatest danger of perversion lies in the direction of the carnal thought of sex, but it is there that this pure stream has been most foully polluted by ignorance.*"[8]

When creative power is stopped in its flowing at the second chakra, or is misused, it does not allow the opening of the other chakras and many men and women are trapped at this point.

Sexual power is physically very close to the first chakra and the ecstasy and high pleasure we feel when engaged in sexual activities are a small experience of enlightenment, if only brief. According to the rishis and masters, misuse of sexual energy is where most human beings get lost in their seeking. All religions have attempted to deal with this strong instinct in various ways from total abstinence from sexual intercourse as a Brahmachara, to use only for the propagation of the race. Others in modern times have gone along with the sexual revolution, the promiscuous use of the sexual energy for pleasure, and birth control devices are encouraged—and well they may be, as the irresponsible use of this energy can bring much suffering to many.

Churches often adjust their teaching to the mores of the populace and seem to have done so during this so-called sexual revolution of the 1960s to 1980s. Whatever the teaching, mankind has continued to get himself tied to desire and responsibilities as a result of his "normal" need to use sexual energy for pleasure, ecstasy experience (momentary), expression of sincere love, propagation, etc. Each person must decide where his emphasis will be made although leaning on the authority of the church and faith has helped many find their individual answer.

It depends on the seriousness with which one is directed, what the solution will be. According to Hindu and Buddhist teaching, true enlightenment, wisdom, creativity, Oneness with the Divine cannot be reached if the sexual energy is misused even in some cases "not spilled" at all in personal gratification as in Tantra Buddhism. The celibate has been honored in the Catholic religion as well as in others. This is a serious decision for the aspirant. Many men of India fulfill their duty to wife and children until they reach 50 or 60 years of age and then leave all to go into the wilderness with the clothes on their back and a begging bowl in their hand to live a celibate life dedicated to the raising of consciousness.

In Matthew 19:11, 12, Jesus seems to deal with this problem, a very human, social one. His answer to his disciples, as to whether man should marry, is veiled but he says, "Not all men can receive this saying but only to those to whom it is given. For there are eunuchs who have been so from birth, and there are eunuchs who have been made eunuchs by men, and there are eunuchs who have made themselves eunuchs for the sake of the kingdom of heaven. He who is able to receive this, let him receive it." My interpretation is that in his loving answer he says to us "You must make the choice. It depends on your goal. There is no hard and fast answer."

As depicted in Revelation, in the message to the church at Pergamum, the use of sexual energy for lust can only bring separation from the Path. Revelation 2:14 is an example: "But I have a few things against you: you have some there who hold the teaching of Balaam, who taught Balak to put a stumbling block before the sons of Israel, that they might eat food sacrificed to idols and practice immorality."

So the sexual power should be used in a balanced way coupled with higher spiritual aspirations of love and wisdom. Those who live alone and have overcome this strong desire are in a perfect place to use this creative power for ascension to the Divine. Overcoming the desire for sexual activity for some may be the greatest stumbling block they have to surmount. Love is the way.

Shakespeare has this to say about Love and Lust:

> Call it not love, for love to heaven is fled,
> Since sweating Lust on earth usurp his name;
> Under whose simple semblance he hath fed
> Upon fresh beauty, blotting it with blame;
> Which the hot tyrant stains and soon bereaves,
> As caterpillars to the tender leaves.
>
> · · · · · ·
>
> Love comforteth like sunshine after rain,
> But Lust's effect is tempest after sun
> Love's gentle spring doth always fresh remain,
> Lust's winter comes ere summer half be done;
> Love surfeits not, Lust like a glutton dies;
> Love is all truth, Lust full of forged lies.
>
> (from *Venus and Adonis*)

Use of the creative force for the opening of all the chakras will give us the Tree of Life in Paradise. Only love can carry us in this direction. We are turned away from the lustful ways of the Balaamites so that we may follow God or find Him to follow. The tree of life, or as some say, the spinal trunk and the chakras on the limbs, will be filled with light and our consciousness will be raised with Him to eternal life when we turn from stopping at the second chakra and look up to the next one and to the next.

Corinne Heline, a Rosicrucian, has this to say as she interprets I John 5:16. "If any man see his brother sin a sin which is not unto death, he shall ask, and he shall give him life for them that sin not unto death. There is a sin unto death: I do not say that he shall pray for it." Quote from Heline: "In the above John is speaking of the sin against the Holy Ghost, or the misuse of the life principle in man which is the one unforgivable sin. It is of such a nature that it cannot be forgiven, but must be expiated through sorrow, pain, and death until the misguided one awakens to a realization of the sacredness of his own divine creative force, and by a life of chastity retains the seed of life within himself. This seed, the very essence of life, may be transmuted into concentrated thought force of tremendous power. When man comes to demonstrate its higher operations he will be able to create a new heaven and a new earth, and also to fashion for himself a new body of light functioning in that new and glorified condition."[9] This sums up, it seems to me, my remarks on the right and wrong use of the creative force.

And what is the reward: Verse 2:17, "To him who conquers I will give some of the hidden manna, and I will give him a white stone, with a new name written on the stone which no one knows except him who receives it." The white stone is consciousness purified. The new name is I AM.

INTELLECT

At the outset of this section I want to make perfectly clear the difference between intellect and intelligence as these two terms are often confused in usage. My position is that intellect is the tool that we each use in our daily life and expression and through it the intelligence, or God's thinking, functions. Intelligence is of God. Intellect bears the marks of the human. We could not think without the creative intelligence functioning and the intellect, or what often is called the mind of man, is the tool which is used. We have control over our thoughts and thus have been given freedom by God to choose our own way. The energy which is used to think is from and of God and herein is termed intelligence. So now let us discuss intellect.

In the seven chakras, I have chosen to designate the third chakra as intellect. The intellect, for me, has been the center that I exercised the most and to which I have given much energy for the last 25 years. Therefore, it has been the center that I thought most important to give me self-confidence, to develop an ego that was false, and to function in the world of men and women. I finally realized that this had to be changed if I were to go higher, and I am in that process now. We gain a little insight about each of our characteristics and as we aim higher and go higher we take energy away from our "stumbling block." Light from the Creative Force is so superior to our intellect that knowing this we can leave our attachment to intellect and move on to wisdom which is intuition. The right use of intellect will carry us to the higher centers of love, wisdom, the Word, and finally Oneness.

As we listen to our inner Self we have real intelligence which can guide us to the highest. Our intellect in our Western society has been given dominance. Power then becomes our desire and the ego is fed which moves us away from the Divine. In Carl Jung's teachings the intellect is given its proper balance with the spiritual or the "self" as he designates it. I shall not go into detail on the ego; the reader may refer to the writings of Carl Jung[10] and Suzuki for ideas about the differences between the Western and the Eastern approach on the ego. Suzuki, a Zen Buddhist, has written many books, the one with which I am most familiar is *Introduction to Zen Buddhism*. Carl Jung wrote the Foreword to this volume. The intellect when over-developed leads man to believe he has all power and wisdom and further spiritual progress is inhibited.

The message to the church at Ephesus seems to be directed to the intellect. Ephesus was at one time a center of learning and commerce. Ephesus, according to historians, was given up to worship of Diana, the divine goddess, with idolatry, superstition, and general materialism. Diana, a symbol of the great mother, had been brought down to the base of human nature. Thus the intellect may reverse the reality of the divine and produce that which is negative and base.

Chapter 2, verses 2 and 3, give high praise to the church at Ephesus but verse 4 and 5 negate this: "But I have this against you, that you have abandoned the love you had at first. Remember then from what you have fallen, repent and do the works you did at first. If not, I will come to you and remove your lampstand from its place, unless you repent." So the church that symbolizes the intellect has fallen away from its first love or faith and is apt to lose the means of raising the Holy Spirit (I will remove your lampstand) which would raise the consciousness to the Divine. In other words, balance has not been achieved between faith and intellect and the Holy Spirit energy has been misused, and to repent is to let go of the old, and have a new Mind.

Balanced use of intellect is a must in our modern society and the development of intellect through education can release man from the physical want which for the Westerner seems to be necessary before the higher values can be sought after. Maslow's hierachy of values points this out. However, like all the other personal characteristics, the Spirit needs to be blended with the intellect if we are to move up. The answer to our questions of "why am I here?" and "what is after death?" cannot be found in pure intellect, deductive and inductive reasoning, the scientific approach. The greatest thinkers, such as Socrates, Plato, and Aristotle have always included the Spirit, or their interpretation of God, as the balance that intellect needs.

We search for the answer to our longing through pure intellect and think we have found it, but we may "knowest not that thou are wretched, miserable, poor, blind, and naked." (Rev. 3:17) As long as we depend on intellect we are blind and cannot see the heights that remain to be scaled. Believing this, we may not activate the other centers.

If the kundalini, the Spirit of God, is activated through voluntary or involuntary means and stopped at a center and is not used for the development of the higher centers and the purpose of centeredness in God, the repercussions can lead to mental or physical illness and perhaps death. This has been authenticated by various aspirants and teachers of the esoteric truth in their observations. If it is misused for self-aggrandizement or ego development, he will "remove your lampstand from its place." This is why the raising of the kundalini has been kept esoteric knowledge for centuries. Centeredness in the Self or "the love you had at first" will give safe guidance in developing the physical, mental, and intellectual power toward Oneness.

We have been warned for centuries about the misuse of our intellectual power. According to Plato, knowledge is valued as a means of power, and power is a means of wealth. Wealth usually brings man an attachment to materialism and desire for the material above all else. It was Jesus who taught us how difficult it is to turn our attention to searching and finding God if we concentrate on wealth (i.e., the young man who was told to sell all and follow Jesus in Matt. 19:16–22.) Wealth is not the problem, but loving wealth and what it buys is the "root of all evil." "For where your treasure is there will your heart (and mind) be also," said Jesus. (Matt. 6:21) Thus, the intellect can lead us away from our desired goals if not balanced with the energy of the Spirit, and, although the intellect is really Spirit, we misinterpret and believe that our intellect is truly our own doing and forget that God is in All and through All. We must pay attention to It and not to our own ego.

Other religions of other lands have spoken of this also. The Upanishads have this to say: "The Self is not to be known through study of the scriptures, nor through subtlety of the intellect, nor through much learning. But by him who longs for Him is He known. Verily unto him does the Self reveal his true being."[12]

The intellect, by definition, contains both the conscious and the unconscious mind, either of which may be negative or positive. Much that we have disliked in our life we have hidden in the unconscious and as we study Revelation we will see how important it is to rid ourselves of this negative unconscious. We need to clean out the unconscious so our perception or consciousness of the Divine is perfect and the unconscious contains only Good.

It is a narrow gate that separates us from our higher good and the intellect is often the block. The lower sense in our body, mind, and emotions is sometimes as high as man goes. The intellect is that which the ego feeds upon and thus is led astray.

Many New Thought religions teach that the intellect is the same as the Spirit and indeed it is, but the misuse of it can be easily adopted. In believing this, their aim is to spiritualize the intellect by an act of will. The will, of course, is a part of the intellect and when attuned to a higher purpose will lift it up. As we think, so are we, and most of us have much cleansing to do.

Positive thinking is one of the hallmarks of the New Thought movement. The world or race consciousness is usually negative and we are fed more negative food each day through the mass media, through fear about our material welfare, through the arms race that goes on in peace time as well as in war time, through the stress and anxiety of our associates, through the so-called rock culture, through our educational system, through government and religion. Thus fear separates us from the right use of our faith or basic energy. It paralyzes the mind, it encourages us to make choices which are self-protective, which bring untruth, guilt, and base actions against our fellowman. Fear feeds on greed and self-aggrandizement and selfishness. To turn our thoughts to the Divine and center on the Good can help to turn this upside down and make the negative into positive. Positive thinking is not Pollyannaism. It is reality; the negative is *maya*. Try it and see.

Now some sects teach positive thinking grounded on human endeavor. This helps, but may not take one to the step of seeking God's strength and love to help in the process. Many people who are not grounded in faith in a higher being will lose heart and wonder why their change to positive thinking has not wrought the rewards hoped for. What reward we are seeking makes all the difference. If it is a reward of more material possessions, for occult and psychic abilities, for greater happiness, we may gain all of these but they will not last, for our faith is placed on "shifting sand," the mental control, the ego. We would not have the relief from fear of losing all of our gains unless we are faithful to our belief in God and not in materialism or the intellect. The Good we desire will come as a by-product of our attention on the Divine and it will be for His use and for His people. Mind control is often used for selfish purposes. Beware!

To cleanse our thinking processes or our intellect, we may start with affirmations of positive thoughts. This is very basic to the New Thought movement. Charles Fillmore believed that the use of denial and affirmations could change the negative in the subconscious and thus the conscious mind would be cleansed for positive thoughts. The unconscious, through our years of living is so filled with the negative that an effort must be made to neutralize these thoughts.

In some cases one may need to go deeper by the help of a Jungian analyst, for our dreams reveal suggestions from the

Divine as to what unknown negatives need to be erased from our consciousness. The inner spirit ever speaks and is always available if we will only listen. In Matthew 1 we have an account of an angel of the Lord appearing to Joseph in a dream and telling him not to be afraid to take Mary as a wife. In the Book of Daniel we read many accounts of dreams as, for instance, the dream of Nebuchadnezzar who said, "I had a dream, and my spirit is troubled to know the dream." (Dan. 2:3) Do not ignore your dreams. They contain much gold. Cleansing of the unconscious is a natural process. The negative may bubble up in sleep through dreams while our watchdog, the conscious mind, rests. A book by Carl Jung, *A Study of Dreams,*[13] would be valuable.

Another method of changing our negative intellect or thoughts to the positive is to take the leap of faith. By this I mean to let go of your conscious will, lean back, let go and let God. Faith is only the start of our adventure, but goes all the way with us on our Journey, and unless we exercise it we will never make it. Most people will not do this unless they have come to an *impasse* in their lives, have used up all human resources at their disposal (including psychiatric help and chemicals) and still have not found a solution to their unhappiness. This usually happens after age forty, although more and more young people in our Western culture are turning to a spiritual "trip" to solve their unhappiness.

Another method taught by some gurus is to meditate and thus release the negative thoughts to come up to the conscious mind and then to let them go in the love of the Spirit, to repent, to release. This usually necessitates active involvement with a teacher or guru who helps the aspirant verify the cleansing.

Turning the mind, the intellect, from the negative to the positive will reduce the dependence on the intellect for our growth and development toward Oneness, for the positive is just an aspect of God, the Creator. Using the mind in a positive way will bring you more than you ever could envision. "But seek first his kingdom and his righteousness (right-use-ness), and all these things shall be yours as well." (Matt. 6:33) He is waiting to give you His good favor, but if you are filled with ego, centered on the intellect which may be negative, you may have to wait a long time for it. "Do not be deceived; God is not mocked, for what ever a man sows, that he will also reap. For he who sows to his own flesh will from the flesh reap corruption; but he who sows to the Spirit will from the Spirit reap eternal life." (Gal. 6:7, 8)

The main ingredient or need for turning from the lower to the higher is the DESIRE to raise conscious awareness of the Good. And DESIRE comes from the use of the intellect. If one makes this decision, the way and means will come to him, for his inner spirit is ever waiting and watching for the ego or small self to turn to the large Self. "Behold, I stand at the door and knock: if any man hear my voice and open the door I will come in to him, and will sup with him and he with me." The promises are all through Revelation.

The reward of the white robe, a symbol of Pure Consciousness spoken of in Revelation, should be enough to lead us on to higher levels of consciousness, taking the intellect along grounded in faith and love. The white raiment is promised and "I will not blot out his name before my Father and before his angels." In other words, there will be a reward that has been promised all along. When we reach the Omega point of Teilhard de Chardin, we will have life eternal.

Each of us has the potential in consciousness to overcome the base and reach to the highest, and it is an individual Path. Find a teacher through books, or teaching centers, or through meditation, or through a guru (which all of the foregoing are), and listen. I believe that the Spirit of Jesus is ever at our side and within us waiting to help us in an inexplicable way, for the Spirit of Jesus is our Christ. Sincerity and desire will help, but belief and dependence on our Faith in God is primary.

As we understand the place of the intellect, our thinking ability and thoughts on our Path, we will inevitably go up higher. With the Grace of God and our own desire, we can go on. If not now, perhaps some time in the future. For God calls us on. "He who has an ear, let him hear what the Spirit says to the churches." Listen with your intellect, and in His Love.

LOVE

I have designated the heart chakra as the love chakra or center. This is the fourth station on our Path, and the middle, with three centers on either side. Love spreads in all directions and is intermingled with the three below and three above. Love is our motivating power to become better, to go higher, to achieve Oneness. It is also the motivator to activate Faith, to balance our creative and sexual force, and to be used to direct the thinking toward the love of our God and of our fellow man. Seeking God is loving God. Wisdom is intellect and love combined, and the Ultimate is Pure Love. Thus, Love should be placed at the heart center of the physical and spiritual body: for it, like the heart, is the very blood of our spiritual and physical existence.

Most interpreters of Revelation who consider the heart center the center of love, place that center at Philadelphia. And so do I, for Verse 7 of Chapter 3 states: "The words of the holy one, the true one, who has the key of David, who opens and no one shall shut, who shuts and no one opens." David is the symbol of love and the I AM. And the promise of the messenger gives us assurance again that if we overcome we will be rewarded, "He who conquers, I will make him a pillar in the temple of my God, never shall he go out of it, and I will write on him the name of my God, and the name of the City of my God, the new Jerusalem which comes down from my God out of heaven, and my own new name." And so love will be our guide and will be our goal.

When we consider the most of what is written to the church at Philadelphia, we are impressed with the positive words and praise that is given it, i.e., the spirit of the church or our own spirit. This is not surprising when we consider that to love is to fulfill the great and wonderful commandment that Jesus gave, to love the Lord thy God and thy neighbor as thyself. (Matt. 22:37–40) Verse 8, "I know your works. Behold, I have set before you an open door, which no one is able to shut;" refers to the opening of the heart chakra which can never be shut and the Christ within has opened it in the grace and love of God. What an assurance that if we come up this high we will never go back or never be without the open door of Love!

And then, verse 9, "Behold, I will make those of the synagogue of Satan who say that they are Jews and are not, but lie—behold, I will make them come and bow down before your feet, and learn that I have loved you." This seems to be saying that there can be no duplicity in love, that the synagogue of Satan (material thoughts) has those within it who say they are Jews (keepers of the law of love) but this is untrue, and they will bow down to the feet (understanding) of those who love in the way that God has loved them. This is not referring to someone else, but to the consciousness that is within each of us that thinks or believes that we are loving and really aren't. Bowing down is an act of humility which must be centered in our Christ.

In verse 10, those who are of Love will not have the hour of trial which comes to those who are of the world, or we will overcome the trials of earthly existence with love. This I shall refer to later as personal love. This is a new state of consciousness, a resurrection, and if completed in a new life, will take care of all the growing toward Oneness that we need. However, most of us do not love with that purity and need more purification as do the Jews mentioned. But those who do love already have the crown that cannot be lost. Then they cast down their crowns in humility.

It is then that the promise is given; "He who conquers, I will make him a pillar in the temple of my God; never shall he go out of it, and I will write on him the name of my God, and the name of the city of my God, the new Jerusalem which comes down from my God out of heaven, and my own new name." (Verse 12) The new name is Love, which is the Christ presence in which we exist at all times. Then again the admonition, "He who has an ear let him hear what the Spirit says to the churches." We must listen with the Christ Spirit to understand all of this.

Activating Love in your life may be as far as you want to go on your Journey and what a wonderful goal even if it is the ultimate of personal love, for, of course, personal love has within it the Ultimate. The Christian has been taught that brotherly love is most important, and so it is. But love of God is primary, and as we love God more and more we want to continue our upward spiral of consciousness. Hence, there are other goals that some may search out and attain.

Love is an abstract term, the meaning of which comes as we experience it. Love is a noun and a verb. We all know what it is, if we have experienced it, but to define it has taken the ages' great thinkers and adepts many words. And still we do not know until we *Know,* for Love is God and God is Love. I John 4:7, 8: "Beloved, let us love one another; for love is of God, and he who loves is born of God and knows God. He who does not love does not know God; for God is love."

Carl Jung has this to say: "But what will he (the psychologist) do when he sees only too clearly why his patient is ill; when he sees that he has no love, but only sexuality; no faith, because he is afraid to grope in the dark; no hope, because he is disillusioned by the world and by life; and no understanding, because he has failed to read the meaning of his own existence. . . . One cannot just think up a system or truth which would give the patient what he needs in order to live, namely, faith, hope, love and understanding. These four highest achievements of human endeavor are so many gifts of grace, which are neither to be taught nor learned, neither given nor taken, neither withheld nor earned, since they come through experience, which is an irrational datum not subject to human will and caprice. Experiences cannot be made. They happen—yet fortunately their independence of man's activity is not absolute but relative. We can draw closer to them—that which lies within our human reach. To experience is a venture which requires us to commit ourselves with our whole being."[14] And so we must live, and live in the fullest sense, not hiding behind the church, our parents, or our commitments to our society, if we are to find the full life of love, hope, faith and understanding.

The scriptures of the world are replete with references to love, although the Christian New Testament probably has the most references. Many feel that I Corinthians 13 is the most complete definition of love. Please read it and question yourself on its application to you and your loving.

If I speak in the tongues of men and of angels,
        but have not love,
I am a noisy gong or a clanging cymbal.
And if I have prophetic powers, and understand all
        mysteries and all knowledge,
And I have all faith, so as to remove mountains,
        but have not love,
I am nothing.

Love is patient and kind;
Love is not jealous or boastful;
It is not arrogant or rude,
Love does not insist on its own way,
It is not irritable or resentful;
It does not rejoice at the wrong, but rejoices
        in the right.
Love bears all things,
Believes all things,
Hopes all things,
Endures all things.
        Love never ends;

As for prophecies, they will pass away;
As for tongues, they will cease;
As for knowledge, it will pass away.
For our knowledge is imperfect and our prophecy
        is imperfect;
But when the perfect comes, the imperfect
        will pass away.

When I was a child, I spoke like a child,
I thought like a child, I reasoned like a child;
        When I became a man,
        I gave up childish ways.

> For now we see in a mirror dimly,
>> but then face to face.
> Now I know in part;
> Then I shall understand fully, even as I have
>> been fully understood.

> So faith, hope, love abide, these three;
> BUT THE GREATEST OF THESE IS LOVE.

Other scriptures treat Love thusly:

From *The Way of Lao Tzu* (the Tao-te Ching), the scriptures of the Taoist:

> "When Heaven is to save a person
> Heaven will protect him through deep love."[15]

Confucius: "All men have a certain sympathy toward their fellows. If you love others but are not loved in return examine your own feeling of benevolence."[16]

The Upanishads: "Whatever you give to others, give with love and respect. Gifts must be given in abundance, with joy, humility, and compassion."[17] And the Bhagavad Gita: "By love he knows me in truth, who I am and what I am. And when he knows me in truth he enters into my Being." And: "Offer in thy heart all thy works to me, and see me as the End of thy love, take refuge in the Yoga of reason, and ever rest thy soul in me."[18]

These all seem to be saying that love is of God and is God and our relationship with people must be based on Divine or Heavenly Love.

And from the New Testament: "Love your enemies and pray for those who persecute you." (Matt.5:44) And: "This I command you, to love one another." (John 15:17)

Love is then compassion, giving, forgiveness of our self and others, is receiving, is the light of the Word and the World, is God, is All. No wonder it is so important and what we all seek. For it is Love that we really seek. All else is illusion. Sometimes we are misguided and believe that love is to "have and to hold" but Love is to Be. Love is a state of Being. Love is that Principle of life that gives us a reality of life, for life is based on love.

Love is the epitome of our search, for as human beings we are ever looking for our own. That is our problem. That is our nemesis, for Love is not to "have" but to release, to let flow. It is like mercury. It goes in the direction of the least resistance. It, like the Tao of Life, is the Journey.

We, of course, all agree with these statements on love if we have given any thought to it. And we believe it. But to put these into practice is what our challenges are all about. We may give lip service and mind service, but heart service is left out when we try to put truisms into practice. We must act on these abstract ideas in order to make them a part of our Being and our life. And we must also meditate on them, concentrate on them, for understanding requires complete silence and quietude, also.

The great law of love given by Jesus is our talisman for it is the Great Law. Mark 12:29-31 reads: "Hear, O Israel: The Lord our God, the Lord is one and you shall love the Lord your God with all your heart, and with all your soul, and with all your mind, and with all your strength." The second is this, "You shall love your neighbor as yourself. There is no other commandment greater than these." The first law is found in Deut. 6:4, 5 and the second in Leviticus 19:18. So Jesus was repeating the law as given to the Israelites by Moses from the Lord. And he taught us again what it means.

"Israel, metaphysically, is the real of man—that consciousness which is founded in God. It requires the story of Israel from Abraham to Jesus Christ to picture the growth and spiritualization of the whole man."[19]

So Israel is being addressed. And if you and I are in the consciousness founded in God the message will come through to us. Our Journey is tending toward Perfect Love, the seventh chakra. Centeredness in God is a prerequisite to attaining that goal. So many do not understand this and believe that if they have achieved personal love they have gone far enough and have fulfilled the Law. But the Law is addressed to those who have "consciousness founded in God" and thus, as I will enlarge upon later, we must go beyond personal love.

David, the forerunner of Jesus Christ who was of the house

of David, represents divine love personalized in human consciousness. David was split temporarily, however, between divine and
human love for instance in the stories of Bathsheba and Absalom.
Jesus Christ was One in the divine. Most of us in our human
consciousness are David—in our ultimate state of Being we will
be completely Divine as Jesus Christ.

The Law says, "The Lord (Jehovah) our God, the Lord
(Jehovah) is one, and we must Love Jehovah (our inner Christ)
with all our heart (emotions), soul (spirit), mind (intellect), and
strength (body)." If we loved in this respect we would be in
Universal Love, the Love that Christ Jesus demonstrated, and the
second law would not be necessary. However, inherent in being
in Universal Love is action toward our self and our fellow man,
and so Jesus, being cognitive of our need for growth toward the
Divine, gave the second law, for through our growth in loving
mankind we learn of the Divine Love.

Most Christians believe that to love our neighbor is the only
law and forget the first law. That is, they practice love based
more on personal love and that leaves them longing for Perfect
Love which is Universal Love. If we, however, love our Self,
then we shall be acquainted with Universal Love and will love our
neighbor in the larger sense.

Let us discuss Universal Love and Personal Love now. Both
are of the Spirit, or God, for God is Love, but one is at a higher
stage of consciousness. Personal Love is expressed in varying degrees of Christ consciousness, but the more pure it is, the closer
it is to Universal Consciousness of Love. Unless you have suffered
from Personal Love, it may be difficult for you to understand
what I am going to say. Most of us have suffered from the results
of Personal Love and cannot understand why love brings pain,
since we have been taught that to love is Divine and will bring
us great happiness. And, of course, that is the crux of the
problem. For we tend to, with personal love, be selfish and expect
love in return, or possession, or are attached to that one we love.
This is illusion! For love does not capture, it frees. It does not
expect something in return. Real Love frees!

What your concept of Universal Love is, will make a difference in your Personal Love. Most of us reach the fourth chakra of love to one degree or another and feel we have arrived at true enlightenment. But there are three more stages to go through, or at least two, seeking God and Wisdom, before we can experience in its highest degree Universal Love.

Universal Love is pure God Love. How do you understand God's Love? Does it limit you? If you believe this, then you have a limited view of God's love, mankind's limited view. God throughout the Bible is pictured as the Divine Essence of all the Good that exists on earth. This Divine Essence is the "glue" that holds the inhabitants of the Earth to the Earth and holds all that is on the Earth. It holds us together. It is gravity. It is what some call energy. All religions of the world accede that God substance is in everything—called by numerous names.

Now this God substance is the Good. It is activated when needed by the entity, but is quiescent and nonattached unless contacted. The mind of man contacts this energy and it goes to work for and through him. How free we are to ask for this direction, this intelligence, and all we are required to do is ask. "And I tell you: Ask and it will be given to you; seek, and you will find; knock, and it will be opened to you. For every one who asks receives, and he who seeks finds, and to him who knocks it will be opened." (Luke 11:9, 10) How simple.

Do you love that way? Are you able to free your loved ones without attachment? To love your neighbor (and "who is my neighbor?" was asked, and the answer was "he it is who does the will of my Father"), as your Self is to free your neighbor to be who he is and not a facsimile of yourself. You free your neighbor to be without any demands made on him by you, and you are freely accessible to him/her when needed. That is Universal Love. That is the kind of Love we are all searching for. Love in the highest sense is Love that is freely received and freely given without strings attached, and that love will bring us freedom from pain. "And there shall be no more tears or death," Revelation reports.

However, to reach that state of being, it behooves us to practice personal love to its limit, and I Corinthians 13 gives us our map, our guide. What a description of Personal to Universal Love! So many times we are mistaken about our love. It is such a muddle for us humans. We are so confused about love when it is not centered in the Spirit. Our present generation, particularly, has confused love with sexual lust or lust for material things. Morality and love have been confused with sexual activity. What a bastardization of love, for love is unselfish, does not seek its own. This is immature love. "When I was a child, I spoke, thought, reasoned like a child." And most of us are still a child when it comes to love. We know in part; we see in a mirror dimly. But when we are mature in love, we give up childish ways and we shall understand fully even as we are fully understood.

Universal Love is our aim! Fillmore defines Universal Love as broad, unlimited, a universal and harmonizing power. Human love or personal love is based on personality (the outer facade) and is selfish, lawless and fickle. "In reality there is only one love; when man expresses divine love in limited ways he makes a separation in consciousness and his expression of love is personal instead of Universal."[20]

Universal Love—love the Lord thy God—will bring all that we need. But to practice personal love will bring us pain for personal love is not centered on "the Lord our God" and so if you are interested you must go beyond the heart chakra which is basically divine love but which also admits the human factor, as David, and continue on your journey of seeking God and His Wisdom in order to find Universal Love.

Love of children, parents, brothers and sisters is often Personal love. They are not ours, they are God's and we eventually will learn to release them to Him and bless them on their Journey and continue on our own. This is a difficult task for many of us, but remember the first law "To love the Lord thy God" takes precedence over the second "love thy neighbor." Let us continue on our Path to Oneness with the Divine and thus *know* Universal Love in all of its glory.

Love your enemies, Love is of God, Love for the less fortunate, forgiving Love, we are all brothers. All of these are basically Universal Love and we all practice it to one degree or another and we are "Right on!" We were made for Love and all negativities of hate, envy, greed, must and will eventually be lost in Universal Love. As we clean the negative from our consciousness it will be infilled with Universal Love and then we will understand. Again, each must do it for himself. As the chakra of love is fully opened we are "half way home." Express personal love and as you progress it will become the Universal, the Love of God. "Greater love has no man than this, that a man lay down his life for his friends." (John 15:13) And "This is my commandment that you love one another as I have loved you."

But why go beyond love, you may be asking. Isn't that far enough? Apparently not for some of us who are into the New Age way. For the New Age will demand love and also total awareness of a God-centered direction to handle our life in all of the changes that come very fast. We will need to be able to use the power of love for others and to have total love we must be One with Him. Turning within to the Source is assurance that we are armed for any catastrophe, uncertainty and pain. If we have the assurance of His Presence at all times, we can face anything and be of inestimable help to others. Churches, ministers, priests are all of great help but at times now and in the future we may only have our own rich awareness of the Divine to guide us.

The New Age holds many surprises and although I do not hold with the disaster claimants, I believe that "we haven't seen anything yet." With all the great communication techniques we now have that bring us instant communication, we are made aware of the joys and sufferings of others in our world and we can tune in with them and help when we are aware of the Christ presence within ourself and within them. It is the same. I believe that our communication techniques are really in a primitive state now. What the future holds will be truly great. We live in a world of new discoveries. Let us be one of those who is prepared for any exigency.

So our next step would seem to be our Seeking of God in the Highest. And where and how do we start?

SEEKING GOD AND WORSHIP

For many, the achievement of the ability to love and act in love is far enough to go, in fact for most who are serious about their spiritual life. Many fine Christians have achieved this level of consciousness and what a blessing they are to the world. They are satisfied and to them this is being at One with God. They may not be aware of the highest level of Universal Love, but well enough. For others, however, there is an incompleteness, a longing for a deeper awareness of God. For some the ability to live and love will not come until they have reached a higher understanding of God. Only when they achieve enlightenment will they be satisfied. For the Buddhist, the Hindu, the Taoist there is more to aspire to: total enlightenment either in this life or the next or the next. They believe that the level of consciousness which we achieve in one life will be our starting point in the next. So they build life on life and ultimately reach and receive the morning star, they believe.

I have chosen to assign to the next chakra or church the personal characteristic of Seeking or Worship. For we must have a desire to go further in seeking knowledge of the Divine and man is that seeker. To this fifth chakra I have assigned the message to the church at Thyatira spoken of in Chapter 2, verse 18–29. Thyatira was a city in Asia Minor and the center of much commerce and also the worship of Diana, the goddess of the moon and a sister to Apollo, who was also worshipped. Apollo was god of archery, prophecy, music and god of the sun. This city was famous for its dye of purple or turkish red. Paul had visited here, and there were Christians there, so the populace was split between worshipping the gods without and the Christian teachings according to Paul.

The words used in the scripture at first are very complimentary and love, faith, service and patient endurance are all used. "I know your works, your love and faith and service and patient endurance, and that your latter works exceed the first. But I have this against you, that you tolerate the woman Jezebel, who calls herself a prophetess and is teaching and beguiling my servants to practice immorality and to eat food sacrificed to idols."

So the positive characteristics are fine but not enough as there is still immorality (incorrect use of spirit) among the members. Again I believe this is referring to the misuse or adulteration of the basic energy or life force in centeredness in the world and earthly pleasures. Sickness, death, and karma ("I will give to each of you as your works deserve"), are mentioned as results. "Behold, I will throw her (Jezebel, the ruling emotion on the plane of physical consciousness) on a sickbed, and those who commit adultery with her I will throw into great tribulation, unless they repent of her doings; and I will strike her children dead. And all the churches shall know that I am he who searches mind and heart, and I will give to each of you as your works deserve." He who conquers this desire and "keeps my works" until the end will be "given power over the nations."

To adulterate is to mix thoughts and actions, to be confused. This brings the unhappiness to each that is their recompense. When we have control over this strong force we can "control" all the forces of our being. And the "Keeping my works until the end" brings us to our fifth chakra or teaching and refers to continuing on, not stopping because we have achieved a certain level of good deeds, not resting on our past good, for the goal of "the morning star" is still to be achieved, the ultimate reality of God, full recognition of the Christ within, enlightenment, the final state of Being. Jesus called this state the kingdom of Heaven.

The kingdom of Heaven is mentioned many times in the New Testament account and is the center of Jesus' teachings. John the Baptist: "Repent for the kingdom of Heaven is at hand." (Matt. 3:2) Jesus' prayer or the Lord's prayer: "Thy kingdom come" (Matt. 6:10) He referred in his parables to the kingdom of Heaven. "Seek ye first his kingdom and his righteousness (right-use-ness) and all these things shall be yours as well." (Matt. 6:33). "The kingdom of Heaven is like a grain of mustard seed."

(Matt. 13:31) "It is like heaven." (Matt. 13:33) "I will give you the keys to the kingdom of Heaven." (Matt. 16:19, 20) "Let the children come to me and do not hinder them; for such belongs in the kingdom of Heaven. (Matt. 19:14) "You are not far from the kingdom of Heaven," Jesus said when he repeated the two great laws of love recorded in Mark 12:29–31. Also, "There is no man who has left house or wife or brothers or parents or children for the sake of the kingdom of God who will not receive manifold more in this time and in the age to come eternal life." (Luke 18:30) And a final one: "The kingdom of God is not coming with signs to be observed; nor will they say 'Lor here it is' or 'There' for behold the kingdom of God is in the midst of you." (Luke 17:20–21) The kingdom of Heaven is the very essence of you, right within you.

So what does this all mean, these definitions of the kingdom of Heaven? To me it is the true abode of all that is highest in my consciousness and I want to achieve that state of being. If you do, continue reading and gain further insight on how to seek God or perfection, for beyond our personal love are more stations or churches: seeking God, Wisdom, Enlightenment.

The keys to the kingdom of Heaven are several. The kingdom of Heaven is a state of balance among our various attributes, mind, body, emotions, and spirit, and to attain this balance we have considered four already. In the fifth state of seeking, the keys are hearing, desire, commitment, will power, meditation, living an exemplary life. Let us discuss these one by one. We will find our keys as we go along the Path, but guidance from a great teacher, Jesus Christ, for the Christian is primary. Others who have great teachers of other religions may wish to follow them. It is all the same Truth!

As we go higher, we must not forget the achievements already discussed, especially love. The New Age will demand love and also total awareness of a God-centered direction to handle our life in all of the changes that will come very fast. We will need to be able to use the power of love, faith, intellect, and creative force for others and to have total love we must be One with Him.

This will give us the assurance that we can seek direction from our inner Spirit in the face of any challenge or catastrophe.

Back to our keys. The first key, it seems to me, is the *desire* for completion. Whether this comes before or after we *hear* the "knocking" is a moot point. The knocking must be heard. "Behold I stand at the door and knock; if anyone *hears* my voice and opens the door, I will come in to him and eat with him, and he with me." (Rev. 3:20) And Rev. 2:29, "He who has an ear, let him hear." When we listen, when we hear, we will then have the desire for completeness where incompleteness exists. Perhaps this is an urge that you have had from childhood; perhaps some great speaker has awakened you; perhaps the reading of a book will catch your ear; perhaps you may have a physical or psychological break; perhaps you will realize that man's laws and wisdom are not enough; perhaps unconsciously you have heard the knocking for years; that will bring you to the desire to go further in consciousness of the Divine. In any case the desire comes and then a commitment is required. The commitment is what so many lack who have heard the truth, who have the desire but allow the world to get in their way.

Commitment to the use of our personal will power until it is centered in His Will, will help us on our Path. Sometimes we are surrounded by obstacles: our daily work which takes 40–45 hours a week; our family which demands time and attention; race consciousness of "eat, drink and be merry"; the fear of being considered strange; the fear of stepping out into new territory of spiritual understanding. And we use many other excuses. There are valid reasons in everyone's life, in our personal thinking, and we should think carefully about making the commitment. Timing is very important. "For everything there is a season and a time for every matter under heaven, etc." (Ecc. 31:8) The right time will come but only if you really desire to start on the Path. You are where you should be, but to continuously stand there without doing something to fulfill the urge to open the door will eventually bring death. And once you have "put your hand to the plow" there may be no turning back.

Will power, our own personal, which of course is really God's, is needed. I have known so many people who hear the truth time after time, but who seemingly cannot put it to work in their life. "Watch and pray that you may not enter into temptation; the spirit indeed is willing but the flesh is weak." (Mark 14:38) Jesus spoke this to his apostles who slept while he was praying in the Garden of Gethsemane. Gethsemane, incidentally, is metaphysically the struggle that takes place within the consciousness when Truth is realized as the one reality. To exercise the will power that you will need requires your attention to the two greatest laws: love of God, and self and neighbor. Loving the Lord thy God means loving the Christ within, the Holy spirit within, the Allness within and throughout all creation. This love used to the highest point will give you the will to undertake this Journey or Path as the Taoists call it. Indeed you cannot avoid it forever and as you put these laws into operation your need and understanding of them will deepen.

The desire, the will when centered in Him, will bring about circumstances in your life that will allow you to seek God to the highest level. Some experiences you may tag as less than good and joyous, but remember that suffering is a must if we are to achieve our goal, for through suffering we reach into the depth of our being for surcease from pain and we go a step higher. Listening during a time of deep suffering may be impossible, but turning to others who can pray and meditate for you will help you on your way. Sometimes this desire and the exertion of your will, centered in His Will, may bring you unhappiness, but perhaps this is necessary for you to "get on with It." Be committed! Only you can take that step. The Bible, Jesus, the Holy Spirit are all great helps. Turn to the Within and listen. This brings me to my most important suggestion: Meditation. "Be still, and know that I am God." (Psalms 46:10)

Meditation, the word, is not used often in the Bible, but it is implied. This is one of the greatest teachings we can get from our Eastern brothers, as meditation has entered into their practice for hundreds, yes, thousands of years. I wonder how we could have missed it for so long. In Matthew 6:6 we read, "But when you pray, go into your room (consciousness) and shut the door (close out the world and thoughts) and pray to your Father who is in secret; and your Father who sees in *secret* will reward you." This, no doubt, refers to meditation.

Prayer has been a part of all great religions although clothed in different dress. Prayer is usually thought of as supplication. Meditation is different; it is Listening.

I feel that meditation is basic to the experience of enlightenment and give much importance to it. It has been of utmost importance in my spiritual life and in the lives of many, many others.

In the scripture of the Eastern religions we find, of course, many references to meditation. The Taoists, the Sufis, the Buddhists, the Hindus all have references to it in their Books. In the Bible we can find in Psalms 1:2 and 119 references to meditating and I am sure there are many others. In the New Testament we may consider the word prayer as the same as meditation, for we know through Jesus' example of going away from everyone into the mountains, a high state of consciousness, that meditation was a way of life for Him. When the prophet, Daniel, "had a dream and visions of his head" (Dan. 7:1) he may have been in a meditative state, in the Spirit.

Some consider meditation a dangerous practice; some say that it encourages one to turn away from outer authority and that is anarchy. Maybe the word meditation was left out of the scriptures, in translation, because the priestly class felt that it was dangerous for people to know about it and to practice it. We must depend on other scriptures for our directions on meditation.

Meditation is religious contemplation; concentration, inner direction. Prayer is extravert or outer directed for some. Perhaps prayer was thought of as meditation and Jesus' words about "going into your room" were understood this way. The scriptures have had so many changes through the years in translation and by the fiat of the church leaders that it is hard to say.

The Hindu religion went through many phases from the gods being in all of nature to the belief that man and God are One.

From the outer to the inner, their worship moved. Meditation is considered primary by the yogi who practices Raja Yoga. In the Bhagavad Gita, Krishna says, "Immerse thy mind in Me alone; concentrate on Me thy discriminative perception, and without doubt those shall dwell immortally in Me."[21] From the Upanishads: "Control the vital force. Set fire to the Self within by the practice of meditation. Be drunk with the wine of divine love. Thus shall you reach perfection. . . . Meditate on Brahman with the help of the syllable OM. Cross the fearful currents of the ocean of worldliness by means of the raft of Brahman—the sacred syllable OM."[22]

From Huston Smith's *Religions of Man* learn this about meditation in the Taoist tradition: "By cultivating 'stillness' through yogic practices paralleling if not actually deriving from India—'sitting with a blank mind,' practicing the 'dawn breath'— a few key individuals in each community could become perfect receptacles for Tao, the basic power of the universe. Thereafter, these persons would radiate a kind of healing, harmonious psychic influence over the communities in which they lived."[23]

From *The Sufis* by Idries Shah we learn: "Man is the microcosm, creation the macrocosm—the unity. All comes from One. By the joining of the power of contemplation all can be attained. This is the Work. Start with yourself, end with all. Before man, beyond man, transformation."[24]

These are just a few examples of the belief and practice of meditation in various Eastern religions. The Zen Buddhist makes it the central part of his life work toward samadhi. It is called Zazen and is the 'gateway to total liberation' and 'only through Zen sitting is the mind of man illumined.'[25]

The interest in meditation in the Western world has inevitably brought the Eastern philosophy to our attention. The Buddha reached enlightenment through austerity, will power, and concentration or meditation. He went aside three times a day for private meditation after his enlightenment.

Many books abound with complete directions on how to meditate and there are groups and individuals who will teach the art. It is an art and the final method must be found by yourself to fit your needs. It is not necessary to have a guru, a mantra that is dispensed for a price, a special method. Just sit down at the same time and in a quiet place and watch your breath. Concentrate on it. Start out by sitting for a short length of time and extend the time as your concentration ability develops. Develop habits of life that will give you a time and place to spend some time centered on God each day. He will take care of the rest.

Meditation for the explicit purpose of contacting the Christ, the Self, the Holy Spirit, God, is of primary importance if you are on the Path. For the purpose of material gain, extra-sensory perception, performing of miracles and other reasons may bring destruction, according to many who have testified. The occult, the miraculous, the out-of-this-world experience is fascinating, and Jesus performed these arts but only to teach people about the Power that was within them. To focus on these powers to the exclusion of the Spiritual is dangerous.

The gain through meditation is the finding of God, your own personal God, as well as the impersonal, for our definition of God contains both and you are well on the road to Samadhi after you have practiced it for some time. Do not be impatient. It takes us all different lengths of time to quiet the mind, to focus on the Christ within, to know His Presence through our feelings of ecstasy, love, joy and Truth.

Carl Jung writes in *Psychology and Alchemy* that the Westerner has avoided meditation because he is afraid of uncovering what is in his unconscious. To improve the whole "starts with himself" never enters his head. If he is troubled he turns to the psychoanalyst of whom he makes a god and who seldom effects a cure. The cure lies within the individual. He also suggests that the Christian viewpoint of dependence on the outer, on the church, on the atonement of Jesus Christ, on "God up there," has weakened a man or woman as it takes the focus of attention away from his/her inner self from which the true guidance must come. As a result his/her soul has not kept up with outer developments, as the outer is split from the inner. Then the person, the

Christian, is not an integrated personality, for his inner and outer thoughts, actions, and beliefs are out of balance. Attention to the inner Self, he believes, is primary if we are to become an individuated personality or an integrated whole.[26]

For our purpose and goal, meditation is a must. If you want to reach a higher consciousness of God or perfection, it is a must.

The Hindu and the Buddhist teach, also, that our *life must be exemplary,* that self analysis must go on all the time to determine what there is about our thinking, our speaking or our acting that is keeping us from our goal—and more importantly, what is clouding our consciousness, so that it can be cleared. The right use of the basic energy, faith, of our creative energy or sexual energy, of our intellect, and of love, must be practiced. We bring the development of each of these along as we go higher. Each of us must sweep our Path clean, must control the mind— the intellect or the Ox, as the Zens put it. We must find our own way.

Other ways that I have found valuable as I seek God are: dream analysis by a Jungian analyst; active imagination (a Jungian term for visualization or listening to the inner voice); studying of New Age literature; studying of the Bible; reading about the world's great religions and their religious scriptures; having times alone away from the world; being with nature as much as possible; being consciously centered on God's direction; and being in the Silence. All of these activities keep my mind centered on God.

As we gradually sink our will (our ego will, the small self) into His will, our life will become filled with joy, peace, energy, bliss, happiness, prosperity, all the Good. There will always be challenges as we clear our consciousness, but I believe that Revelation teaches that ultimate bliss is eventually reached, and in the meantime our life is more peaceful than ever.

Seeking God is a twenty-four hour a day activity and our work, our waking life, our sleeping life should reflect this. As we develop a higher consciousness it will become easier. After retirement, so the Hindus teach, full time may be allotted to seeking God. The will must be strong and concentrated on the goal.

The mystic is the supreme example of this concentration. Very few may want to get to the kingdom of Heaven, but we can add to our conscious awareness of Him whom we seek.

Jesus demonstrated and taught the multitude how they could live and demonstrate the same as he did. He taught them much about prayer. The Lord's prayer, a great affirmation of Truth, is an example. Giving the Lord's Prayer a metaphysical interpretation turns us to the inner from the outer.

And then, of course, the most of Jesus' teachings, through the Parables, dealt with the living of the Christ-directed life to attain the kingdom of Heaven. The Sermon on the Mount gives us the map for an exemplary life, also. The Buddha gave his disciples the Eightfold Path which w̶ ̶ ̶o be followed as they trod the Path to a h̶i̶g̶h̶e̶r̶ ̶

Li̶ ught, as well as being guid ̶ from our Center, is most mber to: 526-4859 ı Chapter 2, Verses 26 an

the ert̶t̶y̶a̶n̶n̶ *eps* my works until he sha 6246 Roadrunner Loop, NE, R̶ ᴐns (thoughts), and brokerone number ̶ ̶n earthen pots are

Father; ̶'̶ In other words, He is ̶essa and control over our thomber to: 382-8480 ır greatest need. This we ᴎon and continue seeking (Father will take us to the ı162 Sotol Court, Las Cruces, ᴐonsciousness!!

So as w 522-2666 reach closer to the Infinitε ght with us the other chara ̶lect, and love. Now all are ̶d Wisdom on our Path to ̶

6

WISDOM

The sixth chakra, as I have mentioned previously, symbolizes Wisdom to me. It is the next to the last stage of development of Enlightenment, and since meditation or seeking God brings Wisdom, this seems both logically and intuitively correct. The church at Sardis, Chapter 3:1-6, seems to be located at this center, the sixth.

The message to Sardis is a warning to those who have almost "made it" and who appear "to be alive but are dead." The speaker says that the work is not perfect in God's sight. He warns them to remember what has been received and heard and to hold fast and repent (of their not being fully alive). They are told to watch for "he will come like a thief in the night" and they may be surprised. Those who have not defiled their garments will be with Him and robed in white. They will be named to the Father and his angels. Again he gives the admonition to listen.

All of this seems to point to the fact that we must continue on, we must listen, we must repent, which is a reversal of mind and heart in the direction of All-Good. When we repent we break the mortal thought and ascend into the spiritual thought realm, the kingdom of God.[27] Repentance is also an admission to God of sorrow over past sin, separation from God, and a resolve to be centered in the Spirit. And repentance is necessary all along our Journey, for we are still human and divine. It is strange that we should be reminded of this all along the way, but not so strange if you have observed yourself, your ego, closely and want a closer consciousness of Him. We continue to have the need to cleanse our perception of Him in order to be at One with Him. And, of course, listening comes in again. Let us now define Wisdom.

There are many definitions in the Bible and here are some: Wisdom is understanding, is intuition, is pure knowing, is fear (awe) of the Lord, is pure mind, is intelligence, is everywhere as pure mind, is understood by God. From these definitions it can be seen that Wisdom is of God and expressed through man. From the Bhagavad Gita, "When Wisdom is thine, Arjuna, never more shalt thou be in confusion: for thou shalt see all things in thy heart, and thou shalt see thy heart in Me."[28] Wisdom, according to Jesus, was hearing the word of God and following His direction. And Jesus' teaching on Love was included in the definition of Wisdom. Wisdom for so long for the antecedents to Christianity, the Jews, had meant an intellectual, logical process. Jesus taught that it must include love and intellect, the mind and the heart as one.

Now Wisdom has been greatly misunderstood. Many people believe that seeking the Lord is the same as Wisdom, but unless we desire to be wise it will elude us. Wisdom comes to those who listen to the voice within their own consciousness. It is a part of the ascension, it is a station, it becomes the way of life for the pilgrim who is seeking nirvana, samadhi, enlightenment. The sage in the forest is sought out by many, for people know intuitively when one has wisdom. Remember Socrates and his influence on the multitude. But many individuals think they have wisdom when they may not. This is what the message is warning against.

Jesus was considered wise at age twelve when he told his parents that he had to be about his Father's business as he taught in the Temple. (Luke 2:49 King James). He knew then that the beginning of Wisdom is the understanding of our reason for being on earth—to be about our Father's business. He had many years of growing and maturing before he reached enlightenment, but he was on the way. Wise sayings come from the mouths of children, from the Christ Child within. "Let the children come to me . . . for to such belongs the kingdom of Heaven." (Matt. 19:14)

Being at One with creative intelligence is our goal and how we reach there is the inevitable question of life. And can we obtain it from those who consider themselves wise? Usually the wise ones are egoless and unaware of their Wisdom except as they hear the voice of God and act on His Intelligence. Wisdom comes from the Inner Center, and until we lose our attachment to the world and really seek God, we cannot express it. When we understand what life is about—that is the beginning of Wisdom.

From the Apocrypha, ancient books left out of the Bible, we read in the Wisdom of Solomon, Chapter 7:25,26: "For she (Wisdom) is the breath of the power of God, and a pure emanation of his almighty glory. Therefore, nothing defiled can enter into her. For she is a reflection of the everlasting light, and a spotless mirror of the activity of God, And a likeness of his goodness." And Verse 28: "For God loves nothing but the man who lives with wisdom."[29] Psalms 111:10: "The fear of the Lord is the beginning of wisdom." (fear being awe). So we turn within and listen if we are to find wisdom.

Remember the story of Solomon's dream? God came to him and asked him what he should give him. (I Kings 3:5-14) His answer was one of gratitude and humility, and he requested an understanding mind in order to be of service to the people. God answered him, "Because you have asked for a wise and discerning mind, I will give you that and also riches and honor." Solomon from that day was known as the most wise.

As we meditate we learn to listen to our Inner Voice. As we listen we learn more and more that man cannot know except he develop the power of God that is inherent. And as we listen and put more and more of His direction into our activities and thoughts we become wiser. To listen to the Holy Spirit is to Know. This takes practice as we at first know not how to discern His voice and we may mistake the small self for the Self. We believe our works are perfect, that we are living in our Center, but we are still not perfect, and if we want to go to perfection we must continue clearing our consciousness of the small self, the ego.

Many pilgrims stop here and live their lives in an aura of wisdom and understanding—being of service to mankind and that is their achievement for this life, and we need them, but if we want to reach the Ultimate we must remember what we have received and heard, and repent. Repent perhaps of our believing we are really alive, that we have arrived, but in reality we have stopped short of the goal.

In seeking God through meditation we have learned to listen, but we may still be unfulfilled, be dissatisfied if we only listen during our times of meditation. It behooves us to listen all the time, day and night, and to be guided by "him who has the seven spirits of God." This means giving up our own ego and allowing ourselves to be guided by Him. Eventually we will turn to Him for all decisions and then Wisdom is our gift. To be intellectual is not to be wise. To be intellectual and spiritual, with love as our guide, brings us Wisdom. Before we can reach the blooming of the Lotus at the seventh chakra we will practice Wisdom. Wisdom is a prerequisite to completion, for the white robe and crown are given to those who hear.

Wisdom also comes as we study the words and ideas of those who have lived before us and have been considered wise. Prov. 19:20 says, "Listen to advice and accept instruction, that you may gain wisdom for the future." And Jesus said, "the Son of man came eating and drinking, and they say, 'Behold, a glutton and a drunkard, a friend of tax collectors and sinners!' Yet wisdom is justified by her deeds." (Matt. 11:18,19) "With God are wisdom and might; he has counsel and understanding." (Job 12:13) So we have man and God. A study of the great philosophers' writings is a must, for their ideas bring us a setting for listening to the Voice within. But be careful, test them by your own intuitive understanding.

The sixth chakra is in the forehead between the eyes and is called the third eye location. According to Hindu and Buddhist teaching the Third Eye, when open, gives the aspirant the power to hear the voice of the Master or the higher Self. The gifts of clairvoyance, clairaudience, visions, awareness of great light are given. There are people in our world who seem to have these psychic gifts but are not spiritual aspirants. If their gifts are used for the materialistic needs and not for spiritual growth and understanding, they may pay a painful price in the future. The Third Eye is opened by those who use the Wisdom that God gives them as spiritual pilgrims in order to bring God's Wisdom to others. We are His mouthpiece and he needs us as much as we need Him. We are His messengers and as we center on the inner Voice, the Holy Spirit, we use this wisdom in love and intelligence for His glory.

Wisdom grows as we are aware of the special place we have in the Universe. In Wisdom we are still at a dualistic stage. By that I mean I, the ego, is listening to the Self and following His intent.

Our goal is Oneness. So we must push on to the ultimate goal of enlightenment, of the I AM.

Proverbs 4:7–9, "The beginning of Wisdom is this: Get wisdom, and whatever you get, get insight. Prize her highly and she will exalt you, she will honor you if you embrace her. She will place on your head a fair garland; she will bestow on you a beautiful crown." And Proverbs 3:13,14, "Happy is the man who finds wisdom, and the man who gets understanding, for the gain from it is better than gain from silver and its profit better than gold." And Proverbs 3:21,22, "My son, keep sound wisdom and discretion, and they will be life for your soul and adornment for your neck."

What we are really talking about is intuition. Charles Fillmore has this to say, in *The Revealing Word,* about intuition: ". . . the immediate apprehension of spiritual Truth without resort to intellectual means. The wisdom of the heart. It is very much surer in guidance than the head. When one trusts Spirit and looks to it for understanding, a certain confidence in the invisible good develops. This faith awakens the so-called sixth sense, intuition, or divine knowing. Through the power of intuition, man has direct access to all knowledge and the wisdom of God."[30]

And from the book of James: "If any of you lacks wisdom, let him ask God who gives to all men generously and without reproaching, and it will be given to him. But let him ask in faith, with no doubting, for he who doubts is like a wave of the sea that is driven and tossed by the wind. For that person must not suppose that a double-minded man, unstable in all his ways, will receive anything from the Lord." (James 1:5–8)

Also, James 3:13: "Who is wise and understanding among you? By his good life let him show his works in the meekness of wisdom." And the same chapter, verse 17: "But the wisdom from above is first pure, then peaceable, gentle, open to reason, full of mercy and good fruits, without uncertainty or insincerity." So our wisdom is based on meekness, understanding, a good life, works, purity, peace, gentleness, reasonableness, mercy, certainty, sincerity, intuition, and the results will be good fruits, fruits of the spirit. "Be ye doers of the word and not hearers only." (James 1:22)

A review of our ascension seems to be in order now since we have been brought to the seventh step, the step of spiritual completion. Our Journey has taken us from faith to creative force, to intellect, to love, to worship, to wisdom. It has taken us from the temporal body to the house of God, the regenerated Spiritual body. For wisdom, personified in Solomon who built the temple in Jerusalem and dedicated it to the eternality of Oneness of God in man, is our last stage of development.

Solomon, symbol of unity of intelligence and love, personifies a state of peace and plenty, a state of rest which surrounded Solomon and he desired to build a Temple within which would be kept the great representation of God, the pillar of Light. Only those who had cleansed their consciousness by gifts, by love, by sacrifice could experience the Inner Light, the Holy of Holies. And this was through the representatives of God, the priestly class. We are those representatives of God in the New Age.

Fillmore compares the tabernacle (the temporal body of man) to the temple (the regenerated body of man)[31] One preceded the other and we, on our Journey, are reaching for eternal existence in the Temple not made by hands. Solomon, our symbol of wisdom and peace, constructed the spiritual body, the Temple, which was a transforming of the physical to the spiritual. I do not wish to go into all the symbology of the Temple construction. (For further information about this subject read the book by Edyth Hoyt.) In any case, true wisdom is ours only when we have given up all materialism for the spiritual and then we are ready for our final state, the goal toward which all of us are tending, to become One with that Pillar of Light.

Jesus, our Wayshower, demonstrated the finding of the Pillar of Light within our own Being. We do not need the outward temple, the temple made with hands. We, in our own body and consciousness, have the temple and we will be allowed to enter the inner Holy of Holies, for we are sanctified by our sacrifices, our prayers, our listening through meditation, our repentance, our renewed mind and the Universal Love that interpenetrates All. We have all Wisdom of God and we are ready to be transformed into His Likeness. So let us experience with John, the seventh step—the ultimate which includes all the six steps that John describes in the messages to the churches. We are balanced in mind, body, heart, and soul. We are ready!

ENLIGHTENMENT

That to which we have been attending is near at hand, at least our guide is going to help us understand what the final stage is like and how we can obtain that state. You will remember that I suggested that the instruction to the seven churches would give us a map. The final stage is really not described in full until we reach chapters 21 and 22. But the map will beckon us on to our own experience.

We have come on our Journey from faith and we are ready for the final step as described by John. For some, the final stage is the reward for having opened the other six centers with Spiritual awareness. For some, the final stage is not really the final but only an experience which is fleeting and gives them a brief ecstasy which draws them on. We will see, as we continue on in Revelation, that we may catch glimpses of the kingdom of God but still have cleansing that is keeping us from total enlightenment. Since we are in the beginning instructions for our Journey, I would expect that more cleansing is required and so I have chosen the church at Laodicea as representative of the seventh chakra or seventh step.

There are those of Eastern religions who hold that there are six chakras that must be opened and when cleansed and energized, the state of enlightenment is reached. In *The Secret of the Golden Flower,* we find this explanation of the seventh chakra opening: "When the pupil keeps the crystallized spirit fixed within the cave of energy and, at the same time, lets great quietness hold sway, then out of the obscure darkness a something develops from the nothingness, that is, the Golden Flower of the great One appears."[32] And: "The thousand petalled lotus flower opens, transformed through breath-energy. Because of the crystallization of the spirit, a hundred-fold splendour shines forth."[33] The Golden Flower is the crown of Revelation.

Indians, Chinese and many others teach us to practice yoga to achieve the Golden Flower or crown. There are different types or schools of yoga, each having the same goal and the appropriate one is chosen depending upon the personality of the aspirant and his/her particular needs. "Some practice Jnana yoga or the way of knowledge; others practice Karma yoga or the way of action or works; others, Bhakti yoga or the way of service or love; and others Raja yoga the way of meditation and raising of the kundalini power."³⁴ Hatha yoga, for physical development is often combined with the others.

It is the Raja yoga that we have been speaking of although many practice one of the others and may reach unity by that method.

The angel addresses the church in Laodicea thusly: "The words of the Amen, the faithful and true witness, the beginning of God's creation. (You see we are back to the beginning of the book of Genesis.) I know your works: you are neither cold nor hot, I will spew you out of my mouth. For you say, I am rich, I have prospered, and I need nothing; not knowing that you are wretched, pitiable, poor, blind, and naked." (Rev. 3:14–17)

Since perfection is our goal we are reminded to not settle for less than that. Being lukewarm will not gain the stone that turns all to gold, metaphorically speaking. Lukewarm is rather peaceful and seems to be the nirvana state but the speaker says, "Either get on with it or get off." He suggests that the aspirant may think that he has reached the highest level of consciousness but he points out that there is still something lacking in it and according to a higher vision, "he is poor, blind, wretched, pitiable and naked." And then he says in verse 18 "Therefore I counsel you to buy from me gold refined by fire, that you may be rich, and white garments to clothe you and to keep the shame of your nakedness from being seen, and salve to anoint your eyes, that you may see." And in verse 19, "Those whom I love, I reprove and chasten, so be zealous and repent."

To study the symbolic meaning of gold refined by fire, one needs to study the teachings of the alchemists who were active during the Middle Ages. Carl Jung, the great Swiss psychologist, has written extensively about them in his book *Psychology and Alchemy,*[35] and according to the account it is believed that the façade of chemical analysis that the alchemists pretended to be doing was really symbolic language for attaining enlightenment. They had to keep it as esoteric knowledge in order to avoid punishment by the church authorities. They were really talking about spiritual growth and development and the Philosopher's stone they speak of was the Christ within that would change the dross of materiality to the gold of spiritual ascendency.

In the scripture, gold refined by fire refers to the symbolic burning away of the dross of our misunderstandings and illusions in order to obtain the gold. This brings enlightenment and then all things follow. Sometimes this is a figure of speech used to denote the need for much suffering due to our own karma. If we do not repent we will never obtain the gold.

The yogis, as mentioned previously, speak of the kundalini force as the fire that burns away the dross in the body, both the subtle and physical body, and opens up the chakras or centers of energy. Flames pictured around the Buddha and high spiritual beings denote the fire of the god Shiva, which comes to meet Shakti, the Holy Spirit or kundalini. Enlightenment is pure light surrounding the physical being and indicates perfection, thus the white robe.

Verse 20 is the famous "Behold, I stand at the door and knock and if anyone hears my voice and opens the door I will come in to him and eat with him and he with me." Let us look at this from the Western and the Eastern interpretation.

Our Western interpretation is that we symbolically feel a "knocking" when we feel the urgency to accept Jesus Christ as our personal savior. If we open to him we will be saved. This may be much the same as the yogi would say but couched in different language. He would say that the Holy Spirit which can be heard in the spinal column is knocking, or the voice is heard by the aspirant on the interior of his body. When this sound is heard and with concentration or meditation on the Light from the Third

Eye, enlightenment may be reached. This is a concentration technique that may be followed and Oneness can be achieved. Our interpretation is based on both, for Jesus Christ has saved us by his teaching and demonstration, and the way to reach a true knowledge of those teachings and demonstrations is to meditate and listen for the knock and open the door to our inner Christ consciousness.

Verses 21 and 22 give the promise of the throne that is described in the next chapter. The throne is the cranial area of the body in which resides the Shiva or male power of All Knowing, the Father or the Self. The speaker says, "I will grant him to sit with me on my throne" or the self is on the throne with the Self and Oneness is achieved.

You know, we cannot really escape the "knocking" nor can we escape the necessity of opening the door, for it is our nature to turn to our Higher Self at some time or another, sooner or later. I should like to quote part of the poem "The Hound of Heaven" by Francis Thompson.

> I fled Him, down the nights and down the days
>   I fled Him down the arches of the years;
> I fled Him, down the labyrinthine ways
>   Of my mind; and in the mist of tears
> I hid from Him, and under running laughter.
>   Up visted hopes, I sped;
>   And shot, precipitated
> Adown Titanic glooms of chasmed fears,
> From those strong Feet that followed, followed after.
> . . . .
>   Still with unhurrying chase,
>   And unperturbed pace,
>   Deliberate speed, majestic instancy,
>   Came on the following Feet,
>   And a Voice above their beat—
> "Naught shelters thee, who wilt not shelter Me."
> . . . .

> "Ah fondest, blindest, weakest,
> I am He Whom thou seekest!
> Thou dravest love from thee, who dravest Me."

And so, when the seventh chakra is opened, we can expect our final reward and we attain that for which we have been longing. Let us review some of the promises made to us in Chapters 2 and 3 when we reach this stage of Awareness:

"To him who conquers I will grant to eat of the tree of life, which is in the paradise of God." So we will be back in the Garden of Eden or a pleasant, productive state of consciousness in which are all possibilities of growth.

"Be faithful unto death, and I will give you the crown of life. He who conquers shall not be hurt by the second death."

"To him who conquers I will give some of the hidden manna, (the secret Word of God) and I will give him a white stone, with a new name written on the stone which no one knows except him who receives it."

"He who conquers and who keeps my works until the end, I will give him power over the nations, . . . and I will give him the morning star."

"Yet you have still a few names in Sardis, people who have not soiled their garments, and I will not blot his name out of the book of life; I will confess his name before my Father and before his angels."

"Because you have kept my word of patient endurance, I will keep you from the hour of trial which is coming on the whole world, to try those who dwell upon the earth. . . . He who conquers, I will make him a pillar in the temple of my God; never shall he go out of it, and I will write on him the name of my God, and the name of the city of my God, the new Jerusalem which comes down from my God out of heaven, and my own new name."

"He who conquers, I will grant him to sit with me on my throne, as I myself conquered and sat down with my Father on his throne."

Seven great promises, and I believe they will be true when I reach the final stage of enlightenment, for I know that these promises are true and from our Heavenly Father. And do you know what accompanies each of these promises? The ear, listening, goes along with them for it is by listening that we find our directions from our Inner Being, our Christ. The ear represents the receptivity of the mind, and it is the spiritual ear and not the physical, for we really only Know when we listen to our inner voice and not all of the outer voices that know answers for themselves but not necessarily for us.

We have now discussed the seven churches in terms of the seven energy centers or chakras in the physical and subtle body and the steps for the unfoldment of our awareness of the Divine. Cross references to Eastern and Western philosophy have been used. The intermingling of both make Revelation a book for all men and women, all of us, a teaching of how each of us can find our way back to the Oneness we once had which will bring us joy, ecstasy, bliss and eternal life. If you are interested, continue reading but remember there are difficult tests for those who aspire to such a high calling. The Hindu and most Eastern religionists teach this as the ultimate goal of spiritual seeking and, of course, so do the Christians, as they gain forgiveness and eternal life through the crucifixion and resurrection of Jesus Christ.

The Christian, as well as the Buddhist and the Hindu, can find much to enhance his own awareness of eternity by the study of the book of Revelation. For the Eastern religionist, the goal must be achieved by the individual through what I have touched on briefly. Perhaps we, the Westerner, and the Easterner are both right, depending on the time and the age, but the New Age seems to demand that we become One World. Should we not use both religious understandings as a focus to bring about that One World? Perhaps so. We can certainly learn from each other.

All of this has to do with evolution, evolution of the spirit, and is like the great Darwinian theory which has been so misunderstood. The natural inclination of all the natural world is a continuous reaching for perfection. Mankind gets side-tracked many times by *maya,* but the natural trend goes on. As we become free from using all our energy for food, shelter, and procreation, we will make faster strides. Change will come faster and faster and a few of mankind will reach the "Omega Point."[36] Jalalu 'd Din has his own description:

> "With Thy Sweet Soul, this soul of mine
>   Hath mixed as Water doth with Wine.
> Who can the Wine and Water part,
>   Or me and Thee when we combine?
> Thou art become my greater Self;
>   Small bounds no more can me confine.
>   Thou hast my being taken on,
>   And shall not I now take on Thine?
> Me Thou forever has affirmed,
>   That I may ever know Thee mine.
> Thy Love has pierced me through and through.
>   Its thrill and Bond and Nerve entwine.
> I rest a Flute laid on Thy lips;
>   A lute, I on Thy breast recline.
> Breathe deep in me that I may sigh;
>   Yet strike my strings, and tears shall shine."[37]

And so it is!

CHAPTER 4

A View of the Throne

Working our way through the messages to the churches or chakras is really a synopsis of the Book of Revelation. Contained in those messages are the directions interpreted by one consciousness, mine, for the attainment of the enlightened state. Each reader may find that for his/her particular needs each station or chakra would have a different characteristic. And the promises given in Chapters 2 and 3 lift our spirits as we come to Know that final freedom from materiality.

Chapter 4 gives us our first view of the throne of God, of the kingdom of Heaven, of that which is and was and evermore shall be. This will not be the last description, however. Oh, no. For throughout the rest of the book we will have other opportunities to "see" the beautiful scene that broke on John's consciousness while "in the spirit," and we, ourselves, may have our own vision which bears some resemblance to John's vision but may be quite different, as I will note in my discussion of the Mandala. And so let us continue on our Path with the goal so beautifully described in this chapter.

In John's description he leans on the Old Testament symbology which takes us back to Egyptian symbology which the Jews picked up while in exile in Egypt. Since Israel during the time of John was an Eastern nation and not, as now, more Western, the Oriental symbology also enters in. So we find Buddhist symbols also. We are all of one great Mind and it should not surprise us to find interwoven in the book of Revelation ideas from all or at least many of the world religions.

John's most holy experience had been with the Tabernacle and the Temple and thus he leaned heavily on that knowledge to describe the scene that came to him in the vision. For further information on this I refer you to the book by Edyth Hoyt, who was a pupil of Dr. Richard Moulton who wrote an interpretation of the Bible in the early 1900s. Her studies with him brought to light her book *Studies in the Apocalypse of John of Patmos,* which is an extensive interpretation.[1]

The first verse calls to John to "Come up here." The trumpet attracted his attention and the trumpet was a symbol of announcing news of the future that was extremely important. To "Come up here" metaphysically means to put attention on something that is above the material, the mundane. Higher consciousness, if you will. "I will show you what must take place in the future," is a directive to the aspirant meaning that he or she will have this experience when reaching the upper level of consciousness of the great One on the throne. John says that he was "in the spirit" which means that he was in a deep state of meditation, on another level or dimension. Thus, we should be "in the spirit" as we find our way and our goal.

The description contained in verses 2–8 will be quoted in full for your own visualization. "At once I was in the Spirit, and lo, a throne stood in heaven, with one seated on the throne! And he who sat there appeared like jasper and carnelian, and round the throne was a rainbow that looked like an emerald. Round the throne were twenty-four thrones and seated on the thrones were twenty-four elders, clad in white garments, with golden crowns upon their heads. From the throne issue flashes of lightning, and voices and peals of thunder, and before the throne burn seven torches of fire, which are the seven spirits of God; and before the throne there is as it were a sea of glass, like crystal. And round the throne, on each side of the throne, are four living creatures, full of eyes in front and behind: the first living creature like a lion, the second living creature like an ox, the third living creature with the face of a man, and the fourth living creature like a flying eagle. And the four living creatures, each of them with six wings, are full of eyes all round and within," etc.

This description, I believe, symbolizes total oneness with that which is most high. This has been painted or drawn in various ways but the most universal drawing seems to be the Mandala. A Mandala is defined as "a circle surrounded by a square with various symbols drawn to depict various religious beliefs." Carl Jung has written a great deal on the mandala. He says "In the light of historical parallels the mandala symbolizes either the divine being hitherto hidden and dormant in the body, and not extracted and revivified, or else the vessel of the room in which the transformation of man into a divine being takes place." In regard to the circle in the center, he says, "According to the Tantric idea of the lotus, it is feminine, and for readily understandable reasons. The lotus is the eternal birthplace of the gods. It corresponds to the Western rose in which the King of Glory sits, often supported by the four evangelists, who correspond to the four quarters."[2]

Jung noticed that when he himself was "in the spirit" (not his words) he was able to paint a beautiful abstract design which was round surrounded by a square. As he started working with his clients he observed the same process. Finally, he was able to understand that when his analysands dreamed of this symbol, saw it in meditation during active imagination, painted or drew it from their creative center, it symbolized unification of the conscious and unconscious, or the beginning of movement of the psyche in this direction, and the opposites in the person's thinking were becoming unified or united.

As he studied the mandala he found that it was a universal symbol depicted in much prehistorical art and in the cultures and religions of the world. A real breakthrough occurred when Richard Wilhelm sent him a copy of *The Secret of the Golden Flower,* in which was described the opening of the chakras and the accompanying figure of the flowers with the mandala depicting the Golden Flower which is revealed at the seventh chakra, the crown chakra. (Notice the Golden Flower is like a golden crown of our description.) *The Secret of the Golden Flower*[3] is a Taoist text for enlightenment. When this was experienced by the meditator it was seen as a mandala. Jung called the mandala an "archetype of psychic integration."

The mandala, a drawing or painting of one, is used by the

Buddhists as a point of concentration in meditation. The Tibetan Buddhists especially have this as a part of their religious ceremony. There are many beautiful Tibetan mandalas depicted in art forms. Many of their mandalas depict the journey of life from the outer to the inner. Other mandalas are geometric figures which bring the attention to one-pointedness. Others seem to be just an abstract design, but they all have many common elements. The Tibetan Buddhist initiate sees the mandala, which his teacher gives him, as a map of stages he must go through to reach the inner awareness, not unlike our Book of Revelation and vision of John.

John's vision indicates a throne in the center (round) and figures "round the throne," twenty-four in all, which is a multiple of four and also of eight, eight being a number that is even, and the perfect mandala has eight radiations from the center. The crystal sea is before the throne but we picture it as a sea of bliss, and on each side of the throne are the four living creatures, which brings the quaternity or the square. The six wings on each of the four creatures, brings us the number twenty-four again, which could be a part of the mandala. In the center circle or on the throne was great light, great sound, the elements with which the primitive has always described the Godhead, an archetype of our past. The Mandala is sacred and concentration on such a sight brought John nearer to the Truth.

In John's description we are told of the "throne that stood in heaven," and on the throne was an indescribable figure. "He who sat there appeared like." It was too great and holy a sight for him to be able to describe in any terms but symbolic ones. Other visionaries have had this same difficulty when attempting to describe a figure that appears to them from another dimension. The bright shining light was like lightening, like the shining of beautiful jewels, like a burning torch of seven fires "which are the seven spirits of God." The seven fires could, of course, refer to the seven chakra centers that have been opened and are designated as the "seven spirits of God," which are the angels of the seven churches. Seven torches are indicative of illumination of the aspirant.

It is interesting to note that the mandalas of different individuals will have a variety of symbols in the center, depending on their religious experience. Jung noted that those of the Jewish faith experienced the Star of David; the Buddhist often depicts a buddha, fire, a fierce image, light, harmonious landscapes, lovely colors and forms. The Christian will usually draw some symbol of Jesus or Jesus the Christ. This may be a Divine Child, a picture of Jesus, a cross, a round circle with a dot in the center. It would be interesting to study all of the great religions in terms of what is central to the teachings and what is drawn in their mandalas.

In John's description, the crystal sea immediately brings to our mind a beautiful scene which symbolizes the allness of race consciousness; the quietness of the Void that surrounds the throne, or the center, as taught by the Zen Buddhists; the all in all of the presence of the One on the Throne. All of these depict the priceless spiritual realization of the aspirant. We are all a part of the race consciousness and universal consciousness and affected by each other. Jesus taught that we are all of one brotherhood. The crystalline sea is a beautiful figure bringing to our mind the quietness and peace that surrounds our own central consciousness when we see it and feel it as a high point in our meditative state.

In the book *Studies of the Apocalypse* by Edyth Hoyt, we find this reference to the crystal sea: According to her interpretation the vision of the kingdom of Heaven that John is describing in Chapter 4 has a direct relationship to the tabernacle built by Moses, and each of the figures he uses are like those referred to in the description of the tabernacle. In fact she suggests that the tabernacle was built to help the people realize that God was in the midst of them. The crystal sea she compares to the laver in which the priests washed their hands before approaching the Holy of Holies. The laver of the Temple was very large and supported by bronze oxen and the priests had to mount up the steps to wash their hands. In so doing, they were reflected in the laver. This she compares to the crystal sea which surrounded the throne and in which was reflected the four creatures, the One on the throne, the 24 elders and the angels of illimination, and all are One in the circle of the crystal sea, circle being a symbol of Oneness.⁴ John would use that with which he was most familiar to describe the wonderful scene in his vision.

Around the throne were "four living creatures." Some translations name them beasts. We must realize that in the time when John wrote, all animals were considered beasts, so the connotation of the term has changed in our day. The four creatures symbolism goes back many thousands of years. It was found in what is considered Atlantis symbology and depicted different aspects of man, so those who have studied such matters say. In Egypt when Horus was the central symbol for God, he was surrounded by an eagle, a cow or ox, a lion, and a man. We note that the sphinx has the body of a lion, with wings of an eagle, the hooves of an ox and the face of a man, and the sacred device, the uraeus, at the third-eye place. The four evangelists have been connected with these symbols and indeed appear in many mandalas of the Middle Ages of Europe. In Chartres Cathedral we have the example with the four shown. So these four are universal symbols and if we continued our search we would probably find them a part of many civilizations in their religion and in their life.

Four is a number of completion as is seven and twelve. There are four great creative forces depicted in the Land of Mu information.⁵ (James Churchward has done extensive research all over the world, in ancient records, to prove the existence of the Land of Mu, an ancient civilization which is said to have existed. He has written a series of books on the Land of Mu. He is described as both mystic and scientist.) Quaternity has always been a symbol of wholeness throughout man's known history.

The interpretation of the meaning of the four creatures varies with the mind set of the interpreter. I prefer the following as it fits most readily with our basic assumption about the Book of Revelation, that it is a revelation to each individual for his own growth and development of spiritual consciousness.

I am grateful to Emmet Fox, the great teacher in America during the 1920s and 1930s. He says the four creatures are the four basic elements of man which we bring to the throne of grace and they become unified into One. He also connects them with the four horsemen of the Apocalypse.

We have four major elements in our make-up: the body, the mind or intellect, the emotions, and the spirit. These four must be taken into consideration any time we talk of man and his strengths or weaknesses. Western science has tried to separate them and has for many years, but now we see in the 1970s a turning to the realization that all four qualities make up man and no one is more important than the other, although we as human beings tend to concentrate on one or the other at various times in our lifetime.

The ultimate is to bring them all together around the throne of the most high in total balance, with each giving its share to the higher consciousness of man. When they are in balance they form a circle or wholeness of a sphere with the Ultimate in the center. The six wings on each symbolize the freedom each has to use the power within as the person desires. Their business is to offer homage day and night to the One on the throne, and All that is in All.

The eyes are symbols of awareness of the inner and the outer. The unconscious and the conscious affect each of these qualities, the mind, emotions, body, and spirit. And we can see both ways as human beings. Sometimes we cover our eyes or instruments of awareness and thus lose understanding of that which is within and without; especially the within. In Jung's teaching we are to bring into balance the inner and the outer, the conscious and the unconscious. This will take work, and since six symbolizes an unfinished state, it will take work (according to Elizabeth Turner in *Be Ye Transformed*) to finish our course, the Path of awareness of the Christ within.[6]

Emmet Fox has this to say about his choice of these four qualities as interpretation of the eagle, the lion, the ox, and the man: "The four beasts of Revelation are really the four horses treated in another and most interesting way. The second beast 'like a calf' represents the body and the physical plane in general and takes the place of the Pale Horse. The third beast 'had a face as a man' and represents intellect or the Black Horse. The fourth beast 'was like a flying eagle' and he represents the emotional nature, or the Red Horse. The first beast was 'like a lion' and represents the spiritual nature, or the White Horse.'''[7]

So, when we bring our four elements to the throne of Grace we will be able to see all, or be omniscient, and each of the elements will be balanced with the others for the work that needs to be done or is incomplete. For you see, enlightenment does not mean that we will sit down and strum on our golden harps. Oh no! Enlightenment is just the beginning of our responsibilities to live in the Christ and to express the Christ to all others.

Some translators have considered the four creatures the four elements that make up our known world: fire, air, earth, and water. In Corinne Heline's translation of the Bible for the New Age, she says this about the four elements: "The mystery of the four beasts conceals the workings of the four elements under the direction of the Lords of the four fixed Signs: Taurus, Scorpio, Leo and Aquarius. Taurus is the symbol of service; Scorpio of purity through regeneration; Leo, of the power of love; and Aquarius, of the new race in which these attributes are to manifest."[8] Corinne Heline was a Rosicrucian who worked directly with Max Heindel who revealed much of the esoteric teachings of the Rosicrucians to all the world. She did an entire interpretation of the Bible based on those teachings.

The adulation the four "living creatures" express in "Holy, holy, holy" . . . in verse 8, is what each individual must come to eventually as each of us brings our offerings and praise to the most High, to the One, the inner Christ, the highest consciousness of all that is.

The twenty-four thrones and elders upon the thrones bring us to the powers of each individual and the need to have them centered around the One. Twelve refers to spiritual fulfillment or completion. Charles Fillmore writes that the twelve powers of man are actually twenty-four as there is a positive and a negative, or a physical and a spiritual side to each of these powers. Notice, according to the scripture, they are closer to the inner circle than the four creatures. Perhaps this is because our powers, which are directed by our will, balance the four qualities.

The Elders so mentioned in Revelation are of the highest order, however. The Elders symbolize the intelligent powers of the spiritual Self. Their high consciousness is indicated by their white robes and the crowns of gold. Elders symbolized, in the Bible, the men who in the Jewish account were the nearest to the Holy of Holies. These men were of the highest rank. Much of this symbolism comes from the Jewish teaching as known by John. So the twenty-four Elders bow down before the throne, cast their crowns before the throne, and sing.

The twelve powers named by Fillmore as representing twelve nerve centers in the physical body are: faith, strength, judgment, love, power, imagination, understanding, will, order, zeal, renunciation or elimination, life conserver or generative function. His book *The Twelve Powers of Man*[9] is one of the most important in the Unity teaching.

So our powers of being must also give praise to Him in thanksgiving, realization of His creative actions, understanding and knowing that we of ourselves can do nothing, and that all things are created by Him. This is what the Elders' Song of Praise indicates. If we could only remember this, and act upon it, our lives would be spent in love for Him, others and ourselves. Thus, when we reach the highest state of consciousness all will praise Him and give glory and honor to Him "FOR THOU DIDST CREATE ALL THINGS, AND BY THY WILL THEY EXISTED AND WERE CREATED." We have lost our personal will in His will and we are humble.

Chapter 4 is a work of art, for it brings to our visualization a beautiful picture that contains all the high elements of the Divine as well as the physical and material. Perhaps this description has not moved you to desire to achieve this high state of awareness but the promise of understanding, peace and joy call us on as we remember the words of the spirit of Jesus in the second and third chapters. We still have some distance to go before we reach the throne in our own awareness, and the next chapters tell us about some of those challenges and rewards.

The Scroll

Chapter 5 begins, "And I saw in the right hand of him who was seated on the throne a scroll written within and on the back, sealed with seven seals: and I saw a strong angel proclaiming with a loud voice, 'Who is worthy to open the scroll and break its seals?' And no one in heaven or on earth or under the earth was able to open the scroll or to look into it.'' (Verses 1-3)

The scroll was the ancient paper or parchment that was used for recording writing. Since we are studying Revelation from the viewpoint of individual consciousness development, let us see what message this chapter has for us.

The scroll was written within and on the back and sealed with seven seals which no one in heaven or earth or under the earth was able to open or look into. This says to me that only the person who is responsible for the writing on the conscious and unconscious, the inner and outer, can open it. What is written upon the scroll is told to us in Chapter 6. But who will open the seals?

Verse 5 refers to the "Lion of the tribe of Judah, the Root of David, who has conquered so that he can open the scroll and the seven seals." It seems to me that the seven seals are those personal characteristics which prevent our knowing the Self and those that help us know our Self. These are akin to the chakra centers just discussed in Chapters 2 and 3. These are the characteristics that may prevent our opening the centers. But we need to know what it is that is preventing the opening. And our own personal Christ, the Holy Spirit within, seems to be the opener of the scroll and the seals.

Most Christian interpretation has placed Jesus Christ as the opener of the seals referring to the Lion of the tribe of Judah, the root of David. This seems to me to be a viable interpretation since Jesus Christ, in his teaching and overcoming of death, has taught us the method of reaching this high estate around the throne. But we each must do it for ourself as He teaches us how, through His words, and through His divine Presence through the Christ within each of us. The Spirit that Jesus personified is the Lion and the Root. Let us study these.

The Root of David is the Holy Spirit in my interpretation. Jesse was David's Father, which might be considered his root in our present day parlance of looking for our roots. Jesse, metaphysically, represents eternal existence, I AM. The word "Root" is capitalized, which is reserved for those words directly related to God or the Universal Energy. In Isaiah 11, we have a description of what comes from the stump of Jesse. "And the Spirit of the Lord shall rest upon him," (Verse 2) So the Holy Spirit shall be his Root, his guide, his beginning. The Holy Spirit, of course, has its roots in the I AM.

The Lion symbolizes strength, sovereignty, princely achievement. Since it is also capitalized it must refer to the Spirit that led the tribe of Judah. Judah, as described in Genesis 49, was the leader of one of the twelve tribes of Israel, and is described as a lion, the highest to be praised. The Holy Spirit fits this description of Judah, the Lion of Judah. Incidentally, Judah means "praising the Lord."

In the *Metaphysical Bible Dictionary,* Fillmore has this to say about Judah: "The tribe of Judah. . . . represents the central faculty of consciousness. It may be roughly described as the focal point of body organization. Its physical expression is the spinal cord, yet this is but the visible aspect of an invisible energy or mind substance at the very center of the man and is susceptible of the highest and/or the lowest. It is the serpent that may resist divine wisdom and crawl upon its belly in the dust of materiality, or it may be lifted up and exalted in the most high place among the faculties of man."[1] (This all fits with the belief in the kundalini power that may be used for the positive development of consciousness or the negative development of materiality or animal forces.)

So the Lion and the Lamb are One and the same, the Spirit, the Christ, the Holy Spirit within each of us.

Then we have reference to the Lamb that was slain and had "seven horns and seven eyes which are the seven spirits of God sent out into all the earth." Again I feel this is referring to the Holy Spirit within the whole earth, within all men. The Lamb was used as a sacrifice during the Jewish dispensation and was symbolic of that which took away the sins of the people. You will note that John, the recorder of Revelation, does not say the Lamb was Jesus Christ. Paul is responsible for identifying Jesus with the Paschal Lamb as he related the death of Christ to the Jewish Passover where the lamb was sacrificed. (I Cor. 5:7) He may have done this in order to influence the Jews toward Christianity. According to the Old Testament, the lamb was to be without spot or blemish and the sacrificing of it restored and redeemed man so his relationship with God was restored. We must remember that sacrificing either animals or human beings is a part of our religious heritage and goes back thousands of years, to the primitives. The Mayans, Aztecs, Aryans and others sacrificed human beings for the sins of mankind. This was a ceremony held by the priests.

Fillmore defines the Lamb of God as the "pure life and substance of Being. Jesus Christ, by His overcoming, restored to humanity the consciousness of this pure life and substance; hence He is called the Lamb of God. In Scripture the divine life is termed the Lamb of God.[2]

Again, Isaiah 11:1 and 2 reads: "There shall come forth a shoot from the stump of Jesse, and a branch shall grow out of his roots. And the Spirit of the Lord shall rest upon him, the spirit of wisdom and understanding, the spirit of counsel and might, the spirit of knowledge and the fear of the Lord." Is not this referring to Jesus Christ who is the Holy Spirit within each of us?

So, following our line of thought, let us discuss the Holy Spirit and how it opens the seals.

As previously pointed out in the interpretation of Chapters 2 and 3, there is Spirit within each of us called by various names in various religions. Holy Spirit is the whole-Spirit. It makes us whole and is symbolized by the circle, the sphere, the throne described in the last chapter. According to Jung, the Holy Spirit is the unity between God and man, created by God in his love for man. "It is total unity between God and man, the father and the son."[3] It dwells in man as the "spirit of truth" to remind him of God's teachings and can lead man to light, wisdom, understanding, counsel, knowledge, love of the Lord. The Holy Spirit is our spiritual conscience and is able to open all the seals of God to teach us what is in our conscious and unconscious mind and how to clean it out. "What? know ye not that your body is the temple of the Holy Spirit, which is in you, which you have of God, and ye are not your own." (I Cor. 6:19)

The Holy Spirit is a part of all great religions. We must be conscious of it in order to free it to do the work within us. The Hindu Pandit, Usharbundh Arya, says, ". . . in the life situation he or she must come face to face with all that lies latent within the subconscious and what flows from the superconscious."[4] It is called the kundalini. It is that fire within the body that opens the chakras and allows the divine energy to be released into our consciousness.

We have sacrificed or slain the Holy Spirit in many ways in our material existence, using this energy for our daily desires and attachments. The sacrifice or slaying brings a feeling of well being for many years until one day we allow our inner Spirit to speak. We may sacrifice our life to pain, problems and tragedy, to accumulate material possessions, to family and friends, to our country, before the Holy Spirit can find an opening to speak to us. Through dreams, through grief, through pain both physical and emotional, through doubt, dissatisfaction, unhappiness, our attention can be caught. Then It may speak to us and we are never the same. It has all power (horns) and all knowing (eyes). When we become aware of It and begin using our Holy Spirit to open the seals and raise our consciousness, then it is being sacrificed for our evolvement to a higher understanding. So we offer our small self to the Holy Spirit in order to know the Whole Spirit, to know our Self. Then we are on the Path.

And so for the purpose of this interpretation, we take the

position that it is we who have slain the Holy Spirit, the Lamb before the throne, by our misuse of It. In much of the literature on the kundalini this is repeated over and over, that we use the energy for the wrong purposes and thus do not reach the throne.

Jesus Christ is our wayshower. The Holy Spirit within Him was given full sway as He reached perfection, omniscience, omnipotence, omnipresence. Thus we can learn about ourselves and what we can do through the offices of Jesus. He said, "God is spirit, and those who worship Him must worship in spirit and truth." (John 4:24)

The singing of praise is natural when we are overjoyed and elevated by spiritual forces flowing from Him. Verse 9, "And they sang a new song, saying, 'Worthy art thou to take the scroll and to open its seals,'" ... and in verse 13, "And I heard every creature in heaven and on earth and under the earth and in the sea, and all therein, saying, 'To him who sits upon the throne and to the Lamb be blessing and honor and glory and might for ever and ever!'" The elders (those who have arrived—our twelve powers), the angels (all our divine ideas and thoughts), all the living creatures are all exultant when the Holy Spirit is found and will open the seals. "The singing of praise in Revelation is always connected with the initiates' overwhelming awareness of divine Presence," so says Elizabeth Turner.[5]

The New Song is sung by those close to the throne, who have reached this high state of enlightenment and can only be sung by them although those on earth lift up their voices later. Annalee Skarin says, "And so the song in the soul is a new song. It is a song of everlasting glory, of divine perfect love, of light and power and peace—it is truly a new song and only those can sing it who will eliminate all darkness from themselves, who will purify themselves and be cleansed from all sin, for the song is pure, celestial, divine love made perfect right within the very being of man. It sings from every cell and fiber of his being—love, adoration, praise, and exaltation."[6]

Annalee Skarin, a mystic and author, wrote and practiced the Realities. According to her editor, "soon after publishing the first edition of this remarkable book, *Ye Are Gods,* the author, Annalee Skarin, according to affidavits in our files, underwent a physical change known as 'translation,' such as did Enoch of Biblical days.''[7]

And so it is! And our worship should go out both day and night as we come to each stage of our life and His love will well up within us and we will know His Presence. Amen and Aum!

CHAPTER 6

Opening of Six Seals

So the Lamb, the Holy Spirit, God incarnate is going to open the seals and we are started on our upward path. The seven seals are stages of progress, states of being, leading us on to the Ultimate goal of Oneness. The way is not easy. We will think we have arrived, we will demand our just reward, but time will pass beyond time before the Ultimate is reached. We will despair, we will have high hopes, we will curse, we will turn our back on the Most High, but it rolls on taking us to our Omega point. Time will stand still. Progress will be made in one life then another, one moment then another, one year and then another. The cycle goes on. The way is bright, the way is dark but dark through our own thoughts, our own intellect. We try this and that. We know with an inner knowing who we truly are and only our thinking sullies this. We are in dis-ease. We are searching for Peace.

Our human nature seems to be composed of four elements or parts. How we feel—our emotions; how we think—our intellect; how we use our body—our physical world; and our Spirit, the Christ within. Each of us seems to emphasize one or another of these elements in our life experience. Or at various times in our life we put emphasis on one or another. Jung calls these functions of the personality feeling, thinking, intuition, and sensation, and when they are in balance they will bring us to our goal of individuation[1] or in our terms, Oneness.

Emmet Fox has designated the four horsemen of the Apocalypse as symbolic of these four elements and it is from him that I have taken this interpretation.[2] He designated the white horseman or the rider of the white horse, as the Spirit, "And I saw, and behold, a white horse, and its rider had a bow; and a crown

was given to him, and he went out conquering and to conquer."
The rider of the red horse he designated as the emotions, "And
out came another horse, bright red; its rider was permitted to
take peace from the earth, so that men should slay one another;
and he was given a great sword," verse 3. The horseman on the
black horse he has named the intellect, and the horseman on the
pale horse he has designated as the physical body. Verses 5 and 6
read, "And I saw, and behold, a black horse, and its rider had
a balance in his hand; and I heard what seemed to be a voice
in the midst of the four living creatures saying, 'A quart of wheat
for a denarius and three quarts of barley for a denarius; but do
not harm oil and wine!'" And verse 8, "And I saw, and behold,
a pale horse, and its rider's name was Death, and Hades followed
him; . . . "

Emmet Fox was one of the early New Thought teachers and
preached for years at Carnegie Hall in New York City as well as
all over the world. He has written *The Sermon on the Mount,*
an interpretation from the New Thought viewpoint, *The Four
Horsemen of the Apocalypse, The Zodiac and the Bible* and others.

The first seal was broken by our Inner Spirit and we saw the
white horse. The Four Horsemen are pictured in most art work
as men riding on horses. However, no translation says that man
is riding the horse. The pronoun "he" is used and "rider." This,
of course, makes the picture more real to us as we read it.
However, the rider may be a more abstract or symbolic object.
The rider may be you and me, it may be an element of our own
personality that is "in the driver's seat." And the rider wore a
crown and carried a bow.

As we awaken to the Truth, however faint, we know that our
consciousness of Spirit is symbolized by the crown. To express
through Spirit only is the Ideal, and will bring us all we desire
and we can conquer anything. We know this subliminally and
must learn it in all of our expressing so that our entire being is
pervaded by this Truth. The white horse is purity and the bow is
the conveyance for the arrow of Truth. The Spirit within each of
us and throughout the Universe will conquer and is conquering.

We have emotions though. The red horse is carrying our emotions, both negative and positive. In this case it is the negative emotion that takes away peace from the earth and we would kill one another either with the implement of death or with our thoughts. This goes on in our everyday life as well as on the immense scale of war. The sword symbolizes the "dividing the truth," judgment, Truth, penetrating Spirit. Since all is Spirit, then the emotions are spirit and may be used for advancement of our consciousness or to its detriment. Emotions that carry hate will bring hate to us, the Law of Karma. Thus our emotions must be free to express through the Spirit.

The third horse carries the symbol of logic, the balances. The symbol can also mean trade, dealing in barter, the marketplace. Since one of the qualities that we each have is reasoning ability I shall use the symbol as intellectual logic. Man prides himself on his logic! That places him higher than the animals!

Man can think and reason. We have controlled nature through intellectual means. We tend to make a god of the intellect. Great learned men handed down to us the word of God, the Law, as understood by the intellect. Books, universities, teachers have been enthroned, especially since the age of Science began. We try to find the fulfillment of our need for peace through the intellect and the education of the mind. But anyone who has tread this way has found out that it lacks the ingredients for peace.

Each of us, however, has an intellect which must be in balance with spirit, emotions and body. The intellect is developed by man, intelligence comes from God. The intellect is a tool to be used as we go on our way developing consciousness of the Is or the One. We often get off the path by use of the intellect for negative purposes. The way we use our intellect definitely affects the outcome of our lives.

The fourth seal is broken and the pale horse carrying Death followed by Hades comes into view. Death is always assumed to be as inevitable as taxes and our race consciousness dictates that we all must die. If this be true, then Hades or Hell is close behind. In studying the lives of the great saints, I think we will realize that Death can be overcome. We have a great fear of death, indeed our life is spent avoiding it. The medical world has been developed because of man's fear of pain or fear of death, that is Western man. The Eastern religions have taught that Death is not to be feared as it does not carry the idea of punishment or Hades in most of its teaching. Reincarnation and rebirth of each soul in another body give hope that the future will hold Oneness. Our Christian view has given man much fear even though Jesus Christ demonstrated that we can overcome death. Revelation written by John again carries the Christian philosophy and indeed it is true: we will die again and again until we reach Perfection.

Most of the time we think of our body as separate from our inner Self. We claim it as "my body" but when a part of it gets diseased or ill we separate it from our self and disclaim it. How correct that is. But it is a part of the Self. Our body lives and breathes with the essence of the Holy Spirit and is healed by it.

Death, riding the pale horse, can also refer to our concentration on things of this world, on materialism, money, position, honors, sexual pleasure. If given too much emphasis or attention, these may bring death to the body or the mind or both. A balance with mind, emotions, and spirit is necessary for life. We may experience Hades while in this life. Indeed, some say this *is* Hades. But we can be Whole.

The Self is never ill. The Self is all health, and if our thoughts and emotions are centered on Self the body will have the health of the Spirit. We need to love our body, each separate part. An exercise each day of bringing love thoughts to each part of the body could help keep it in balance. Our body is perfect; it is our mind that causes the tension in various parts and the energy is blocked that flows through our body causing illness. Then the body chemistry changes in order to balance the imbalance of energy. Chronic illness follows.

Norman Shealy, in his book *Ninety Days to Self-Health,*[3] points out that change first occurs in the endocrine gland centers when the body becomes ill. The endocrine centers are related to the energy centers we call chakras. He also says that imbalance in the mind, the emotions, the spiritual functions, are usually responsible for the beginning of the imbalance in the body. This substantiates the acupuncturist belief that illness is the result of blocked energy flow throughout the body. Acupuncture or Shiatsu Therapy, ancient Oriental methods of healing, are designed to relieve these blockages or imbalances of energy flow. But as a preventative measure, we should love our body, feed it in a balanced manner, keep our emotions and mind at peace, and center in the Spirit.

Someone has said, "Health is a result of what we put into our minds and into our mouths." But Jesus said, "Hear me, all of you, and understand; there is nothing outside a man which by going into him can defile him; but the things which come out of a man are what defile him." (Mark 7:14–16) So it is with mind, body, emotions, and Spirit.

The four, Spirit and mind and emotions and body, in coordinated effort makes the whole individuated person. Each out of balance can disrupt the functioning of the others. The Spirit, on the white horse, however, "had a bow; and a crown was given to him and he went conquering and to conquer," verse 2, and the power is really *there*.

The opening of the fifth seal is another lesson for the individual as he finds his Path to Unity. The vision places a large number of entities at the altar begging God for revenge on those who have persecuted them. There is much learning in this for us.

The opening verse states that these souls have been slain for the word of God (the Aum or Amen) and the witness they had borne. This seems to hold several ideas for us. Many times we must suffer and not understand why, and why we have lost our Peace. We believe that we have done all that is necessary and that we should be rewarded. We are following our high Self, the Aum, the Holy Spirit; we have let go of much of the world but still are not able to find that total Peace and we cry with a loud voice, "When, oh, when will I be released? I have been mistreated. When will I be revenged for what my enemies have done to me?"

"Wisdom" can often be misinterpreted. As we turn to our Intelligence we may allow our ego to do some interpreting and we blame others for the mistakes, the sufferings that come to us. We are perfectly honest, we think, and cannot see our error. We are angry with others, we cannot look within to our own responsibility for the dis-ease. This misinterpretation, this error, must be corrected while we live our earthly life if we are to go higher. We cannot reach the Ultimate until we have let go of ego, quit projecting our shadow onto others and accept our own responsibility for gaining the crown, the ultimate reward. And self-pity, directed by the ego, can remove our Peace. When our consciousness is puritied, self-pity will cease.

The answer to these souls who cried came gently but firmly. Love sparkles in every word. "Each was given a white robe and told to rest a little longer until the number of their fellow servants and their brethren should be complete," verse 11. Each was given attention and a reward, a white robe, which is near to the final reward of the crown. They should rest and wait for the other inadequacies to be "killed" and perfection reached so that they could join them. The sacrifices of earthly attachments is not complete and they must wait and learn that more cleansing needs to be done.

Each of us must cleanse from our consciousness the self that dictates to the Self what our reward should be. Humility is a primary requisite to reach wholeness. As we go up the ladder of consciousness, we may decide we are due our reward, but only our inner consciousness knows when that time will be.

In like manner we must let go of hate and revenge motives against those faculties in each of us which are not perfect. We have to love and let go of the grievance we have against ourselves and others whom we blame for our condition. We have more overcoming before our final leap.

Love and understanding must mix to bring us wisdom and only the Holy Spirit can know when our final reward will come.

Verses 12–16 give us the account of the opening of the sixth seal. The important figure when it is opened is the "fig tree that drops its winter fruit when shaken by a gale" or as the King James version reads "and the stars of heaven fell unto the earth, even as a fig tree casteth her untimely figs, when she is shaken of a mighty wind,'' verse 13.

The stars of heaven refer to the seven stars or the seven spirits of God and I have designated as the seven chakras. The Holy Spirit which contains these seven stars fell to earth or were used for earthly purposes, or human purposes. The fig is a phallic symbol referring to the sexual organ. ''She'' is the pronoun used to indicate the kundalini. The mighty wind is the spirit, the *nous*, the All Knowing. So what do we have?

The opening of the sixth seal shows the aspirant what the results are if the Power is deflected to the use of sexual needs. There are those who discover the kundalini and use it for psychic purposes and selfish aims. It may be developed through the various chakras but peace and ecstasy and a sense of Oneness eludes them. They are misusing the energy for sexual or earthly gratification. The results are:

''A great earthquake, the sun became black, the moon became blood, the heaven departed, and every mountain and island were moved.'' In other words, the world caved in. The usual interpretation gives us a picture of what will happen to the outer world, a Cataclysm. But we know that this refers to the individual consciousness. Even if the Energy has not been misused, this same feeling may occur. It is called ''The Dark Night of the Soul'' by the mystics. It is a natural reaction to all the positive steps we have taken and we must overcome this if we are to finish our Course. The opening of the six seals seems to have brought us chaos!

The Dark Night may come as psychological depression, as physical illness, as loss of those that are near and dear to us, as guilt over the misuse of the Power, as a period of chaos in our thinking processes, as extreme physical and psychological pain, as complete negativity in our thinking, as non-production in the creative sense, as a falling apart of our world. But we know that we still have some overcoming in order to be given the crown, and all is Good. We have come up higher if this happens to us and we should look at it as a period of transition. We sometimes go lower to come up higher. Fillmore calls this chemicalization. So what can we do?

We can surrender! "Oh, no," the mind worshiper will say, "If I surrender I will go down in utter defeat." "I'll hide from the face of him that sitteth upon the throne and from the wrath of the Lamb." And also they might say, "For the great day of his wrath is come; and who shall be able to stand?" The pain is unbearable. But it isn't. Remember Jesus and Buddha and ask them for help, or some other teacher or Master. And He is always there and if you cannot reach out to Him in prayer and meditation, then turn to thy neighbor and ask him to help.

If you need professional help to understand what is in your unconscious, hidden from you, that may be blocking your progress, find a Jungian analyst, or a Holistic doctor. But better yet is to work it through by yourself, believing all the time that Good will come again. Know that Love is in the world and in you. Look to yourself and your behavior, your works. Have you misused the Power for selfish pleasure? Have you misused the Power for selfish gain? How is your spiritual pride? If it is alive, then that may be your problem. Maybe you are attached to some person or some thing. Ultimately we have to give up all in order to make Unity with our Father.

The rich, the powerful, the military man or woman, every slave, every freeman, are affected by the "Dark Night." Many go down to defeat and will rise in another lifetime to start on the Path where they got off. But if you believe that you are not given "more temptation than you can bear" (I Cor. 10:13) you will rise up, grow in understanding and wisdom and overcome this interference with your progress. But do not turn away from the challenge and bury it in your unconscious. Look at it. See and hear! And be aware of your own responsibility.

In a book by Grace Faus, *The Eternal Truth in a Changing World,* we read: "Yes it is by overcoming the little difficulties that we make our lives big. The first thing we must do is to recognize that nothing can come into our lives unless we draw or attract it. . . . It is a matter of a change of consciousness that brings about a new luster and a new beauty in life. After the sand, comes the pearl."[4]

So what is being said is that we must suffer, surrender to His will, accept our responsibility for the defeats, lose much of what is *maya,* and realize this is an "intervening period of chaos between an old state of equilibrium and the establishment of a new state of balance. It is for them (the mystics) the gateway to a lighter state."[5] (Thus says Evelyn Underhill, the writer of the classic, *Mysticism,* which recounts the experiences of many mystics. It was first published in the early twentieth century and has affected religious understandings worldwide.) And so we rise above it to continue on the Way. Remember even after Enlightenment or Illumination we have much experience on this earthly plane to reach the Unitive Life.

Six seals have now been opened in our account. The mind, body, emotions and spirit are pictured as either attacking or conquering. Achievement of harmony and peace will come with balance. Our spiritual pride, our ego, must be cleansed a little more, and depression (The Dark Night of the Soul) is difficult to understand, and the destruction that it brings is almost overwhelming. But there is still faith and still our inner Christ, the Holy Spirit, and all these negatives will be overcome for we remember the promise: "To him who conquers I will grant to eat of the tree of life which is in the Paradise of God." And so it is!

CHAPTER 7

Those Around the Throne

The Book of Revelation seems to be very repetitive and we may think, "Oh, I have read that before" or "I understand that already." Do not forget that great teachers, Jesus for instance, repeat and repeat a particular truth in order to give us additional opportunities to learn the depth of the knowledge that may be strange and unacceptable at first hearing, but will gain strength and clarity if repeated. Then, perhaps, the "big bang" will occur and we will exclaim, "Oh, Yes. Now I understand!!" The Path to Total Consciousness bobs up and down like a hot air balloon, but it goes higher and higher and finally goes out of physical sight. This is it—we are in the up and down stage now. Later—out of sight!!

After we have gone through the great tribulation, we are given a view of those who have succeeded, of those who bow down before the throne and sing praises to Him and the Lamb on the throne.

The aspirant is standing aside and observing this and "the four angels held back the wind from the four corners of the earth so none might blow on earth or sea or against any tree." Wind symbolizes the Spirit that moves across the "face of the waters." This feeling of nothing happening, a plateau of spiritual development, happens many times as we ascend and especially after a particularly difficult time in our lives. It is as if we have to gather our forces again.

Verse 2, "Then I saw another angel ascend from the rising of the sun, with the seal of the living God, and he called with a loud voice to the four angels who had been given power to harm earth and sea, saying, "Do not harm the earth or the sea or the trees, till we have sealed the servants of our God upon their foreheads." The angel from the East comes from the Ultimate Reality to seal those who are servants of God on the forehead. If we follow the analogy of the raising of the kundalini we, the servants of God, receive the seal on the forehead which indicates that we are closer to total awakening and this seal has been depicted as the Third Eye. Yogananda equates the Third Eye with total centeredness of the consciousness on God. East refers to Spirit. The Third Eye is Christ Consciousness.

The Third Eye has been depicted in much esoteric art and written about in the world literature for thousands of years. The Egyptians showed a Uraeus, which represents spirit, eternal fire, in the center of the forehead of the Sphinx and on the drawings they made of highly evolved people.[1] The Hindus speak of the Third Eye. The Third Eye is mentioned in Matthew 6:22, "If therefore thine eye be single, the whole body shall be full of light."

According to Paramahansa Yogananda, the spiritual force is in the *medulla oblongata* at the base of the skull and is connected with the center of the forehead which, when that point is activated, causes the aspirant to become all seeing, all knowing, all powerful. He describes it as a luminous sun, with a dark round spot inside it and a star inside the dark spot that can be seen when consciousness is concentrated on the Third Eye location.[2] Also, "During deep meditation, the single or spiritual eye becomes visible within the central part of the forehead. This omniscient eye is variously referred to in scriptures as the third eye, star of the East, inner eye, dove descending from heaven, eye of Shiva, eye of intuition, etc.[3] (This reminds me of the figures drawn in the center of various mandalas.)

The Third Eye, when opened, indicates that the pituitary and pineal glands have joined forces. Activity in the seventh chakra contributes to the activity of the Third Eye. However, the Third Eye, like the spiritual body, is not a definite organ of sight and may extend as an aura around the entire head. This is depicted in the large golden halo around the heads of the Buddha statues.

When the Third Eye is opened we can receive intuitive and

instinctive messages from the Self, from God, and it is a focal point for directing impulses from the Oversoul into the level of normal consciousness. Through it healing may occur as well as insights and understandings from planes of life that we are not usually conscious of.

The methods of opening the Third Eye vary with the religious teaching. It has been an esoteric teaching for thousands of years and was used by soothsayers and sorcerers, who were incidentally condemned as in Revelation 21:8 and will not enter the kingdom of God. A soothsayer or sorcerer works completely from the psychic world and does not center in the Spiritual and so is out of balance. Again when the consciousness is centered in the Christ, the use will be spiritually impregnated. Generally meditation, centeredness on the Third Eye location, and opening the mind channel to receive will help to activate it. All of this, of course, is an indication of the movement of the kundalini or Holy Spirit which comes to that location and activates the two glands. Intuition and wisdom then become part of our KNOWING.

In any case, the seal of God is going to be given to those who have achieved some measure of enlightenment.

The twelve tribes of Israel before the throne has been described symbolically as the wheel of the Zodiac in astrology. Reference is made to the positioning of the twelve tribes in the encampment of the wilderness during the exodus of the Jews from Egypt. The twelve tribes were chosen of God and were placed at twelve positions. Some interpret the twelve tribes as twelve characteristics of the aspirant, as did Charles Fillmore.[4] The twelve powers of man, he says, must bow down before the Divine in order to reach completion. (See chapter 4)

Verse 4, "And I heard the number of the sealed, a hundred and forty-four thousand sealed, out of every tribe of the sons of Israel, twelve thousand sealed out of . . ." and all the tribes are named.

According to Corinne Heline, the twelve tribes of Israel represent the entire human race who came under the influence of the twelve zodiacal creative Hierarchies. The added digits of the number 144,000 give nine, which signifies mystically that portion of the human race found worthy to receive the spiritual illumination known as the nine Lesser Mysteries. The 144,000 are the elect of the pioneers of the New Age.[5]

The number 144,000 has been made very significant by those who are interested in numerology, since twelve, symbolizing completion is the base number of 144,000. Another way of interpreting it is to realize that zero is symbolic of infinity. So 144,000 could be an infinite number reaching completion. Whatever the meaning, we must realize that John chose the twelve tribes of Israel as being of a high state of spirituality. They are also mentioned in the 21st chapter of Revelation as having the names of the 12 tribes inscribed on the twelve gates that open into the City of God. Israel, according to Fillmore, symbolizes spiritual consciousness, the thoughts that have been wrought in Truth and righteousness.[6] 12,000 of each of the tribes of Judah, Reuben, Gad, Asher, Naphtali, Manasseh, Simeon, Levi, Issachar, Zebulun, Joseph, and Benjamin, all offspring of Israel, spiritual consciousness.

There were people from "every nation, from all tribes and people and tongues, standing before the Lamb clothed in white robes with palm branches in their hands." (Verse 9)

Down through the ages the religionists, especially the Christians, have tended to teach that only those of their faith and doctrine would inherit the kingdom. This has given them great missionary zeal. It seems to me that this verse should be studied by them to open up their tolerance and love for people of every persuasion as being chosen of God. Revelation was written for *all* of mankind and the people before the throne makes us realize that this climb to perfection has been going on many, many centuries—an eon of time. The angels, the four creatures, and the elders were around the throne.

They were before the throne and before the Lamb. Again the Lamb indicates Jesus Christ consciousness that has come home to the Throne. The Comforter, the Holy Spirit, is with the Father. If one reads the history of the great religions, the primitive religions, the ancient religions, he will find the theme of God, man, and the Holy Spirit running through them as gold thread through a tapestry. The names may be different but the theme is the same. The tapestry of man pictures many conditions and climes but the same precious gold thread of obeisance to the inner power, the inner spirit, runs through all. And the eventual condition is Oneness in God. Symbols in the outer were originated by those who had the inner experience of enlightenment to indicate to the worshipper the truth of Universal Power. Many of these symbols were then worshipped by the multitude and the original intent was lost. The priesthood has often known the Truth. But we are all of the priesthood now, and as the Silent Revolution goes on we will KNOW this.

The paeans of praise that fall involuntarily from all those around the Throne is natural. As one gets closer to the Perfection he/she can only shout, laugh, dance, sing, and experience the great ecstacy of being so close to Allness.

Angels symbolize, according to the Taoist, spiritual beings; to the Buddhist the angels are Boddisattvas (an arm of the Buddha representing oneness and manyness) and are seen in visions during Zazen, meditation. The Suffi recognized them also:

> Lord, is this sweet scent coming from the meadow of the soul or is it a breeze wafting from beyond the world?
>
> Lord, from what homeland does this water of life bubble up? Lord, from what place comes this light of the attributes?
>
> Amazing! Does this clamour arise from the troop of the angels? Amazing! Does this laughter come from the houris of paradise?
>
> What concert is it, that the soul spins around dancing? What whistle is it, that the heart is coming flapping wings?
>
> What a marriage feast it is! What a wedding![7]

The dictionary definition describes them as one class of spiritual beings. Fillmore says they are divine ideas, spiritual ideas, guardian thoughts, intentions which dwell in the presence of the Father. Each of these definitions has some merit. The Christian artist has often painted them surrounding the highly evolved man or woman. We are all drawn to the angelic figure knowing intuitively that this same loveliness, simplicity, innocence lies within each of us, and besides they have wings and can fly and man has always wanted to fly!

Verse 11 reads "And all the angels stood round the throne and round the elders and the four living creatures, and they fell on their faces before the throne and worshipped God." I should like to choose "spiritual thoughts" or "intuition" as the interpretation of the symbol of angels. When we are before the throne of God and centered in the Holy Spirit, our thoughts become intuitive and able to touch the very essence of Truth and our thoughts worship God with "our face to the ground" with our mind centered on Him at all times. We move in and by Him and thus turn within, and with our faces down. I should like to call your attention to the worshipping position of the Muslims, the Hindus, the Buddhists, the Christians in prayer, and others all showing obeisance to Him on the Throne by pointing their thoughts to the One and shutting out all else from their awareness.

And verse 12 gives us an affirmation that we should repeat at all times, day after day: "Blessing and glory and wisdom and thanksgiving and honor and power and might unto our God forever and ever. Amen" (or "Aum"). Seven worshipping thoughts.

These are seven, our magic number of completion. To worship our God in meditation by taking one of these words into the Silence for a period of time will bring us closer to Oneness and will bring ecstacy and bliss to us. One might also make up his own list and dwell upon each word of praise for a long period, for instance a year, while invoking the presence of the Most High. Love, Peace, Selflessness, any positive attribute would be valuable.

Verses 13 and 14 give us more clues as to who are these, clothed in white robes, and whence they have come. "These are they who have come out of the great tribulation, they have washed

their robes and made them white, in the blood of the Lamb.''
As mentioned elsewhere, the Lamb was used as a sacrifice to
satisfy the gods, and the figures of speech refer to that. The
sacrifice of the Lamb is our using the Holy Spirit either to bring
us more worldly pleasures or to raise our consciousness to God.
Blood is turned into semen and milk. The propagating energy of
woman comes from blood. Blood is energy.

As we are washed in the energy of the Holy Spirit we reach
higher and higher consciousness. Being washed in the blood of the
Lamb could only mean being washed by the energy of the Holy
Spirit as we live on earth in a body of blood. The Lamb could
of course be symbolic of Jesus Christ who lived and was resurrected from the dead so that we might know the secret of the
ages, how to attain Oneness. But our life on earth is washed
in blood and this experience, life after life, may be gone through
in order to reach Perfection. But remember, Perfection can be
reached in this life, if we follow Jesus' teachings.

And a further description of those around the throne is given
in verses 15-17. Serve him day and night within his temple; he
who sits upon the throne will shelter them with his presence;
no more hunger nor thirst; they shall be shaded from the sun or
scorching heat; the Lamb will be their shepherd; he will guide
them to springs of living water; God will wipe away every tear.
What a wonderful description of Love of God that comes to us
when we are admitted to the vision of the throne. Can you imagine
what a beautiful state of consciousness we would have. Our
reward will be protection and shelter from all the fears, griefs,
negative forces in the earth plane. We will hunger and thirst no
more—our material needs, as well as our spiritual will be cared
for. This seems to bear testimony to Jesus' words: "Seek first
his kingdom and his righteousness, and all these things shall be
yours as well.'' (Matt. 6:33).

"The Lamb in the midst of the throne will be their shepherd"
etc. All of our psychological and spiritual needs will be taken
care of. What love sounds through these verses. The kingdom of
Heaven has come! The Holy Spirit, the Lamb, will be our

shepherd. Jesus referred to himself many times as the shepherd who cares for the lambs, a very appropriate simile in a sheep-raising culture as He spoke as simply as possible in order to be understood by the common man. The shepherd is aware of all the needs of the flock and cares for them. Our shepherd is the Holy Spirit within the temple of God, our body, our consciousness. Bow down before Him! And no tears. Thank you, Father.

Living water was a term used by Jesus many times. In John 4, we have an account of Jesus at the well with the Samaritan woman, discussing there the living water as Truth that will take away thirst and "the water that I shall give him will become in him a spring of water welling up to eternal life." (John 4:10–14) This it seems to me refers to his baptizing with the Holy Spirit to activate the Holy Spirit within to give eternal life. Gurus do this also.

The above description of the state of those who are around the throne is what we have fondly called Heaven and have placed far away in the sky where we shall go some day when we live the right moral life, worship God as our own religion dictates, tolerate all the unhappiness and ills of the world, and support the teachings and the needs of the leaders of our religion. I suggest that we should wait less and expect more NOW. The kingdom of Heaven is on earth, is in your consciousness, can be reached in this lifetime—indeed will be reached some time, some place, as we raise our consciousness to Him on the throne. But we do not have to wait until we die. We can touch, we can be that Kingdom of God. The choice is ours here and now.

The vision of the throne and all the beings around it is a vision of our own consciousness and what lies within each of us. Jesus said "the Kingdom of Heaven is like a mustard seed," etc. (Luke 13:18). The Kingdom of Heaven is like leaven to raise bread (Luke 13:20). He gives a promise of "you may eat and drink at my table in my kingdom, and sit on thrones judging the twelve tribes of Israel" in Luke 22:28. In John 3:3, he speaks of being born anew to enter the Kingdom of Heaven. John 3:5 says "You must be born of the spirit and the water to enter the Kingdom of Heaven."

We must be born of the water, have an earthly birth, and then be born of the spirit in new consciousness of the Holy Spirit.

Jesus says, in Matthew 7:13, "to enter through the narrow gate, few will seek to enter and will not be able." Luke 12:32–34 gives us directions "Sell your possessions (do not be attached) and give alms (give to Him on the throne), provide yourselves with purses that do not grow old, with a treasure in heaven that does not fail, where no thief approaches or no moth destroys. For where your treasure is, there will your heart be also."

Jesus' life and teachings tell us how to inherit the Kingdom of Heaven, the method will be of your own choosing, but *choose,* being neither hot nor cold, but be one of the chosen around the throne.

We have almost made it, it would seem, although the seal has not been placed or the crown given. This view of the throne and what to expect when we join the 144,000 will lead us on as we go through our cleansings. The promise, we know intuitively, is true and this will be our inheritance, the throne and all its glory. Amen.

CHAPTER 8

Seventh Angel, Burning Dross

> Silence is the sweetest music
> In our raucous world
> Silence fills with love and wisdom
> These cannot be told
> Silence comes from God the Father
> He in silent ways
> Makes grass grow, roses bloom
> And joy within to stay.

The first verse of the eighth chapter should be included with chapter seven as it is an account of the happenings when the seventh seal was opened. When the other six were opened there was great activity: singing, praising, action of a great multitude, use of intellect, words, eyes, feelings. But when the seventh seal was opened we have silence. "When the Lamb opened the seventh seal, there was silence in heaven for about half an hour." (Verse 1)

Silence is the activity of the Lord and is beyond our physical hearing ability. The voice of the dolphin is sounded at a higher decibel than the human ear can hear. There are many sounds beyond the human range of awareness but so far as we are concerned there is silence. And in the silence is where great thoughts, ideas, teachings begin, where creativity, wisdom, love, intelligence combine. We have forgotten the goldness of silence, the need for it physically, mentally, and spiritually. It is the sound of one hand clapping, a koan of the Zen Buddhists.

The high point or lowest depth of meditation is complete silence. "For God alone my soul waits in silence; from him comes my salvation." (Psalms 62:1) Isaiah 47:5, "Sit in silence, and go into darkness." And Habakkuh 2:20, "But the Lord is in his holy temple. Let all the earth keep silence before him." Only in the silence can we really be at One with Him.

The high point of meditation is closing out the world awareness through concentration on Him. Concentration on the Aum, the divine vibration humming within our body; concentration on the light that flows from the Third eye position or is all around and through us; concentration on God. All of these, and others, bring us to the point of silence. When we are experiencing ecstasy we are not silent, for we are responding emotionally. We are cut off in our awareness at that moment when all is silent. Being silent is the act of Being, the Isness of Him, the Void. Silence is gold and gold is the purity we are seeking.

Enlightenment, Nirvana, Samadhi are each a state of silence. He is silent and our touch with Him is silent. Seek the silence. Let go of the noisy world for all is in the Silence. Quiet or silence, according to Evelyn Underhill, is but the outward silence essential to inward work.[1] Quiet, according to St. Teresa, is a form of supernatural contemplation and the final step of quietness brings in Perfect Love, that which has been our goal throughout our search, our longing, our finding.[2]

The Bhagavad Gita, chapter 4, verse 18 defines silence: "The man who in his work finds silence, and who sees that silence is work, this man in truth sees the Light and in all his works finds peace."[3] So the Silence is active in Work which brings Light. From the Tao-Te-Ching, number 16: "Attain complete vacuity. Maintain steadfast quietude."[4]

The seven angels before the throne are now given seven trumpets which will bring seven messages of truth to the earth. Before this happens, however, there is a worshipping before the golden altar by an angel. Verses 2–5: "Then I saw the seven angels who stand before God, and seven trumpets were given to them. And another angel came and stood at the altar with a golden censer; and he was given much incense to mingle with the prayers of all the saints upon the golden altar before the throne; and the smoke of the incense rose with the prayers of the saints from the hand of the angel before God. Then the angel took the censer and filled it with fire from the altar and threw it on the earth; and there were peals of thunder, voices, flashes of lightning and an earthquake.''

The worship is reminiscent of the ceremony performed by the Hindus and others in the temple as a worship of the Holy Fire which brings to mankind life, both spiritual and physical. Man lived for eons without the use of fire, but it was an evolutionary advancement when fire was used for the comfort and feeding of human beings. So fire worship was a part of the primitive worship and still holds great charm for us as we gaze into the flames of a campfire or fireplace. Great terror too as fire can destroy. It also purifies and gives life.

According to Jung, fire in ancient times was an attribute of the Deity and signifies life.[5] The alchemists saw fire as an archetype and related to Pneuma which is the Christ.[6] So the ancients used fire as a sacrifice and as a symbol for God.

Incense needs fire to burn it and incense burning has long been a worship ceremony by many people of many lands. The tabernacle and the temple had the incense altar. The incense smoke carries to the heavenly throne the prayers of the people, and incense in its loveliness of odor and the spiritual quality of the smoke rising from it gives an aura of love and Otherworldness. It is used in most of the Eastern religious worship as well as in the Roman and Greek orthodox churches. It is an archetype going back through the ages.

''Then the angel filled the censer with fire and threw it to earth and there were peals of thunder, voices, flashes of lightning, and an earthquake.'' (Verse 5)

Fire is a symbol of soul, life, attribute of the Deity, esoteric Christ, Holy Spirit, serpent energy. The serpent fire is so called because of the intense heat that is generated at the base of the spine and throughout the body when the serpent energy or kundalini is aroused. The serpent has had a connotation of the negative since we have studied the serpent in the Garden of Eden in Genesis, but the serpent energy can both rise in the spine and take us to Oneness with all joy and light or it can be reversed and become our enigma, our Achilles heel as we spill it in earthly activities, in sexual promiscuity, in attachment to the material.

So the fire from heaven is that Holy Spirit and when our earth bodies become aware of it our whole being is changed and it is like a great storm, voices from another world, our whole world is shaken up and we seem helpless before the earthquake. We search for words to describe the experience and can only come up with those that are given in the text which are earth-related and in the experience of everyone.

The history of mankind contains the positive as well as the negative. It is a bloody account of destruction, killings, wars, hate, floods, evil rampant in our world. It is an account of the evolvement of mankind toward the Good. We still have this going on. It is in the collective unconscious. According to June Singer, a Jungian analyst, the collective unconscious is an extension of the personal unconscious to a wider base and encompasses contents held in common by the family, society, group, nation, race and all of humanity.[7] It is a part of our inheritance. It is that which we must rise above in memory, in personal activity, and be aware of.

Our race consciousness, or unconscious, can pull us down more quickly than anything. In its negative sense it is continuously battling the positive aspects of our consciousness. We are barraged by it if we pay attention to the media, TV and radio; to reading the newspapers and magazines; to listening to sermons of the fundamentalist Christian minister who preaches fear and develops guilt within his hearers; to personal conversations with others; to our educational system which breeds the negative aspects of our thinking by the development of the intellect without the balancing effect of love and faith and spiritual aspects. All of these are preventing us from rising to the Oneness but are good for they are a part of our challenges which we can overcome in order to advance spiritually. Our living on earth is necessary and when we can turn all of these negative aspects of race consciousness to the positive we have made long strides back. Let us consider what we have done with fire, for we are all in it having lived many times on this earth and been a part of the history.

Fire through war has destroyed human beings, trees, green grass, man's achievements in building cities, and has destroyed the earth. Need I remind you of Vietnam? Certainly hail and fire mixed with blood was part of that. How about America's use of the atomic bomb on Japan? Was that not a mountain of fire that destroyed people? And man's continued experimenting with the bomb by testing it in the ocean, and deep within the earth, has done untold damage. Destroying of our fresh, clean water goes on all the time and has for generations. The environmentalist movement has been warning us for years that we are turning our streams to bitterness.

The account gives us the impression that some outside force is giving mankind all of these disasters. They are called, in everyday parlance, natural disasters or an act of God. If we read the passage carefully we will see that the fire was blessed by the saints around the altar of God and was holy. So this fire is holy. It is not what God has done with it but what we, mankind, have done with it. It has been used for much advancement on this planet and has released man from much drudgery. Now is the time to make a holy use of fire, the serpent fire. Let us see how it can be used in a holy way.

The fire, the kundalini power, the Holy Spirit is misused and then we may have emotional or physical illnesses. These illnesses can bring about a cleansing, a spiritual cleansing if we understand them as being for that purpose. Many people who report high spiritual experiences with the kundalini power or Holy Spirit, report a spiritual cleansing accompanied by experiences like thunders, lightning, voices and a feeling of an earthquake as they seem caught up in something they cannot control. Usually, however, if these experiences are intense the aspirant has not conditioned his body, mind and spirit around the throne of God and used the fire power in a holy way. The exercise of Yoga with meditation will bring these experiences to many. The angels of the seven trumpets are ready to announce the earthly aspects and our challenges.

Verses 7–9 read: "The first angel blew his trumpet, and there followed hail and fire, mixed with blood, which fell on the earth; and a third of the earth was burnt up, and a third of the trees were burnt up, and all green grass was burnt up. The second angel blew his trumpet, and something like a great mountain, burning with fire, was thrown into the sea; and a third of the sea became blood, a third of the living creatures in the sea died, and a third of the ships were destroyed."

If earth is taken symbolically as the conscious mind and the sea as the unconscious mind reference to both is a description of what may happen to the individual when the fire power is misused. There is much destruction both physically and emotionally. The conscious, the earth part of our consciousness, gets too heavy and the destruction is necessary in order to grow in consciousness of the Divine. This is also true of the unconscious in which we have stored away those memories and beliefs that bring us separation from the Spirit.

When we read these passages we are reminded of our own life and the seeming destruction that occurred when we were maturing and growing in our awareness of the Christ. Later, we knew that the fire that burned out the dross was a blessing. As we cleanse our conscious mind and our unconscious we are coming closer and however painful it is, sacrifice must be made if we are to advance. The sacrifice may occur in the body or the material side of our life; in the emotional by perhaps losing someone we have loved deeply with a personal love and which must be transferred to a spiritual love; in the mind, through giving up our negative thinking and worship of the intellectual side of our nature; or sacrificing our old concept of the Spiritual. All of these will bring pain but it is worth it for suffering brings "feet of burnished bronze or refined gold," understanding that comes through trial by fire. The Crucifixion is real for each of us but the Resurrection and Ascension are also possible.

Then the "third angel blew his trumpet, and a great star fell from heaven, blazing like a torch, and it fell on a third of the rivers and on the fountains of water. The name of the star is Wormwood. A third of the waters became wormwood, and many men died of the water, because it was made bitter.'' (Verses 10,11.)

Water is symbolic of the unconscious containing, as I have said, memories of the Spirit and of the man's life on earth. Some of this unconscious needs to be destroyed by revelation through dreams, visions, meditation. The star is a symbol of divine intervention and He is a part of our own unconscious, and the race or collective unconscious. Dying to the negative in our unconscious cleanses us for our next step in evolution to our Goal. The star, being named Wormwood, is our perception of the divine intervention and the third of the waters becoming bitter refers to our thinking about our experience in a negative way.

Edyth Hoyt in her interpretation of this section suggests that Wormwood is ''counterfeit thought'' and refers us to several passages in the Old Testament that define Wormwood as bitter. Jeremiah 9:13–15: ''Because they have forsaken my law which I set before them and have not obeyed my voice, neither walked therein; but have walked after the subbornness of their own heart, behold, I will feed them with wormwood.''[8] And, of course, any thought separated from the God of our Being is counterfeit. Current false practices and teachings can poison us and make our life bitter. And when we experience bitterness we are then separated from our Inner Knowing, our Good.

When the fourth angel blew his trumpet ''a third of the light was darkened; a third of the day was kept from shining, and likewise a third of the night.''

Our way does become darkened when we are faced with overcomings. We become depressed, our light of happiness seems to go out, and if it is only a third we still have enough light of truth to lift us up. Faith in the goodness of our experiences will pull us through and we will be cleansed.

Verse 13: ''Then I looked, and I heard an eagle crying with a loud voice, and it flew in midheaven, 'Woe, woe, woe to those who dwell on the earth, at the blasts of the other trumpets which the three angels are about to blow!'" And we may respond with fear as we continue. The eagle, a messenger from God which is the same as an angel,[9] is warning the seer about the future of those dwelling on earth, who have an earth consciousness. I should like to point out that the eagle also symbolizes the transforming substance,[10] is a coordinate of gold according to the alchemists,[11] and is like the unicorn and lion who represent Christ or the Holy Spirit.

And so John's inner spirit was telling him to pay attention. The eagle, the unicorn, the lion are all symbols of eternal Goodness, Christ Spirit, and the eagle is sometimes called the Phoenix which is a very old symbol of ancient Egypt, a symbol of overcoming, of the fire of the Christ, the Holy Spirit, the kundalini. The Phoenix rising from the ashes is symbolic of our Christ spirit rising from the destruction of our earthly consciousness. So we should listen carefully to the messages of the next three angels as they are being announced by our Christ Spirit. If we have fear engendered in us by this announcement then our Faith and Love must be sought in order to keep us on the Path. At times it seems more expedient to give up but once on the Path, getting off is not easy. And Love always accompanies us!!

CHAPTER 9

Burning of Dross Continued

Chapter 9:1,2: "And the fifth angel blew his trumpet, and I saw a star fallen from heaven to earth, and he was given the key of the shaft of the bottomless pit; he opened the shaft of the bottomless pit, and from the shaft rose smoke like the smoke of a great furnace, and the sun and the air were darkened with the smoke from the shaft."

It seems that we are going to have more of the same, becoming aware of unconscious contents and suffering from them.

Another star falls from heaven when the fifth angel blew his trumpet. It was different from the one in Chapter 8. This star was given the key to the bottomless pit. The star in Chapter 9 is the Christ consciousness that comes to the individual and he becomes aware of his earthly desire, pains and dissatisfactions. If we did not have within us this heavenly force we might never realize what our potential is. To know our potential we must also know our negatives, our shortcomings. We are still dualistic and as we become aware of Heaven we are also aware of Hell. But remember, heaven and hell are states of consciousness, not a place in the sky or in the earth. They are both in our own inner consciousness.

Verse 1 gives us a description of a bottomless pit. Now what could that be? No bottom. As we are using the analogy of Heaven and Hell, heaven has no limit to its "upness", and hell has no limit to its "downness." Let me then suggest the following:

The psychologist has named the "downness" the unconscious, personal and collective. What is being revealed are the forces that have been collected through the ages, through this lifetime, through former lifetimes and are bringing us pain. Smoke obliterates the sun. Smoke comes from fire and the more smoke the less free-burning the fire. The sun is symbolic of God or Christ consciousness and since the air is polluted by our negative attitudes our consciousness of God is veiled. When God is dimmed to our conscious mind our life is threatened for God is life. Somehow we are heirs to all that which has gone before and must go through the suffering in order to gain release so our potential, our perfect Being, our inner Spark of the Divine is in full view. Let us look at some of these negatives that must be overcome.

A terrible deluge of locusts (Verse 3) fly out of the bottomless pit. In our metaphysical dictionary they symbolize worry, suffering, enemies, ill health, negative thinking, problems of all kinds. And how all of these can sting!

They are told not to harm the grass or trees or anything that was growing. Grass and trees are green and green denotes nature, growth, rebirth and hope. So the locusts are not to harm the positive in our conscious mind, that which is growing. All of the above negatives can be overcome and as we overcome them the bite will become less, so as we start on the Path we will be given surcease from these "locusts" for we are growing. The Lord loves us and as soon as we open to His knocking we are given protection and our growth begins. He is Love. Growth within us will get rid of these negative "beings." They were to harm "only those of mankind who have not the seal of God upon their foreheads."

The seal of God upon the forehead has been dealt with elsewhere. The seal on the forehead designates illumination of the consciousness. When man has arrived at this state, his suffering is no more, for he has risen above the desires and attachments of the flesh, which is what brings suffering.

The Buddha taught four great truths which came to him after his forty days of meditation under the Bo Tree in India. His first sermon taught near Benares, about 500 B.C., outlined them. (1) Life on earth is suffering. (2) Suffering is caused by desires. (3) As we desire we become attached. (4) To overcome suffering we must meditate and live the right kind of life and thus give up our attachments to people and things. So to overcome suffering we must rise in consciousness to the Wisdom of God and stay in that Center. Become unattached to the locusts of worry, suffering, ill health, negative thinking, and have faith that God cares and is strengthening you, and fly to freedom.

Verse 5 indicates that the locusts were allowed to torture them five months but not to kill them. The torture was like a sting of a scorpion; death will be sought but "death will fly from them." The number five refers to the physical man or materialism and the scorpion is symbolic of the spirit of darkness in a man's consciousness compelling his soul to fulfill all his sinful tendencies.[1] It is deadly poison. The scorpion is also a symbol of the transforming of the vital spirit in man into the Divine. It stings itself to death.[2] So the negative becomes the positive as we learn through experience that being separated from our Spiritual heritage is so painful that we are turned toward the Divine. There is good in everything.

At this point I feel we should discuss Karma, for what mankind is experiencing is the Karma of his own thoughts and deeds. Not only mankind but each of us. Karma is a very ancient religious law and according to some historians came down from the Aryans who invaded India, Greece and many parts of the mid-East and Europe. It was also a part of the Egyptian religion. It is believed in and accepted by most Eastern religions.

Karma defined is: *Hinduism,* one's present and future existence is determined by the Law of Karma (karma meaning "deeds" or "works"), the law that one's thoughts, words, and deeds have an ethical consequence fixing one's lot in future existence. Karma is the cause of what is happening in one's life now.[3] *Buddhism,* Buddha gave the Law of Karma more flexibility than most later philosophers. In his view a man of any caste or class could experience so complete a change of heart or disposition as to escape the full consequence of sins committed in previous existences. The Law of Karma operated remorselessly and without remission of one jot or tittle of the full recompense upon all who went on in the old way—the way of unchecked desire—but it could not lay hold upon a man completely changed, who had achieved arhatship, "the state of him who is worthy."[4]

Jainism, the doctrine of Karma is interpreted strictly in accordance with their idea that the consequences of one's deeds are literally deposited in and on the soul. Various kinds of karmas are accumulated during this and previous births like layers of foreign substance and must be worn off by the process of living.[5] *Sikhism,* the Law of Karma can be overcome by "thinking only of God, endlessly repeating His name, and be absorbed into Him; in such absorption alone lies the bliss known to Hindus as Nirvana. Salvation is not going to Paradise after a last judgment, but absorption—individuality extinguishing absorption—in God, the True Name."[6]

Yogananda, the great teacher who came to America to combine Eastern and Western religious thoughts says: "The equilibrating law of karma, as expounded in the Hindu scriptures, is that of action and reaction, cause and effect, sowing and reaping. In the course of natural righteousness each man, by his thoughts and actions, becomes the molder of his destiny. Whatever universal energies he himself, wisely or unwisely, has set in motion must return to him as their starting point, like a circle inexorably completing itself. An understanding of karma as the law of justice underlying life's inequalities serves to free the human mind from resentment against God and man."[7]

Some passages from the Old and New Testament of the Bible also teach the Law of Karma, I believe. The Golden Rule: "Do unto others as you would have others do unto you." Also, Genesis 9:6: "Whoso sheddeth man's blood, by man shall his blood be shed." And Matthew 7:1,2: "Judge not, that you be not judged. For with the judgment you pronounce you will be judged, and the measure you give will be the measure you get." Our own actions come back to us.

The Golden Rule given by Jesus is a law of life and acts and reacts inexorably. As given in Matthew 7:12, it reads "Whatever you wish that men would do to you, do so to them; for this is the law and the prophets." Our Karma may bring positive as well as negative results. According to Hindu teaching the Karma of the family, society, or nation into which we are born is a part of our Karma. The race consciousness is something we have to overcome.

Overcoming negative Karma is for the growth and development of the individual consciousness, for if we accept this and believe it as Truth, we will live our lives centered in the Spirit and become the Christ-like person we were meant to be. Thus we rise in this lifetime and in a golden chain of lifetimes to Ultimate Perfection. If we are to reach Oneness in one lifetime we must sacrifice all the materialism that has encrusted our consciousness, and this is possible. It is up to us.

A corollary to Karma is reincarnation, which most Christians discount. However, according to a note from Yogananda, "The early Christian church accepted the doctrine of reincarnation, which was expounded by the Gnostics and by numerous church fathers (of the 3rd century), and St. Jerome (5th century). The doctrine of reincarnation was first declared a heresy in A.D. 553 by the Second Council of Constantinople. At that time many Christians thought the doctrine of reincarnation afforded man too ample a stage of time and space to encourage him to strive for immediate salvation. But truths suppressed lead disconcertingly to a host of errors. The millions have not utilized their 'one lifetime' to seek God, but to enjoy this world—so uniquely won, and shortly to be forever lost!'"[8]

The truth is that man reincarnates on earth until he has consciously regained his status as a son of God. In I John 3:1 we read, "Behold, what manner of love the Father hath bestowed upon us, that we should be called the sons of God." There are many Biblical passages that suggest reincarnation. At the end of the Old Testament we read in Malachi 4:5, "Behold I will send you Elijah, the prophet, before the great and terrible day of the Lord." (This was written long after Elijah's being translated into a whirlwind into heaven.) And in Matthew 17:12 Jesus said, "Elijah does come, and he is to restore all things; but I tell you that Elijah has already come, and they did not know him, but did to him whatever they pleased." (He was referring to John the Baptist.)

As for me, I believe in the Law of Karma and reincarnation

because of Jesus' teaching and from my own inner Christ. He said, "Judge not, and you will not be judged; condemn not, and you will not be condemned; forgive, and you will be forgiven; give, and it will be given to you, good measure, pressed down, shaken together, running over, will be put into your lap. For the measure you give will be the measure you get back." (Luke 6:37,38)

The Old Testament teaching was of an unforgiving, authoritarian Jehovah that acted on man from the outside. In the case of Saul, for instance, he was never able to feel forgiven. But Jesus taught the love and forgiveness of God and taught man to forgive seventy times seven times. Could Jesus expect more of man than we can expect of God? God is forgiving and would not, I believe, give us only one life to determine where our soul would spend eternity. The grand goal is Oneness, and if we do not make it in this lifetime, perhaps the next, and what gains we make in this lifetime will carry over into the next.

It is my belief that we reincarnate as human beings on this plane or another. There are many variations of the Law of Karma in reincarnation. It brings me hope and logical understanding of the long Path which each of us must tread. Keeping our mind centered on the Christ within will carry us far on our Eternal Path.

And what does all the foregoing have to do with Revelation? It seems to me to fit in with the destruction of the negative that lies within our consciousness that must be destroyed so that the ego can become one with the Spirit. If what we have done in this lifetime does not explain the challenges and problems we face, the law of Karma may explain it to us. Many people look to astrology to learn more of their past lives. However, observing the unfolding of this present life will tell us much about our past lives. When we are Centered, there is no need for the outer pseudo science of astrology to guide us.

In verses 7-10 we are given a description of the appearance of the locusts. They were like horses (instinctive drives that can erupt from the unconscious) arranged for battle. The crown on their heads would symbolize our very human perception of these instincts which we might count as good. We are often misguided and living an instinctual life from our unconscious, perhaps from habits of our past lives, which elevates our own view of ourself.

The locust's face was as a human one which brings the negative aspects of our unconscious as a very human aspect of our being. The locusts had the hair of women, which refers to the emotional strength of our subliminal consciousness. The lion is symbolic of strength, "their teeth were like lion's teeth." Scales, "they had scales like iron breastplates," refer to the dragon symbolic of the divine serpent which may be material or spiritual energy. Wings, of course, refer to that which allows the being to move on land or in the air. All of this is symbolic of the appearance of the negative and its potential for destruction.

We will never make growth toward the Divine until we learn how to overcome negativity in our own thoughts which are fed by our personal unconscious and those of the collective unconscious. To be a prey to the stinging reality of the negative that bubbles up in us and surrounds us is to know pain, suffering, Hell. That is Hell on earth and we will not go very far on our Path until we have overcome the negative in our thinking, speaking and acting; in our emotions; in our lack of faith; and in our not trusting in God. Wisdom is always positive if it is real wisdom, for God is positive in spite of all the teachings that He is a revengeful God.

Some of us are born with the propensity to be negative about everything, or another term is analytical. And how our scientific gods have taught the greatness of analysis as has our educational system. Knowledge, wisdom, intelligence requires analysis we are told. Our radio and TV commentators are always analyzing. Analysis itself carries the connotation of negativity, for it is to break apart, to tear down. We educated ones have prided ourselves on our ability to analyze and have moved further and further from perfection, for perfection is synthesis, is bringing together of all into Oneness. And so we live in a state of analysis which we must rise above. It is through our own thinking that we analyze, not through our spiritual mind, for God speaks from Truth and analysis is not necessary. Truth just IS!

When you become convinced that negative thinking brings negative actions and results and you accept the law of Karma, then you will understand the sting of the locust, the strength of his teeth and the iron breastplate that resists the thrust of Love. Be aware of your thoughts, turn them to the positive, raise your consciousness and the consciousness of the world by positive, synthesizing and life-giving thoughts, words, and deeds. To analyze is important on the earthly plane, but to synthesize is a must on the spiritual. All is One! This includes you and me and God. And so we bring together into Oneness by our positive thoughts, our mind centered on the Most High, and thus Wholeness accrues.

Verse 11: "They have as king over them the angel of the bottomless pit; his name in Hebrew is Abaddon, and in Greek he is called Apollyon." Abaddon means destruction, the angel of the bottomless pit, or Apollyon, destroyer. So the bottomless pit of the unconscious is ruled by the destroyer and the material coming up out of it can destroy the glimmer of hope and light we see in the star from heaven. Use the star from your heaven, the Christ within, to help you unlock the realization of the negative in your life, the unconscious that is keeping you from your good, and continue on in joy and peace.

Verse 13 introduces the sixth angel and "I heard a voice from the four horns of the golden altar before God." The four horns were on the brazen altar of the tabernacle which was the altar symbolizing the "willingness to give up the most valuable human interests in order to go on to complete communion" and was at station two of the tabernacle. The horns on the altar are symbols of complete power, symbols of all that IS; the One on the throne or golden altar gives them power and voice. The voice said "Release the four angels who are bound at the great river Euphrates." (Verse 14) This is another warning that an attack is coming, as in ancient times when the four angels of the river were released, it dried up and then the attack came from their enemies.

The great river Euphrates was one of the four rivers that had their beginning from the one river in Paradise or the Garden of Eden and so has the qualities of that one river which flowed there. (Genesis 2:10–14) The one river was created by God so had the essence of God. So we can then look at the river Euphrates as the life line of the people of the Near East for thousands of years and when it was dried up they were open to attack.

From the viewpoint of the individual development of consciousness of our Oneness with God, I believe that the River Euphrates is symbolic of the spine and Holy Spirit using it as a highway to reach all cells, nerves, energy centers of the body and mind in an effort to transform the body into a body of light which develops as we impregnate the cells with the spiritual essence from God. The kundalini power at the base of the spine does just that as we grow in wisdom, love, and understanding of God. If it is dried up, then we are subject to enemies of our desire to become One. As we are purified, the dross of the unconscious may rise to the top and we will be cleansed.

Verse 15: "So the four angels were released who had been held ready for the hour, the day, the month, and the year, to kill a third of mankind."

Angels refer to spiritual thoughts and ideas straight from Jehovah and are often interpreted as the work of Truth which can overcome our limited ideas and conditions. So this next is for our good. Four, from ancient times, symbolizes the unity or perfection of God and man as a whole. Jung's contemporary and student, M. L. von Franz, says, "We have seen that symbolic structures that seem to refer to the process of individuation (of becoming the individual Self) tend to be based on the motif of the number four . . ."[9] So even though a battle is imminent, we know that Good will overcome the negative.

There is forever occurring on earth the battle between our spiritual and our earthly desires and some will be killed depending on what is uppermost in our consciousness, in our mind. The mind of man is his greatest nemesis and his greatest glory. A paradox!

The instinctive drives that come from our unconscious may attack that good which we are attempting to reach. Perhaps as a result we will suffer death to parts of our being. Death has always been looked upon as negative to mankind and well it should as we need life to grow and evolve toward Oneness. But death also brings resurrection and an overcoming of the material by the spiritual. So it is in our upward Journey. Much must be overcome in our mind, body, emotions in order for the spirit to function. To resurrect that Truth that lies dormant in us requires the defeat of that which is not Truth. So we must go through a period of cleansing, of getting rid of the dross and filth of our material life.

As this spiritual essence is released through the spine the fine qualities of energy lift the physical body and the consciousness to a higher level and the old, useless, dead cells and ideas drop off. This is why it is very important that our body be in perfect condition in order to receive fully the effect of the Holy Spirit. Much of Yoga is concerned with the development of the body, raising of its effectiveness and strength, giving it balance so it can receive the high charge of spiritual energy without deleterious effects. Many accounts of raising of the kundalini power tell of the terrible pain, heat, loss of weight, weakness that occur. At the same time that the body is being cleansed the same cleansing must occur in our conscious and unconscious mind. And so a cleansing takes place.

Throughout this discourse I have interpreted symbols in terms of mythology. At this point I should like to discuss mythology and its place in our understanding. For it does have meaning for us. So many of the figures in Revelation are mythological and it is almost impossible to be sure of the meaning since these figures come from our primordial beginnings and are still a part of the collective unconscious.

According to the teachings of Carl Jung, the understanding

of mythological characters is basic to our understanding of dreams and visions which come from our unconscious. The unconscious is that with which we carry the memories of the past and the Hindus would say of our past lives. Because they come from our primordial past and are a part of the earlier part of our evolution and reincarnation, they carry a message for us and are sometimes beyond our interpretation, indeed each of us must find our own meaning as we encounter them in dreams, visions, or active imagination. Once we interpret them, however, they become a part of our direction for future evolution toward our goal of Oneness. According to Jung, they are a necessary part of our unconscious which must be made conscious if we are to become individuated, or Whole.

Jung has written a great deal on myths and his associates have done so also. Maria von Franz, in her book *Fairytales,*[10] goes into this more deeply. The language of symbology is to a large extent based on mythology which has very important messages for modern man, she believes.

So to continue our understanding of Revelation, Verses 16–19, with this in mind, we would analyze many of the figures in the vision in terms of mythology. A very important book by Jung and his associates is *Man and His Symbols* and I shall be drawing on it for some of this interpretation.

Animals are symbolic of instinctive drives which is reasonable since we accept that animals live largely by instinct and so do men and women until they replace them with something more reasonable and/or spiritual. The instinctive side of our nature is usually neutralized by our parents as they discipline us and we gain self-discipline but even in adulthood we may live our life by instinct. Inevitably we get into trouble, for if we are focused on our lower instincts, society as a whole will not tolerate our behavior.

There are, of course, higher instincts which we ignore many times, and we would do well to give them more attention. Much has been written by psychologists about instinctive behavior and agreement on what are the basic instincts has not been totally reached. Some of these instincts are hunger, self-preservation, sexuality, and the power drive. Various psychologists have dealt with these in their theories. Freud with the sexual and Adler with the power drive. Fillmore said that so long as animal (instincts) rule the man is a slave. The I AM must take charge.

Jung dealt with the need to have contact with a Supreme Power or Being, but I do not know that he classified it as an instinct. None of these horses would seem to represent that, however.

Let us then discuss the cavalry of horses from the viewpoint of instincts. Each animal carries several interpretations based on mythology. Horses symbolize the instinctive drives from the unconscious and because these have riders, we can assume that we are the riders, or should I say our will power, for we begin controlling our harmful instincts by the use of our own will power which ultimately becomes the Will of the Self, or should.

The riders are flashily dressed and so is our will power. Our imagination is called upon as we observe the scene. We see a very proud rider directing his instincts toward death. Our will can be very egotistic and this, of course, takes us from our desired goal since humility is a must on our Journey.

The personal will is very important in our work. Yogananda says in a series of talks that Will is volition. Volition causes a series of continuous, undiscourageable, unceasing determination and acts around a desire until it becomes dynamic enough to produce the much craved result. Will and act until victory, he says.

Progress presupposes the existence of the power of growth from within. We must will to move or think. So as the will is focused on the desire for personal peace, love, wisdom, Oneness, we will make progress; but if the will is ego-bound, then our instincts will get out of hand and our fate is death. "Seek ye first the kingdom of Heaven and his righteousness and all these things shall be yours as well." (Matt. 6:33) Then our will becomes His Will and we can pray in Truth: Thy will be done on earth as it is in heaven. And Jesus also said: "Not everyone who says to me, 'Lord, Lord' shall enter the kingdom of Heaven, but he who does the will of my Father who is in heaven." (Matt. 7:21)

"And this was how I saw the horses in my vision; the riders

wore breastplates the color of fire and sapphire and sulphur, and the heads of the horses were like lions' heads, and fire and smoke and sulphur issued from their mouths. By these three plagues a third of mankind was killed, by the fire and smoke and sulphur issuing from their mouths. For the power of the horses is in their mouths and in their tails; their tails are like serpents, with heads, and by means of them they wound." (Verses 17–19)

These verses give us our closest view of the mythological character of the horse figures. Briefly the symbol of sulphur refers to a use made of suphur, when burned, for fumigating and bleaching. The serpents on the tails are blind force, extra human quality in man, divine fire, sense consciousness which seeks satisfaction through the appetites. I have dealt earlier with the double nature of the serpent energy.

So coping with the animal instincts that arise from our unconscious, through our own will and ultimately the Will of God, can overcome death.

Verses 20 and 21 are plain enough for us to understand without resorting to symbology, for it is a recounting of the negatives by which the majority of mankind live. "The rest of mankind, who were not killed by these plagues, did not repent of the works of their hands nor give up worshipping demons and idols of gold and silver and bronze and stone and wood, which cannot either see or hear or walk; nor did they repent of their murders or their sorceries or their immorality or their thefts."

We as individuals do not usually accept the responsibility for the negative in our lives and blame it on some outside force. We also worship idols of gold, silver, bronze, stone in our materialistic world. The car is often considered the god of many; also the house, the things that cannot see or hear or walk. Gold, at this time, is being bought to hedge against the expected cataclysm in the financial world. Jesus said, "Where your treasure is there will your heart be also." (Matt. 6:21) And because we do not repent of our murders, sorceries, immorality or thefts we can expect negatives to occur in our lives.

Many of us will not agree that we worship idols or commit

any of the evils listed. But since we must be cleansed of all our dross we would best look into our shadow nature to be sure we are clean. Von Franz deals a great deal with the shadow in *Man and His Symbols*.[11] She explains that one of the best methods to learn about our own shadow is to look at what disturbs us in other people; also if a friend points out a fault to us and we react very strongly, emotionally, against the suggestion, we might take a good look to see if that is our shadow. Our shadow, the dark side of our nature, separates us from our Good, and when recognized is neutralized.

So we coninue to be aware of the unconscious and the cleansing that needs to go on before we can reach that high estate at the throne of God. Most of us will probably not attain the very highest level in this lifetime, but as we clean out our unconscious, go through the pain and suffering of realization, we will inevitably rise higher as our whole being is focused on Him. Thank you, Father!

So the fifth and sixth angels have brought the woes that must be overcome if we are to continue on our Path. Our consciousness has been barraged by the negatives of the locusts (the negative in our unconscious) and the power of the cavalry (the horses that represent our instinctive drives). And we have more to come, but we must remember the promise and expectation: "To those who overcome I will give . . . !" Let us be strong in our faith as we continue.

CHAPTER 10

The Inner Christ

We are being given the vision of another angel, a mighty one "come down from heaven, wrapped in a cloud, with a rainbow over his head, and his face was like the sun, and his legs like pillars of fire." This is a mighty messenger, we know, because of this description. He is more than "man"—He is also "God." Could this be the Cosmic Man written about in many religions? This is an important symbol and I should like to quote from *Man and His Symbols,* the chapter on "The Process of Individuation" by M. L. von Franz:

"The Self frequently appears in a form that hints at a special omnipresence; that is, it manifests itself as a gigantic, symbolic human being who embraces and contains the whole cosmos. When this image turns up in the dreams of an individual, we may hope for a creative solution to his conflict, because now the vital psychic center is activated (i.e., the whole being is condensed into oneness) in order to overcome the difficulty.

"The Cosmic Man appears as Adam, as the Persian Gayomart, or as the Hindu Purusha. This figure may even be described as the basic principle of the whole world. The Cosmic Man—the gigantic, all-embracing figure that personifies and contains the entire universe—is a common representation of the Self in myths and dreams. The Chinese call the Cosmic Man or the colossal divine man, P'an Ku, who gave heaven and earth their form.

"In the East, and in some gnostic circles in the West, people soon recognized that the Cosmic Man was more an inner psychic image than a concrete outer reality. According to Hindu tradition he is something that lives within the individual human being and is the only part that is immortal. This inner Great Man redeems the individual by leading him out of creation and its sufferings, back into his original eternal sphere. Also, in old India, Purusha lives within the heart of every individual, and yet at the same time fills the entire cosmos.

"According to the testimony of many myths, the Cosmic Man is not only the beginning but also the final goal of all life—of the whole of creation. In our Western civilization the Cosmic Man has been identified to a great extent with Christ, and in the East with Krishna or with Buddha. In the Old Testament this same symbolic figure turns up as the 'Son of Man' and in later Jewish mysticism is called Adam Kadmon. Later he was called Anthropos (the Greek word for man). Like all symbols this image points to an unknowable secret—to the ultimate unknown meaning of human existence.

"From the point of view of the Hindu, for example, it is not so much that the external world will one day dissolve into the original Great Man, but that the ego's extraverted orientation toward the external world will disappear in order to make way for the Cosmic Man. This happens when the ego merges into the Self.''[1]

All of this points, I believe, to the following interpretation of Chapter 10: that the figure is a representation of the Christ, the Self, which is within each of us. This, the Christ, which is within each of us, is a part of the Whole, the Godhead, the Energy of the Universe. It is the divine-idea man, according to Fillmore. He embodies all divine ideas, such as intelligence, life, love, substance, and strength. We must look to our Christ in order to realize our divine origin. And toward oneness with the Christ we are tending. The Cosmic Man, the angel that "came down" is calling us to Wholeness.

The phrase, "coming down," may have given the Christians the idea that heaven was high above us geographically while indeed it is a high estate containing the throne of God, but as Jesus told us ". . . for behold, the kingdom of God is in the midst of you," (Luke 17:21) or as the Amplified Version reads, "For behold the kingdom of God is within you and among you." So the Cosmic Man, our Christ, has a message for us through the Seer.

This High Being is surrounded by a cloud according to the

text which is the etheric light that surrounds a vision of pure
light and is the fine energy that makes up our world. The rainbow
brings to our mind the promise of God to Noah, that flesh upon
the earth would not be destroyed again by water. (Gen. 9:12-17)
The rainbow also symbolizes the total spectrum of colors that
are the races of the world. So the Christ is a promise and in all
men everywhere.

"He had a little scroll open in his hand." Again the scroll,
but the former one was written on "front and back" and we
interpreted it as the unconscious. Again I feel that the scroll is
about the unconscious but at a different level from the first, since
no writing is mentioned on this scroll. It is above the words
of man. It seems to deal with some Truth from a higher level
and since we are being prepared for the great revelation "of the
trumpet call sounded by the seventh angel, the mystery of God
should be fulfilled" this scroll must be for the purpose of
preparing us.

Let us recapitulate. The angel that has the scroll stands on earth
and sea or he encompasses our entire world, the conscious and
unconscious worlds. These are opposites and as stated previously,
must be brought into coordination if we are to reach Wholeness.
This Cosmic Man, the Christ, is doing just that and will do it
for us. The Christ was in Jesus also and it was not until his
resurrection that he was called Jesus Christ, man and God as one,
the Cosmic Man. This is our goal also. So the scroll is held by
the Cosmic Man and the instructions will follow.

He cried out with a loud voice and the seven thunders sounded.
Using the idea of the opening of the seven Chakras and the sound
of the Christ being the Aum sound of the Universe, we could
conjecture that the seven Chakras resounded with Aum vibration.
Centering on the Christ is a necessity if we are to open the seven
Chakras or grow in consciousness through the seven stations of
faith, creative force, intellect, love, worship, Wisdom and the final
station of Oneness.

"And when the seven thunders had sounded, I was about to
write, but I heard a voice from heaven saying, 'Seal up what the

seven thunders have said, and do not write it down.'" This is, perhaps, one of the most important directives—secrecy. When we are developing our consciousness, each breakthrough is very exciting and we want to tell the world about it. As we grow in consciousness we have experiences that we feel we must share. However, there is danger in sharing too much. First, because the one or ones you share with may not be at the same level of development that you are and may play the reductionist game of "That is nothing but. . . ."

Experiences such as we have spiritually do not always bear logical explanation. In fact, most of them do not. Therefore, we must be very choosey about our hearers. Also, some experiences should not be shared, but should be kept in our most secret place so that our energy is not dissipated in the telling. Focusing the energy of our understanding on them will help us understand them. Some dreams are so personal and spiritual that we should not write them down or tell them. We must not spread our "pearls before swine."

Jesus brought out this need for secrecy in other places. As for instance, in Matthew 6:1, "Beware of practicing your piety (a dutiful spirit of reverence for God) before men in order to be seen by them, for then you will have no reward from your Father who is in heaven." Also, "Thus when you give alms (good deeds), sound no trumpet before you. . . . do not let your left hand know what your right hand is doing." This is not to say that a group that is on the Path should not share some experiences. Just be sure you have gone to your Center and asked what you can share.

The "mighty angel" shows his obeisance to the Highest Being by swearing by Him who made all, "who lives forever and ever, who created heaven and what is in it, that there should be no more delay, but that in the days of the trumpet call to be sounded by the seventh angel, the mystery of God, as he announced to his servants and prophets, should be fulfilled." (Verses 5 and 6) This brings our mind to the Creative Force and the Word. He, God, is all in all, the creative force. And this Cosmic Man, the Christ, bows down before Him. We are ready for our instructions.

The voice from heaven or the inner voice of God, which the vision symbolizes, tells us to "Go, take the scroll which is open in the hand of the angel who is standing on the sea and land." Unless you, the reader, have allowed yourself to enter another state of consciousness as you read these words, it will not seem reasonable that the revealor could actually take the scroll and eat it. But we must remember that visions have more reality to the seer than the seen that surrounds him in his everyday world. A vision is truth from another level and many report that they are convinced without a shadow of a doubt and believe all that they see. Besides, remember that this is a symbolic account.

And the angel said, "Take it and eat; it will be bitter to your stomach, but sweet as honey in your mouth." This scroll has to be eaten, taken into the inner being, digested, not read. It is sweet then bitter. It must be a message to reveal the highest. What then could it be that requires the highest of Truth to be digested? And you may ask, why sweet and then bitter?

Well, as pointed out previously, the Journey to Completion has its ups and downs. It is as if we are being played with but it is really important that we experience the bitter and the sweet for it is not truly sweet until we become Complete or in Unity with God, and the bitterness will ultimately bring us to the sweet. Often when we eat of the Truth our first reaction is the experiencing of great ecstasy and liberation. Sweet has always symbolized, for man, that which is most wanted—candy, a sweet person, anything that gives us great physical and emotional satisfaction is sought after. So when we eat the scroll from heaven our first reaction is that we have experienced the sweetest and as usual the momentary experience of sweetness satisfies us. Some say that this happens to the "Born Again" Christian.

The bitter comes when the sweetness is digested and experienced and we realize how our life must change, what responsibilities we have as individuals to maintain the sweetness, what we must give up if the sweetness is to last, for our consciousness still needs cleansing. Pleasure in sweetness may be lost as we cleanse the inner self, the ego. The ego, our own personality, is always there ready to become strong and overshadow the Self. And when we have a high spiritual experience, it is sweet, and we must remember that it comes from God, is given freely through His Grace and not because we are special, except in the sense that all of us are special.

When we eat something in a physical way the stomach is an organ of assimilation taking the strength from the food for the body and discharging the useless, the bitter. Sometimes the stomach rebels at that sweetness if it is not purified beforehand. The same is true of our consciousness. At times it is not lofty enough for the sweetness of the spiritual food that is given us, as was the scroll, and in order to be purified, the experience of bitterness must be gone through. So we must digest what our mind and body have eaten and enjoy the sweetness but know that the bitter will not be neutralized until we are ready in our spiritual consciousness for this beautiful love message, this divine child, this all knowing of the One who made heaven and earth and all that is in it.

We are given the commission in the last verse to "prophesy about many peoples and nations and tongues and kings." To prophesy is to declare or to foretell by divine inspiration. We are to prophesy to all people everywhere, or rather the seer is to do this. So the message is for all people and the Cosmic Man is the symbol of all people, for we have come from Oneness and to Oneness we must return.

This chapter has brought us a message from our Christ about our Path. We have been given the sweetness experience of the message from our Christ, we have found it can become bitter, we have been given a commission for all people. And we are being prepared for the "mystery of God" when the seventh trumpet is sounded. Amen.

CHAPTER 11

Two Witnesses

Chapter eleven opens with the revelator being given a measuring rod like a staff, and told to measure the temple of God and the altar and those who worship there. Since the temple referred to is our own temple of the Holy Spirit, it would seem that the need to measure our consciousness level is necessary before the mystery will be revealed to us. The rod, according to some authorities, refers to the spine up which the kundalini courses. Perhaps the spine must be at a certain level of development before the force can reach the higher state of consciousness. He, John, is instructed then to not measure the outer court of the temple, "leave that out for it is given over to the nations, and they will trample over the holy city for forty-two months." The outer court is our outer vision of reality which will trample the Truth underfoot.

Then Verse 4: "These are the two olive trees and the two lamp-stands which stand before the Lord of the earth."

It is interesting that Zechariah 4:3-5 has a like description of the two olive trees or the two witnesses. If this scripture is read from the viewpoint of raising of the kundalini power to bring forth perfection of the Lord, it is more understandable. Verses 12-14 of Zechariah 4 read: "And a second time I said to him, 'What are these two branches of olive trees, which are beside the two golden pipes from which the oil is poured out?' He said to me, 'Do you not know what these are?' I said, 'No, my lord.' Then he said, 'These are the two anointed who stand by the Lord of the whole earth.'" The oil referred to, I believe, is the kundalini or the Holy Spirit.

This interpretation of the two olive trees brings us to the center of the teaching of Revelation, that the way that the physical body is changed into the Spiritual is a raising of consciousness or the kundalini power which transmutes the physical to the spiritual. The next few verses speak of how it may be misused, and we are taught this before we can learn of the mystery.

It is necessary at this point to discuss in more detail the raising of the consciousness, the raising of the Kundalini, the raising of the Holy Spirit. Because Revelation is supreme in its use of symbology its interpretation has been either left alone or those who have interpreted it have taken it at face value, usually, and being unaware of the symbolic meaning, have interpreted it in the light of their own limited understanding and knowing. Interpretations have been written which approached the core of Truth but the time for their acceptance had not arrived. I pray that "those who have ears, let them hear, those who have anointed their eyes, let them see." This interpretation is also written from the level of the author's consciousness. The future may hold much more Truth from those who understand, from the Light and Love flowing in and through them.

We have described elsewhere the chakra centers in the body and the changes that occur in the body, mind, and spirit as each of these are opened. Little has been said about the spine and the part it plays in this process. So I shall quote from *The Chakras* by C. W. Leadbeater. This describes the raising of the kundalini.

"Ida and Pingala (two currents that flow on either side of the spinal column, which is called Sushumno by the Hindus) play along the curved wall of the cord in which is Sushumna. They are semi-material, positive and negative, sun and moon, and start into action the free and spiritual current of Sushumna."[1]

Again from the same book: "The spine is called in India the Brahmadanda, the stick of Brahma."[2]

The raising of the kundalini through these centers is to bring together the two powers, the Shiva and Shakti. The Shiva, according to John White in *Kundalini, Evolution and Enlightenment,* is "our consciousness which retains its static quality and remains identified with unmanifest consciousness. This is the objective consciousness, and has the power to be but not to act or manifest. Shakti is dynamic, energetic, creative aspect, the great Mother of the Universe and manifests herself in matter, life and mind."[3]

And "Shiva resides in the crown chakra and Shakti (the kundalini) lies dormant at the base of the spine with a small part dynamic in the body. It is thought that Shakti contains latent energy and latent memories, both personal and transpersonal. It is called the unconscious by modern understanding. Yoga union is the meeting of Kundalini (Shakti) with pure consciousness (Shiva). When united this is the experience we call enlightenment."[4]

So the two witnesses are Ida and Pingala on each side of the spine up which the kundalini power or Holy Spirit courses as it does its cleansing and consciousness-raising work. Many there were and are in the hierarchy of religions who understand this. Just now it is beginning to be revealed to Western seekers of Truth in its esoteric sense. And for good reason.

Time after time, as we read authorities on the kundalini raising, we are warned against disturbing the Power at the base of the spine. By we, I mean the Western man and woman. In the East, India particularly, there have been gurus, yogis, who have helped awaken this kundalini in their disciples so that they may raise their consciousness of Brahma or God. However, the Master or Teacher was always sure the disciple was ready for this high charge of energy active in his body and passed on to the disciple, by touch, the awakening of kundalini or we would call this baptism.

Remember that Jesus baptized with the Holy Spirit as he touched or was touched. But first he always asked "Do you believe?" Matthew 9:28 relates his questioning of the blind man before he was healed. And in John 20:22, "He, Jesus, breathes on them and said to them, 'Receive the Holy Spirit.'" When Jesus asked "Do you believe?" and the answer was in the affirmative he baptized, he healed, he created abundance out of little, he quieted the storm, he raised the dead. All was done by his passing his Essence into the situation. He knew how to use the Holy Spirit power and he came to teach us how. By all accounts his awareness of the God within and in the world was higher than any religious leader before or since. So if Jesus baptized by the Holy Spirit, what does that mean to us? What are we to do? Let us turn back to our scripture. Could our protection be faith?

It is pointed out in Verse 5 that if anyone should harm them (the two witnesses) "fire pours from their mouth and consumes their foes; if anyone would harm them, thus he is doomed to be killed." The great powers they have are recounted, which are descriptions of great woes to come on any of mankind who misuses them. This warning is appropriate, for this power that courses up the tree of the body, the spine and all of its branches, cannot be played with or misused. It must be used for spiritual growth and faith is a prerequisite to its development if it is to be used right. Misuse may bring disaster. Pain, suffering and even death may accrue as a result of misuse.

In *The Twelve Powers of Man* Fillmore has this to say: "The ego, through its recognition of this life stream, sets it flowing to every faculty. Being by nature formless, the life stream takes the mold and character of that into which it is poured. It is the servant of the ego, the I, which man is, and through his failure to recognize the divine intelligence, which should show him how to use it in the right way, he blunders ahead in his ignorance, and the Lamb of God is slain from the foundation of the world."[5]

I should like to refer the reader to a book by Gopi Krishna, *Kundalini: The Evolutionary Energy in Man*. Gopi Krishna, a Hindu living in Kashmir, through meditation activated the kundalini and went through some difficult experiences. He has since established a research institute in Nishat, outside the capital city of Srinagar. In this book he gives an account of the sudden awakening of the kundalini and its negative effect upon him. Later the bliss and ecstasy came, but at first he had a nightmare of a life. "The days that followed had all the appearance of a prolonged nightmare. It seemed as if I had abruptly precipitated myself from the steady rock of normality into a madly racing whirlpool of abnormal existence." And, "The nights were even more terrible. I could not bear to have a light in my room after I had retired to bed. The moment my head touched the pillow a large tongue of flame sped across the spine into the interior of my head."[6] He recounts many other negative experiences as the kundalini began to flow due to prolonged meditation. It seems to me that he was not Centered at the time, but later events brought him surcease from pain and suffering and he is now considered an enlightened person.

Alice Bailey, a Theosophist, gives this reassurance and warning: "He who directs his efforts to the control of the fires of matter is (with a dangerous certainty) playing with fire that may literally destroy him." To overcome this danger she adds: "Let a man apply himself to a life of high altruism, to a discipline that will refine and bring his lower vehicles under subjection, and to a strenuous endeavor to purify and control his sheaths. When he has done this he will find that the development and functioning of the centers has pursued a parallel course and the work has proceeded along the desired lines."[7] (Sheaths refer to the various bodies surrounding and interpenetrating the physical one.)

This very clear description of the misuse and the right use of the Holy Spirit power makes us aware of the danger of misuse.

The account says in Verse 7, "The beast that ascends from the bottomless pit will make war upon them and conquer them and kill them. . . ." Here it is assumed that the two witnesses have to be destroyed in order to prevent their destructiveness. The beast has been interpreted as the ego from the unconscious. Ego is materially based and separates us from the Spirit when it is given control. Ego here used means *self* consciousness and not *Self* consciousness. The small self is the beast.

Verse 8, "and their dead bodies will lie in the street of the great city which is allegorically called Sodom and Egypt, where their Lord was crucified." Sodom symbolizes burning, consuming with fire and according to the *Metaphysical Bible Dictionary,* Sodom signifies a state of mind that is adverse to the law of the Spirit, and since it is also a symbol of burning, I would add that the burning sensation of the serpent power is cleansing the spiritual body and the physical body. Egypt symbolized a place of misery, restraint, tribulation. It is a land of darkness and mystery, yet it is the realm of substance and life in the depths of the body consciousness. The Lord of the two witnesses is Shiva which dwells in the higher mind and is crucified if the Ida and Pingala are misused. Great rejoicing will occur in our earthly consciousness if the raising of the Divine Substance is defeated. However, our account tells of their resurrection.

Verses 9–11: "For three days and a half men from the peoples and tribes and tongues and nations gaze at their dead bodies and refuse to let them be placed in a tomb, and those who dwell on earth will rejoice over them and make merry and exchange presents, because these two prophets had been a torment to those who dwell on the earth. But after the three and a half days a breath of life from God entered them, and they stood up on their feet, and great fear fell on those who saw them.

This is an account of the Crucifixion, Death, Resurrection and Ascension of the two witnesses which of course reminds us of the life and resurrection of Christ Jesus. The three and a half days is a mystical symbol meaning half way between one (god) and seven (man) and signifies mystically a covenant between God and man.[8] The kundalini is also said to be coiled three and a half times at the base of the spine. So the witnesses are resurrected and Verse 12 gives us that account.

When we turn our attention to the voice from heaven, to the Being on the throne, to our Inner Voice, the Aum, we hear "Come up hither," a command. "And in the sight of their foes they went up to heaven in a cloud." (Verse 12) This, of course, is what we really want and when we pay attention to the Inner Voice then we will be in Heaven. The foes, earthly desires and attachments, will fall away and the Holy Spirit will become One with God on the throne. The kundalini will then flow throughout the spiritual and physical bodies.

Verse 13 has been an enigma to many translators and difficult to understand. If we continue with our analogy we can see that the verse is more easily understood. "And at that hour there was a great earthquake, and a tenth of the city fell; seven thousand people were killed in the earthquake, and the rest were terrified and gave glory to the God of heaven." This passage seems to refer to the magnificent experience of reaching the kingdom of Heaven by the two witnesses, or the marriage of the Shakti and Shiva. When this happens, many of our former beliefs and activities will fall and our material consciousness is killed in our experience.

And many of our faculties will give glory to God. Our earthly consciousness is really "shook up."

Verse 14: "The second woe has passed, behold, the third woe is soon to come."

So we have passed the second woe and well it is described, for the woe is to earthly thoughts, activities, desires and attachments. The glory of Heaven is still around and when the seventh angel sounds his trumpet we are given a taste of It. "And God saw that it was good." (Genesis 1.)

Finally the seventh angel sounded the vibration of the trumpet which affected the body, mind and soul of the aspirant. When the kundalini reaches the seventh chakra the whole body and consciousness responds and is filled with energy of a very high vibration. The loud voices in heaven, said, "The kingdom of this world has become the kingdom of our Lord and of his Christ, and he shall reign forever and ever." And the Shakti and Shiva have entwined in the spiritual marriage and the world has become the kingdom of Heaven. Then the entire organism, mind, body and soul responds in pure praise.

Praise is a very important action on our part and is involuntary when we reach such a high consciousness. However, along the way we should pray with praise and thanksgiving at all times for the glorious warmth of His love pervades our being when we thank Him. We can sing, play a musical instrument, create our own music; for music is the sound of celestial spheres and is straight from the creative center. Creative acts come to us when "in the Spirit." "And thus the 24 elders who sit on their thrones before God, fell on their faces and worshipped God, saying:

> (Verse 17)   "We give thanks to thee, Lord God Almighty,
>   who are and who wast,
>   that thou has taken thy great power and
>   begun to reign.
> (Verse 18)   The nations raged, but thy wrath came
>   and the time for the dead to be judged,
>   for the rewarding of thy servants, the prophets
>   and saints,

and those who fear thy name,
    both small and great,
    and for destroying the destroyers of the earth.''

Verse 17 refers to the great power which is the will power of the self, the small self, which has been lost in the Great Self. The nations refer to the material desires and attachments of each person. The wrath mentioned in verse 18 is actually the "blessing of God" for the outcome becomes a blessing for the aspirant. The dead to be judged are the remaining limitations which the aspirant has not lost. So the Great One has come and become our own consciousness. We are at One and we get a glimpse of the temple in Heaven and the ark of His covenant which brings flashes of lightning, voices, peals of thunder, earthquakes and hail. All of these are man's symbols for a holy act. (Verse 19)

The mystics who have attempted to write a description of the experience of enlightenment, nirvana, samadhi, are always at a loss to describe the experience. It is so superconscious, above the mundane, that words seem inadequate. Evelyn Underhill says, "Insofar as I am acquainted with the resource of language there are no words in which this realization can be described."[9] And, "We might describe it as a sudden, intense, and joyous perception of God power and splendour of that larger life in which the individual is immersed, and of a new life to be lived by the self in correspondance with this now dominant fact of existence."[10] Optical disturbance, auditory experiences that seem to come from Heaven, and the sense of levitation are some of the results of the shifting of consciousness.

It is clear that the experience can only be realized by way of participation. "It has to be felt to be known."

For Jesus, it is reported, a white dove appeared and landed on his head. The dove symbolizes the Holy Spirit, the Self, the divine law, peace. Paul on the road to Damascus had a vision of Jesus Christ which was so bright that he was blinded. The apostles at Pentecost were in another dimension of consciousness. (Acts 2)

Verse 19: "Then God's temple in heaven was opened, and

the ark of his covenant was seen within his temple and there were flashes of lightning, voices, peals of thunder, an earthquake and heavy hail.''

In our Seers description, the ark of the covenant gives his best analogy. The ark of the covenant, the holy of holies for the Jew, was the most sacred symbol of God or of Jehovah. Each person will choose for the symbol that which is most meaningful to him and his religious life. John ''saw'' the ark of the covenant which privilege was given to the priests only. This is the ray of God, the inner Pillar of light, the divine-man in the holy place within each person. And so his Christ shone ''round about him.''

My imagination brings me this description:

> Enlightenment?
> 'Twould be:
> As the cooing of the dove
> Which brings me
> Paeans of love.
> The pheasant flying
> The whir of wings,
> Brilliant hues.
>
> 'Twould be:
> The silence,
> Nothingness.
>
> 'Twould be   His Light
> Light beyond all
> Knowing.
>
> ''Twould be . . .
> And there is silence. . . .

And so we have our warning of the misuse of the sacred power, the Holy Spirit. We have the announcement of the kingdom of our Lord and of his Christ. We have the praise given by all of the faculties of the consciousness of man, and we have a glimpse of God's temple in heaven. And all of this has prepared us for the ''mystery of God'' which shall be revealed.

The Revelation

We are ready for the Revelation. We have been prepared. We have seen the beginning, the cleansing, and a scene which depicts our goal. Now the climax is in view: The Revelation for our teaching and our direction.

Chapter 12 opens with a view of a "great portent appeared in heaven, a woman clothed with the sun and the moon under her feet, and on her head a crown of twelve stars." We know from ancient mythology that the sun (masculine) and the moon (feminine) depicted together indicates wholeness, completion, perfection. This woman is luminous and has a crown of twelve stars. So we have the sun, the moon, the stars. Twelve signs of the zodiac, it is said by astrologers, must be completed before we can gain Illumination. This tiara would indicate that the consciousness has been completed.

Now woman is, of course, indicative of the female, the intuitive, the spiritual, the feeling side of our being. We are both male and female and birth of the child brings forth an androgenous being. The feminine side of our nature brings forth the divine. And men and women both have this capacity. "In the beginning male and female created He them." And we were created in the image of God, so God, being both male and female, gives birth to a Divine Child, who although designated male in our scripture, is both male and female, being a facsimile of God.

The woman "was with child and cried out in her pangs of birth, in anguish for delivery." We are all aware that "being with child" or being pregnant with an idea requires delivery eventually and many times brings us anguish and pain. This is called a portent, a holy act, bringing forth of something Divine.

Our dramatist introduces another portent—"a great red dragon, with seven heads and ten horns, and seven diadems upon his heads." We have faced dragons before, but what could this symbolize? Some interpreters suggest that it is a symbol for lust, the extreme of emotion used for the opposite of spiritual development. Others suggest that John was referring to Rome and perhaps for the early Christians that would be the best explanation. The Leviathan, which is designated as the dragon, is discussed in many parts of the Old Testament. In Job we read the description of God pointing out to Job that he created the Leviathan. For our purposes, however, I should like to designate the dragon as some quality in our own personality which might make us afraid to bring forth our Divinity. The woman, you see, is the female aspect of God, the Sophia, the kundalini, the Holy Spirit which through Oneness with God brings forth the Divine Child.

The vision that is recounted is a view of heaven and in that consciousness the woman appears who is the female aspect of God, who is considered male in the writings of the Bible, or should I say in the interpretations of the writings of the Bible. The woman can be taken for Sophia in mythology. In Greek mythology, which influenced the Old Testament writers, Sophia symbolized Wisdom. In Proverbs 8 we have a discourse by Wisdom and her advice. Verse 1, "Does not wisdom call, does not understanding raise her voice?" And Verse 14: "I have counsel and sound wisdom, I have insight, I have strength."

Jung speaks a great deal about Sophia in Psychology and Religion: "Holy Ghost and Logos merges in the Gnostic idea of Sophia."[1] And, "The feminine nature of Sophia who frequently represents the Holy Ghost."[2] And, "This Sophia, who already shares certain essential qualities with the Johannine Logos, is on the one hand closely associated with the Hebrew Chochma, but on the other hand goes so far beyond it that one can hardly fail to think of the Indian Shakti."[3] In writing of the "sun woman" he says, "The sun woman is the feminine anthropos, the counterpart of the masculine principle."[4] And another, "Like God, she has her throne in heaven."[5] Since she is female, and about to bring forth a child, she has achieved Oneness by the male principle, the God power, the subjective mind, the Holy of Holies.

As we reach higher dimensions we are often assaulted by the negative. As we are conscious or still attached to earth, *maya* we have fear. So the dragon reaches our consciousness.

Since this is a "how to" book, the dragon may symbolize different dross that is left in the unconscious of the aspirant that prevents him/her from completing the Journey. Each must decide what that is. This dragon is fierce and always comes to those who are highly evolved and ready for deliverance. It is the shadow that has lurked in the unconscious to strike at the 'nth hour. If we have been evaluating ourselves and cleaning out our unconscious the overcoming will be easier. The dragon, it is said, appeared in heaven so that the dragon, defined as evil, or a symbol of evil, is an indication of our condition of duality —both heaven and earth. Perhaps we are too attached to our earth life and not ready to give up those attachments for the heavenly experience. The power of the dragon is symbolized by the horns, the heads, the diadems. It is mighty. The tail brought down a third of the stars, which are high aspirations, to the earth. So he waits to "devour her child when she brought forth." (Verse 4)

When the male and female principles come together there is a birth, the birth of the Divine Child, or the Christ Child. The Christ Child is that holy of holies which is within us—we are all pregnant with it—desiring to be born. The Christ Child is the beginning awareness of our Being, of our Potential, of the I AM. "It is the beginning in the inner realms of consciousness of a higher set of faculties that, when grown to full stature, saves the whole man from ignorance and sin." So says Jung. Toward this birth we develop our consciousness, and the revelator has given us his account.

This then is the mystery of God—the birth of the Christ Child. The Christ Child is born from the vibrations of earth which becomes One with God in the kingdom of Heaven which is within, which is at hand, which desires fulfillment.

According to Jung, "The Christ Child, the Divine Child, is of the New Age. The future birth of the divine child who, in accordance with the divine trend toward incarnation, will choose as his birthplace the empirical man."[6] June Singer, a Jungian analyst, writes in her book *Boundaries of the Soul,* "The Divine child's appearance recalls the marking of the aeons of history of the world which were heralded by the appearance of an infant who overthrows an old order and begins a new one. As for example: Moses, Oepidus, Krishna, Jesus."[7] It would seem then that the Divine Child which is born of Wisdom, or the Holy Spirit, comes from within our own consciousness and not from a prophet, master, or teacher or organization such as the church.

So we have here an account of the meeting of the Shakti (the female principle) and Shiva (the male principle), the Indian symbology for kundalini (Shakti) and the male power (Shiva) within the cranium. Some suggest that the pineal and the pituitary conjoin and the "result is a Third energy. This is the child of the inner Mystic Marriage."[8] The portent appeared in heaven, which is the head or the cranium according to this philosophy. The male power is a vibration that lies dormant until activated by the female to bring forth the Christ Child which is defined as a symbol of the beginning of total consciousness of the Divine, Enlightenment, Nirvana, Samadhi. This is pure Love.

Could this be what is called being "born again"? Jesus speaks of this in several passages: "Truly, truly, I say to you, unless one be born anew, he cannot see the Kingdom of God." (John 3:3) And John 3:5-7: "Truly, truly I say to you, unless one is born of water and the Spirit, he cannot enter the kingdom of God. That which is born of the flesh is flesh, and that which is born of the Spirit is spirit. Do not marvel that I said to you 'You must be born anew (from above).'" The "born again" Christian can attest to the necessity of a new birth and also to the difficulty one has in retaining that high state. The new birth is ours and the Divine Child is brought forth and the dragon waits.

Verse 4, "And the dragon stood before the woman who was about to bear a child, that he might devour her child when she brought it forth."

Well, as anyone knows, when it is time to complete delivery of a pregnancy we have no choice. It must come forth. And since we have set the stage of completion the child must be born. "She brought forth a male child, one who is to rule all the nations with a rod of iron," the account reads. And so the male child, a small facsimile of God, will rule the nations (our earthly thoughts) with a rod (perhaps an allusion to the spine and the kundalini) of iron.

"But her child was caught up to God and to his throne." (Verse 5) The Child is saved by the intercession, the grace of God, and was caught up to God and his throne. Again this is a simile for the results of the uniting of the power within each of us that becomes one with God. This Holy Spirit, this power within our body and consciousness brings forth the child and makes us One with Him and with All. And He is always there to help us when the concept of the Divine Child is attacked by the negative.

"The woman fled into the wilderness." Now the wilderness is symbolic of withdrawal from the world and brings to mind Rama, from Hindu mythology, who wandered for years as recounted in the epic poem, The Ramayana. The Bible gives us many examples of those who reach a high state of consciousness and then flee into the wilderness. The most famous example is that of Jesus, who after his baptism by the Holy Spirit through John, went into the wilderness to be tempted by the Devil for forty days. The Devil, the dragon, tempted him with power, materialism, and personal ambition. (Matt. 4:1-10) We know that this all happened within his consciousness as he raised himself above the material world and realized his mission. And so must we. Jesus' first words, after the temptations, recorded in Matt 4:17 were "Repent for the kingdom of Heaven is at hand." And indeed it is, for the aspirant to whom the Christ Child has been born. It will often be true of us, also, when we reach a high level of knowing, we may be frightened, or uncertain that we want to accept a higher state or awareness, and the negative forces within as well as the race consciousness, all mighty, will barrage us after we reach this high state.

The wilderness is also symbolic of a place of quiet away from the world. This could be a state of meditation, the silence. Meditation, centeredness on the One within, is our only safe barge that will carry us through the troublesome time and God will nourish us.

The Bible account says the woman fled into the wilderness "where she has a place prepared by God, in which she was to be nourished for 1,260 days." This number, like many others in Revelation, can be evenly divided by 12 (the symbol of completion) and in numerology the number adds up to 6, which is a symbol of work. So meditation and work will complete our search.

The next verse tells of war arising in heaven, the inner consciousness, and "Michael and his angels fighting against the dragon and his angels" and the dragon was defeated. Michael symbolizes a noted angel, like Gabriel, the man of God and his angels. For us this means that when we turn to Him in prayer and meditation He intercedes and we are restored to our pristine consciousness as we meet our adversary. But since we are still of this earth we can expect the dragon to attack again.

At this point I should like to discuss good and evil. "And the great dragon was thrown down, that ancient serpent, who is called the Devil and Satan, the deceiver of the whole world." The words Devil and Satan, are the names used for this dragon. We have said that the dragon was within our own conscious or unconscious. The dragon, or the opposite of the evolved woman, is around and ready to attack.

The Christian interpretation has always placed the Devil in the outer world and blamed him time after time for the downfall of man. The Hindu has his evil gods which lurked around waiting to pounce on the unwary. The primitive "runs scared" most of the time until he participates in certain ceremonies to placate or dilute evil that is all around. Other religions have developed other means of protecting their adherents from the forces of evil.

For all of mankind's known existence he has discussed the forces of good and evil. I should like to offer a few quotes relative to the stand taken by New Age teachers that "There is nothing good or bad but thinking makes it so."

"All evil, regardless of its name or nature, is the product of a universal hypnotism or malpractice based on the belief in two powers, which Paul described as the carnal mind."[9] So says Joel Goldsmith, a New Thought author and practitioner, who passed on in 1964.

"All of Buddhism, all worldly concerns, all notions of good and evil will have disappeared, like last night's dream, and your fundamental Buddha-nature alone will manifest itself."[10] (This is a Zen quotation.) Thus, both are dissolved.

"One must take evil rather more substantially when one meets it on the plane of empirical psychology. There it is simply the opposite of good."[11] Carl Jung's view.

"Good and Evil are opposite poles of a moral judgment which, as such, originates in man." Again Jung.

"Good and evil is the challenging riddle which life places sphinxlike before every intelligence. Here and there, a towering lonely figure never cries defeat. From the maya of duality he plucks the cleaveless truth of unity."[12] From Yogananda.

"Good and evil states of consciousness form the heavens and the hells of the race."[13] So states Fillmore.

Since our philosophy of the New Age has turned our attention from the outer to the inner, from the shadow to the anima/animus, from projection to introjection, we should look at evil as the lack of good. It is a part of our own consciousness and it becomes most apparent when we are ready to give deliverance to the Christ Child within. Incidentally the Christ Child is born usually in the presence of animals (our lower state of consciousness).

Let us go back to the chapter on the opening of the Chakras, to the messages to the churches. As we interpreted that we spoke of faith, sexual-creative force, thought, love, seeking God, wisdom, and total Oneness. We also spoke of the narrow gate that leads to a higher consciousness. I should like to propose that the dragon is lurking in those lower three Chakras, faith (lack of use of it or fear), sex energy (wrong usage), thought (ego), and may be, at times, apparent in the next three. The dragon, separation from good, is always there, not completely obliterated as long as we live on earth. Our complete overcoming is not reached until the body vibrations are raised to pure spirit and our earthly attachments are dissolved. This will remove us from the earth plane. As long as we are on earth we are subject to the opposite of good. But we can be safe through the intercession of God's grace and love and our attention is centered in the peaceful knowing of the inner Good.

I do not hold with those who say evil does not exist, only good. It is true that what appears negative often brings about our evolution to a higher level, but only if our aim is focused there. Evil is in the mind of the beholder just as beauty is. It is a force that has to be dealt with but it is a force within each of us. Evil is in our thinking and thought is powerful. But we know that God or His representatives will give us the strength to overcome.

The voice from heaven comes again! The great Aum! The Word! "And I heard a loud voice in heaven, saying 'now the salvation and the power and the kingdom of our God and the authority of his Christ have come, for the accuser of our brethren has been thrown down, who accuses them day and night before our God. And they have conquered him by the blood of the Lamb and by the word of their testimony, for they loved not their lives even unto death. Rejoice then, O heaven, and you that dwell therein! But woe to you, O earth and sea, for the devil has come down to you in great wrath, because he knows that his time is short.'"

This verse is a recapitulation of salvation, power, and the kingdom of God and the authority of Christ (the Holy Spirit) that have come. We have reached the state of totality. The accuser, our Karma, our burden of guilt, our fear, our earthly desires and attachments all have been overcome by "the blood of the Lamb," the living on the earth in our earthly body of the Lamb (the Holy Spirit). "And by their testimony" refers to "our brethren" meaning you and me. "For they loved not their lives even unto death" means that we were willing to give up our life for this great overcoming. Again paeans of rejoicing and then a warning to those who dwell on earth, who are in materialistic consciousness.

The dragon does not give up easily. He pursued the woman who had borne the male child. Because this was written from the consciousness of John, the Christian, the child would be considered male as the male was dominant in that society. The Christ Child, as I have said, was both male and female. This reminds us of Jung's account of the Alchemist's use of the Philosopher's Stone as symbolizing perfection and as a living being of hermaphroditic nature,[14] and Jung continues, "it was recognized from prehistoric time that the primordial divine being was both male and female."[15] The Philosopher's Stone is understood by Jung to mean the total consciousness of the Divine.

So verse 10 reveals the mystery. The great mystery of God is that through the Christ Child consciousness, which we develop through overcoming the difficulties of our earthly life, we are given salvation, power, and the kingdom of our God and the authority of His Christ. And the negative, the evil in our thinking has been thrown out of our heavenly domain and we should rejoice. The warning is there, however, to those of us who think the earth life is all there is. Then trials will be intense. But to raise our consciousness to Him on the throne will bring us Perfection. Amen!

In verse 13 we are told that the dragon, when he saw that he had been thrown out of heaven, pursued the woman. "But the woman was given the two wings of a great eagle that she might fly from the serpent into the wilderness to a place where she is to be nourished." The wings of the eagle are a symbol of the power of the Spirit. There are many symbols from ancient times depicting the flight of the soul as a circle with wings. This is a very old archetypal symbol that is a part of the race consciousness and our invention of the airplane may have been urged along by this symbol in the unconscious. Perhaps the space technology is symbolic of our ability to go direct, under our own inner power, our own Christ spirit, to dimensions beyond the earth. The soul is symbolized by the sphere; the eagle signifies height; wings symbolize intuition or spiritual potentiality.

In a book by Paul Brunton, *A Search in Secret Egypt,*[16] he points out that the birdman is symbolic of a freed human soul. Churchward, in his book *Symbols of Mu,* gives us examples of a winged circle from symbols of Mexican archeological diggers.[17] And Joseph Goodavage in *Astrology: The Space Age Science,* says: The eagle, like the phoenix, represents the endless continuity and eternal nature of the Life Force. It symbolizes the upward flight of Man's evolution and soars to tremendous heights, out of sight."[18]

The serpent did not give up easily. Water issuing from his mouth would be the subtle thoughts from the unconscious (water) that attacks our new state. A flood is symbolic of the overwhelming pressure of negatives from our lower chakras. The second chakra is often referred to as the water chakra. Carl Jung spoke extensively about the second chakra as the water chakra in a seminar reported in Spring magazine and he related it to baptism: "Therefore the very first demand of a mystery cult has always been to go into water, into the baptismal font. The way into any higher development leads through the water, with the danger of being swallowed by the monster. Baptism is symbolic of drowning. It is a world-wide symbolism of the baptism by water with all its dangers of being drowned or devoured by the makara. So the second chakra could be called the chakra or mandala of baptism or of rebirth, of destruction, whatever the consequence of the baptism might be."[19] This seems to support the following:

Baptism by water, in the religious sects, has been most important throughout the ages. In this case—the woman being swallowed up by the water—is used as a warning that it may not save her and the earth saved her and swallowed up the flood.

And so the earth, or materialism which has been depicted as negative, reverses its symbolism and becomes Good. Now that the Revelation of the Christ Child has been given and received, everything negative becomes reversed. Revelation, the birth of the Christ Child, reverses everything and we see all is Good. And the conscious mind is cleansed!

The subtle thoughts of the unconscious needed to be cleansed and the earth, motherhood, substance of faith, the feminine, the conscious mind, love, all of these symbols of earth, saved her. I would choose the symbol of Love as being her rescuer. For the earth, as Love, gives us everything we have to sustain our physical life. It is the great mother and nourishes the heavens and us. It is that which brings us together with our good, that gives us the chance to live and to pursue our goal of Oneness. So earth, Love, swallowed up the water and the woman was saved. May I remind you that love is the fourth chakra after our consciousness has passed through the narrow gate from the lower three centers. Love saves and heals us and only through consciousness of it and meditation can we overcome the dragon.

The dragon is still around and "makes war on the rest of her offspring." So we, her offspring, may be continually barraged, for the Christ Child is your consciousness and mine. We are the Christ, we have the kingdom of God within, which is subject to attack as long as we are on earth. For as we keep the commandments of God and bear testimony to Jesus we will be attacked.

Gaining enlightenment does not mean we are through with our Journey on the Path. Enlightenment is a state of mind, of the consciousness of the glory of that dimension which exists but is reached very seldom. Jesus faced his temptations after his enlightenment and through his teaching we learn they can be overcome in our lives. Perfection is not reached in a day or a flash. Enlightenment gives us a view of heaven as described in Revelation 4:1–6 and that leads us on to be in that state forever.

"Bear testimony to Jesus," from verse 17, is not a one-time-only act either. Bearing testimony to Jesus is the following of his example, of his life, as depicted in the Bible and interpreted by our Inner Knowing. He taught us how to overcome our earthly attachments and to free the Holy Spirit to act through our life. This we must do and this will bring us through the final Satori.

"And he stood on the sand of the sea;" that is, the dragon stood on the sand of the sea. He was angry with the woman and went off to make war on the rest of her offspring, the Christ Child in each of us. There are multitudes of us, like the sand of the sea. And so the dragon touches all of us.

And so, what is the mystery of God? What does all this mean to us on our Journey?

It seems to me that Chapter 12 is a great love poem, an assurance to all mankind that God is ever at work in man's consciousness, that the birth of Divine Illumination comes to each of us when we are prepared and ready. Although we may be afraid that we have unloosed the dragon we can be assured that Divine protection lies all around, and within us. We are loved. We love, and no force can overcome that great and wonderful power containing the totality of what we term God. We must not forget, however, that our God is man's interpretation of the Great Force that holds the world together. It is still limited to the size of our own consciousness and thus we must continue to grow in order to climb the ladder of Pure consciousness. Love, the Holy Spirit, the awareness of pure goodness may be challenged but in the end the God of all creation will ever be in heaven, the Kingdom, in our conscious awareness. Love, the great benefactor, wins always.

And so the Christ Child has been born and is with God where the maturing process will take place. Our growth and Becoming is just beginning. Let us press on.

CHAPTER 13

The Beast

Now begins the most difficult section of the book to interpret in the light of New Thought as the account of the plagues are so real to our human existence, and the beast may be considered a plague, that they touch off fears and it is difficult to see how we can interpret them spiritually. We shall begin, however, and let the Spirit speak from within.

The chapter opens with an account of the beast rising out of the *sea*. It is powerful and is at its apex of becoming. The horns and the diadems indicate this. The seven heads indicate the intelligence with which it acts and it has a blasphemous name on its heads. Blasphemy is irreverent thought toward God such as sickness, poverty, death. Each of us must now find out what it is in our *unconscious* (the sea) that the beast symbolizes and the name which is blasphemous.

"And the beast that I saw was like a leopard, its feet were like a bear's, and its mouth was like a lion's mouth," (Verse 2) The mythological description of the beast is, of course, from the collective unconscious. Leopard is an animal of great stealth and cunning and kills for his physical needs. "The feet being like bear claws are symbolic of the chthonic element,"[1] (the opposite of good.) The mouth was like a lion's mouth which has great power to tear to bits that which is desired, like the king of the jungle. Perhaps this is describing the use of our own mouth for the expression of thoughts that tear apart. According to the dictionary, beast is defined as the animal nature of man.

"And to it the dragon gave his power, and his throne and great authority." (End of verse 2) We have identified the dragon as evil, as the absence of good, in the experience of the aspirant. In the twelfth chapter we seemed to reach the apex of our search, but evidently there is some other dross we must experience and rid ourselves of. Perhaps it will be the temptations of Jesus. Perhaps our own personal overcomings will become apparent as we study. Each then must find his own answer as to what these revelations mean to him, for it is the individual soul that must become aware of Oneness with the Divine and the veils must be removed, one by one. The dragon then is using the Holy Spirit for giving attention to the negative, to what man has titled evil. Since this is a human condition we must deal with it.

"One of its heads seemed to have a mortal wound but its mortal wound was healed, and the whole earth followed the beast with wonder." (Verse 3) So it has the power of evil and is marked with a mortal wound which is of this earth and could bring death but it was healed.

The dragon has a long history in the annals of mythology. It has symbolized many different conditions and thus has been a world-wide figure. The dragon in the Near East symbolizes evil; in Greece the Hydra possessed both protection and terror-inspiring qualities; in the Far East it was a beneficent symbol, the material symbol of China; in Japan it can change its size; in Taoism it is the deified force; in the Bible it is the same as the subtle serpent of Genesis; the Christian has interpreted it as the anti-Christ, sin, Paganism. So there is nothing to be done but to decide for ourselves what it symbolizes. Perhaps it is all of these, for all is Good; and negative or positive, it can bring us a lesson for our enlightenment.

As for the anti-Christ, it is said that when we do not recognize the God within, then we have rising within us the anti-Christ, the "son of chaos," the evil doer. Then we are captured by this world, the materialistic, the *maya* of nothingness and thus suffer.

As we go along our Path it will be necessary to look at our self straight and openly to determine what must be eradicated. For me, there have been many. One that comes to mind now is negative emotions, thoughts, and body ailments that I recognized and called real. These negative characteristics were in my unconscious and I once worshipped them in the name of egoistic diadems. To me, the negative of which I was aware, was my intelligent coping with the world. Critical analysis, criticism, judgment of myself and others, came from the other beast, the conscious mind. The scientific age and education encouraged it. The psychological analysis of aberrant behavior seemed truth to me although I knew in my inner knowing that Freud was limited in his approach. The literary report of the negative in human behavior seemed to be truth. So I worshipped the beast from the unconscious as well as the conscious and gave much attention and energy to it.

Verse 5 mentions the beast uttering haughty and blasphemous words. This was true of me. My ego was in the driver's seat, and the words that I uttered were against the God of which my body is a temple. Oh, of course, I did not take God's name in vain, I gave bowed reverence to the commandments, I kept the outer laws of morality, but the other side of my nature, which was split from the Good, came forth. The seven heads, the seven chakras, were all centered in the judgmental center of the unconscious.

Now this is my confession. What is yours? What do you worship? What is your human condition? The Zen Buddhists have created many beautiful rock gardens in Kyoto, Japan. They are symbolic of man's journey to Oneness. The one at the Daisenin Monastery has boulders and stones that symbolize various stumbling blocks in the life of the aspirant. The last scene is an open sea of fine gravel, smoothly raked, but two piles of gravel in the center are said to symbolize greed and hate—the last two blocks that man must flatten into the sea of peaceful consciousness if he is to reach the goal of peace and joy with the Eternal. Ask yourself, are either one of those my block? The life of the aspirant must be cleansed one step at a time and the veils are removed one at a time from his conscious awareness of God. Only you can know this for you are the "captain of your fate."

Verse 7 indicates that the beast overcame the saints and conquered them. The saints are understood to be those who stand in awe of the Lord God, who symbolize our very positive qualities, our representations of the Spirit within, the qualities of the Holy Spirit without blemish. The authority given it was over all the personal characteristics that are a part of our world. "And all who dwell on earth (within the consciousness of *Maya,* illusion) will worship it." (Verse 8)

Those whose name "has not been written before the foundation of the world in the book of life of the Lamb that was slain," will worship the beast from the unconscious. Many Christians refer to this last quote as a testimony for predestination and that we have no control over what will happen to us. To me this is a most inhuman, unspiritual philosophy, for if you are not of the chosen, according to their interpretation, there is no reason for you to try to grow in conscious awareness of the Higher Self that lies within you. How illogical is a God who would visit such condemnation on you! In other words, following our analogy, we had just as well give up to the authority of the negative in our unconscious because we are not chosen.

It would seem that Charles Fillmore is correct when he says in the *Metaphysical Bible Dictionary:* "Jesus Christ, the world's deliverer and Savior, calls for a company of tried and trained and spiritually developed people to work with Him in establishing His glorious kingdom of righteousness and peace upon the earth; these people are now being made ready." If you are reading this book with a serious intent to follow Jesus' teaching, then you are one of the elect, and people of all nations and races have the opportunity to do likewise. Fillmore also using "chosen people" symbolically suggests that our "chosen people" are our spiritually enlightened and obedient thoughts and as we make these thoughts continuous in our lives we will be the "chosen people."[2]

Verse 8 also refers to the Lamb who was slain. This is the Holy Spirit that each of us has used for riotous living, separate from our Divine Source, for materialistic desires.

Verse 10 reminds us that if we are to be taken captive or if we use the sword, the law of Karma will react. For if we allow ourselves to be captivated by our unconscious desires which are in oppostion to our Good, then like will attract like.

Now let us see what the next challenge will be. But let us remember, "Don't reason about evil, but give it a glance and pass beyond. It is *Avidhya,* ignorance, something merely to be outgrown and left behind, transcended and forgotten,"[3] (William James in *Varieties of Religious Experience).* And from the same book, "Much of what we call evil is due entirely to the way men take the phenomenon—the sufferer's inner attitude must be changed from fear to faith." And, "Since you make them evil or good by your own thoughts about them, it is the ruling of your thoughts which proves to be your principle concern."[4] So don't dwell on these weaknesses, just give them your attention with deep honesty for a moment and then pass on, deciding with deep conviction that your behavior will change, that your thoughts and actions will be controlled. Jesus says, "For out of the heart come evil thoughts, murder, adultery, fornication, theft, false witness, slander." (Matt. 15:19)

Align your thoughts with the Christ within and ask God to divinely guide you. To continually be unforgiving to yourself and to be afraid that you will repeat the behavior you dislike will only draw you to what you fear. Love yourself as God does, center on Him and continue on. This is only an awareness of a stumbling block that can be removed and the inner Christ is reached through meditation and will ever bear you and strengthen your resolve. Thus the challenge will be overcome.

Let us go on to verse 11, which is another epic dealing with the beast, the animal-like nature of man, the anti-Christ. As an aside, before we discuss verse 11, it is a psychological truism that the conscious awareness of the mind, is always filled with some thought, some idea, some feeling awareness. If it is not positive, it will be negative. And strangely enough we get much pleasure out of dwelling on the negative. It is the human condition to enjoy in an odd way the sorrows, depressions, joylessness of life. One would think that such painful apparitions would be fled, but it is like touching a sore spot on your body, there is some pleasure in it. Thus we are subtly drawn into deeper pain. It is a trap!

Turning our attention to the good, the true, the beautiful should be our immediate desire. Philippians 4:8 gives us food for thought: "Finally, brethren, whatever is true, whatever is honorable, whatever is just, whatever is pure, whatever is lovely, whatever is gracious, if there is any excellence, if there is anything worthy of praise, think about these things."

Verses 11-15 give us the view of another beast arising, this time from the earth. *Earth,* as has been pointed out, is the creative female principle and is very much of this world. So the beast rises out of the *conscious* mind and has two horns, and it speaks like a dragon. It has the authority of the first beast and makes all to worship the first beast. The two beasts, one out of the sea and one which rose from the earth, are symbolic of the unconscious and the conscious mind. The dragon does not give up easily and he gave authority to the first beast. The beast from the earth had two horns like a lamb, which was pure deceit. How the conscious mind does deceive us!

The conscious mind, of course, is in the driver's seat and determines what we give attention to or worship. It is often difficult to determine whether our thoughts are good or evil, but we can be sure the worshiping of that which is negative or evil will not raise our consciousness of Good. The mind has psychic abilities which people of less than spiritual stature will use to capture the attention of the populace, as fire from heaven illustrates here in verse 13. Remember Jesus was tempted in the wilderness to use signs and wonders to gain man's favor. The psychic is a part of great mystic knowldege, and as we become further enlightened we have these abilities, but they should come from and be used for the glory of God and not for our own egoistic desires. Then they will be used rightly.

The "conscious mind beast" uses all his wits to bring us to worship the powerful unconscious beast. He even made the image of it come alive and speak and to cause those who would not worship to be slain. Again the mind can turn unreality into reality and eventually our spiritual awareness can be slain.

It occurs to me that worry is much like this. Worry is a condition of the "normal" person while anxiety is a stronger term and is a condition of the sick soul and is based upon nonreality. How insidious they both are. Worry can give reality to that which is dead, in the past. Worry is the opposite of faith. Worry can undermine our faith in God and man. Worry engenders fear which separates us from faith. And worry can eventually turn into anxiety, a sick state, if we continue on that course. The antidote is, of course, checking out the realness of what we are worrying about, taking action when we can, and leaving the rest of the solution to God by faith.

So the beast from the earth which does obeisence to the first beast is the materialistic view of our life, our goals, our needs. Magic is always attractive and if we believe that what the earthly experience has to offer is to be our guide to happiness, we will be blinded.

Further the mark of the first beast must be on us else we will not be allowed to buy or sell. Verse 17, "so that no one can buy or sell unless he has the mark, that is, the name of the beast or the number of his name." And in our earthly existence, how can we survive if we do not buy or sell? That is the stuff of our earthly experience.

There have been many interpretations of what the mark of the first beast was: "This calls for wisdom; let him who has understanding reckon the number of the beast, for it is a human number, its number is six hundred and sixty-six." (Verse 18.) The King James translation calls it the "number of man." The Amplified version uses the phrase, "calculates the number of the beast for it is a human number."

These are some explanations I have found: From an article by J. M. Pryse, in *Kundalini, Evolution and Enlightenment,* we find the number 666 decoded as the lower mind or the beast.[5] Elizabeth Turner says it is "the false prophet." The Christian has connected it with Emperor Nero, the first to persecute the Christians. She also says that spiritually interpreted the number stands for that which is in violent opposition to the spiritual.[6] William James reports, "The mark of the beast is fear which is self-imposed or self-permitted suggestion of inferiority."[7] Using numerology it converts to nine. According to Violet Shelley, who writes from the Edgar Cayce Center, nine is a number of mystery. "Because it is the last of the digits, Nine is the symbol of that which brings things to an end and prepares for a new manifestation."[8] She also points out that nine is often considered the number of the initiate. So perhaps we should take the mark of the beast in a positive way. Perhaps the number of the beast symbolizes opportunity to reach completion of the number ten or Oneness. It is the earthly consciousness ready to become heavenly.

Jung reminds us that the number nine is the number of Heimarmene which translated is fate or natural necessity.[9] According to the Chinese Alchemical book, the *I Ching*[10] nine has great tension within and needs to change to ten or one. So the number 666 has within it the potential for completeness but is incomplete, as the conscious mind, the second beast, is of the earth. Tension that leads to completion is good and our problem from the conscious and/or unconscious contains within it the good that is potential. The 18th verse, "This calls for wisdom," is our clue. Our recognition of the need for Oneness is wisdom as we go on our Path. Since buying and selling are necessary for our earthly sojourn, it is imperative that wisdom be used to understand our need for completion. And Wisdom is Divine.

So what is the conclusion to be gained from this chapter? It seems to me that self-analysis, centeredness in our Good; promotion of faith and not fear, belief in good coming from evil; and realizing that we are the elect and so are all who follow the Path of Jesus by developing our Self awareness, should be considered. Again, our individuation process, our search for pure Joy and Happiness, our own overcomings are all an inside job. It is worth the effort. Just listen to all of the great teachers of the Bible. It is Worth It!! The kingdom of God or the kingdom of Heaven which lies within us and needs to be revealed, is our goal.

And verse 10 of this chapter gives us a clue of how to proceed: "Here is a call for the endurance and faith of the saints." Faith again, our beginning and our end!

CHAPTER 14

Warnings and Harvesting

Again, true to form, we are going to be blessed by the Heavenly angels and He who is on the throne. Growth in consciousness goes in cycles and when we overcome the negative then we are rewarded with the positive. We have just gone through a growth phase, now our reward. As usual we are encouraged and made joyous, after we have realized the negative of the earth life, and turn again in our consciousness to Mount Zion and the 144,000. Verse 1: "Then I looked, and lo, on Mount Zion stood the Lamb, and with him a hundred and forty-four thousand who had his name and his Father's name written on their foreheads."

Mt. Zion is a symbol of the house of God, heaven as the final gathering place of true believers, the highest place of man's consciousness. We have discussed 144,000 elsewhere, but I should like to add that we are again reminded of the number 12 which is a symbol of perfection in spiritual matters. These could be our own spiritual powers that are perfect for eternity, that have reached perfection as the scripture reads, "who had his name (the Lamb's) and his Father's name written on their foreheads." (Verse 1) In other words, the Father and the Holy Spirit have come together and the Third Eye mark or the Wisdom mark is upon all these spiritual powers.

The Lamb, as stated elsewhere, is the Holy Spirit, which was personified in Jesus, and the Father is the Universal Spirit or what we call God. The mark is of the third eye open as a result of raising the personal consciousness, the Holy Spirit, to the Heavenly Throne. Jesus speaks of the eye being the lamp of the body and when it is sound our whole body will take on the glow of light. (Luke 11:34) It is good that this scene is repeated, as for our learning we need much repetition.

Verse 2, "And I heard a voice from heaven like the sound of many waters and like the sound of loud thunder; the voice I heard was like the sound of harpers playing on their harps." From Yogananda's writings we learn that the vibratory activities of each chakra center produces a characteristic sound. In meditation the yogi may hear first the hum, as of a bumblebee, emitted by the coccygeal center at the base of the spine. The sacral center has a flute-like sound; the lumbar center a harplike sound; the dorsal center a bell-like sound. The cervical center at the base of the neck or throat emanates a sound as of rushing waters; and at the medulla oblongata connected to the third eye is heard the symphony of all sounds together—the oceanic roar of the Aum vibration. The kundalini sings in our inner ear.

Verse 3: "And they sung as it were, a new song before the throne and before the four living creatures and before the elders." Again glorifying God after the vision of heaven comes to us is our very human and divine way of worshipping. Indeed the whole earth worships the God of Creation each day. I often think of Handel's "Messiah" as the outstanding example of praise and it has been so performed for hundreds of years and the Allelulia Chorus brings us all to our feet in one great volume of praise. How it rings in my ears as it resounds from the rafters of the room or the skies! Allelulia! Allelulia! Allelulia! O how beautiful is the song of love for the Father. We vibrate it and it vibrates us. The joyous ecstasy of love that comes as we comprehend the light of our Christ is a melody of love. "There's within my heart a melody," an old hymn describes it perfectly. We are the musicians for we are gentle, understanding, pure, forgiving, compassionate. We are love!

Verse 4 describes the 144,000 as those who have not been defiled by women and so have not partaken of the opposites: the lusts of the flesh or of the mind. Perhaps 144,000 is a real number. Perhaps that is all who have withstood this test. We hope a few more have been added in the last 2,000 years. "It is these who have not defiled themselves with women." Is this a case for chastity? Chaste also means pure.

Again "they have followed the Lamb" and "they have been redeemed from mankind as the first fruits for God and the Lamb." So there is hope for us as it does not read "all fruits for God" but the first. It is still open, the invitation, "Come unto me." Notice "these have been redeemed from mankind." In other words, they have had the experience of being on this earth and have followed the Lamb. They have been forgiven all their impurities. They were once like you and me. They have followed the teachings of Jesus and as God loves with an everlasting, impersonal love, He is waiting to add our consciousness, our new name, to the thousands who have reached the throne before us.

Verse 6 starts the angelic messages again with repetition. But we need to hear this heavenly thought many times if we are to be one of the chosen. We already know, of course, that angels symbolize high spiritual thoughts and if we will but listen we will hear. Since the description is one of the transcendent throne and glory we all know the gospel (the good news) and it is for all men everywhere, not just for the chosen religious group. Someone has said that if it is true that only adherents of a particular religion will make it to heaven, it will be sparsely populated, as most professors of a dogmatic religion, which might claim this, are not able to live up to its tenets. The ideal is possible, of course, and that is what we are aiming for.

Verse 7 reads, "Fear God and give him glory, for the hour of his judgment has come . . ." The judgment of God has been a strong point made by the Christian religions and has been used as a whip or a club over the members of the congregation by the priests, the preachers, other members of the church, the high church officials assuming the place of God and passing out the judgment in the form of persecution, censor, excommunication, abandonment, separation to a lonely existence, damnation to a burning Hell, etc. It was and is by and large the male members who assume the throne of the Most High in these matters. The "fear of God" as mentioned in this verse was taken literally to mean the "fear of man and God."

We know from our understanding of Karma that if we are to

be punished it will come naturally. That is probably the reason that the Hindus have never fought a religious war. They neither evangelized the world, for they believe that in due time each will be taught what he needs for his cleansing and it does not have to be taken care of here and now, that each has many lives ahead. I have never feared God, but I have been in awe of God, which is another meaning from the dictionary: "have reverential awe of." Being subject to the instinct of fear, we persons have fallen into the trap of fearing the Lord instead of loving Him. The evolutionary process has taken us to a place physically which has much less fear, but psychologically we are still burdened. To throw off the yoke of guilt taught by churchmen who lay this "trap" upon us is next to impossible for many Western Christians.

Buddha did not teach of a future life in heaven after death. He taught people to live in the now and free themselves of that which they fear, i.e., he taught non-attachment. Other world religions have not held this whip over their members as Christianity has. Its history is filled with violence because of the churchmen believing that the world should understand God through the Christian interpretations. Rather we are to worship God. He made all, all is good "and worship him who made the heaven (spiritual), the earth (material or conscious mind), the sea (the unconscious) and the fountain of water (the Holy Spirit)." Fear indeed! Let us worship!

Verse 8 is recalling to our mind the symbol of Babylon and to remember Babylon and what it stood for will help us understand this verse. "Fallen, fallen is Babylon the great, she who made all nations drink the wine of her impure passion."

Babylon was a great center of materialism and intellectual pursuits about 2000 B.C. It was the center of commerce, a center of the world in that geographic region. The Jews were exiled from Jerusalem to Babylon about 586 B.C. It was a place of great unhappiness for them. Immorality, following of lust, following the lower passions, accumulating wealth, separation from any religious belief was the life of many of its inhabitants.

Now we have suggested that Jerusalem is the symbol of the Holy City, of Higher Consciousness, of the throne of God. Babylon, on the other hand, is symbolic of all that is opposite to Jerusalem. And so it is used in this verse. Verse 8 is a report card for each of us who are on the Path. For those who are not it is a warning. For materialism cannot last. It must fall. The very presence of God within the creation will bring this about. And so it will in your consciousness as you realize the futility of centeredness in "impure passions" and you will have to decide what that means for you. Verse 9: "And another angel, a third, followed them, saying with a loud voice, 'If any one worships the beast and its image, and receives a mark on his forehead or on his hand, he also shall drink the wine of God's wrath, poured unmixed into the cup of his anger.''

The mark of the beast has been discussed previously. If we assume the mark of the beast to be the mark of man in the earthly consciousness as opposed to the spiritual consciousness, we can then gain some insight into the meaning. Verses 9–13 deal with the results of worshiping the beast, the conscious and unconscious of the mind of man and leaving out the higher consciousness. The Christian has interpreted these passages as a description of Hell which will come to those who do not live a moral life and believe in Jesus. I should like to suggest that it refers to the here and now as well as in future lives. Raising the kundalini power or the Holy Spirit for purposes that are bestial will automatically bring us great discomfort, great burning sensation either in body or in mind, and we will be tormented as never before. It is a powerful force we are dealing with and always must be centered in the good or God.

God's wrath is man's interpretation of what happens to him, for man often blames God for that which he himself is responsible. We make the choices and use our own will in making them. If they are for the Good, the True, the Beautiful then God is working in and through us for their completion. If we are separated from our consciousness of Him and going our own way, then we feel wrath which we project on God. Man has always been a great projectionist and the shadow of our own lack is often projected onto God and others.

Our endurance through this time of testing is spoken of as "endurance of the saints or those who keep the commandments of God and the faith of Jesus."

The commandments of God have been different for different generations and cultures throughout the ages. As social, political, and religious circumstances have changed, man has reinterpreted the commandments of God. "God assumes different forms in different ages to serve the special needs of the time."[1] It is very confusing to him who tries to follow outer interpretations. Most of mankind finds it easier to give up his own independent will and interpretation of the commandments to an authority of the state, the church, or an educational institution. Ancient authorities do not always fit the evolutionary statutes of man. The New Age requires that we find that authority within ourselves, for we are facing many choices: overturning of morals and everyday routines, changes in families, changes in nations and their governments. The safe and sure ways of the past just do not fit.

It has come so fast, the changes of the last few years, that the "authorities" in medicine, politics, economics, world relationships, personal relationships, have given up many times and are replying to our questions and problems, "I just do not know." So the New Age requires that we go to our inner authority, our Christ within, contact it, listen and act. The faith of Jesus is needed for this task as His faith was always strong and apparent in all His teaching. And what was that faith based on? Matthew 11:27: "All things have been delivered to me by my Father." Time after time he directed man to look within to the Kingdom of God for answers to his questions. He demonstrated to man how he, Jesus, was keyed in to this power and what any of us could do with it. So we need the commandments of God and the Faith of Jesus.

A book, *The Aquarian Conspiracy* by Marilyn Ferguson, is a very complete report of these changes that are occurring in all levels of our society. The looking inward to an inner guide through

meditation and yoga, and the development of a new consciousness is a quiet revolution, she says. "The great shuddering,
irrevocable shift overtaking us is not a new political, religious,
or philosophical system. It is a new mind—the ascendance of a
startling worldview that gathers into its framework break-through
science and insights from earliest recorded thought."[2]

Verse 13 gives us the impression that dying in the Lord to
rest from our labors is the ultimate. Verse 13: "And I heard
a voice from heaven saying, 'Write this: Blessed are the dead
who die in the Lord henceforth.'" "Blessed indeed," says the
Spirit "that they may rest from their labors, for their deeds
follow them!" The Lord, in harmony with our basic thesis of
baptism by the Holy Spirit, is the Holy Spirit. As we die to all
that the world offers and raise our consciousness of the Divine
Self through the releasing of our small self to it, we are released
from our labors. In other words, we do not have to work at
our task. If we flow by the Spirit or through the Spirit as Taoism
teaches, then all will come to us and our deeds will naturally
happen without conscious work. "Therefore the sage manages
affairs without action, and spreads doctrine without words.[3]
(From the *Tao te Ching*)

Flowing with the Spirit is so foreign to us who live in the
limited world of time and space that we discount it as a possibility
at all. But oh what peace it brings. As we meditate, keep our
mind on seeking God, move and breathe in his wisdom, "the
peace that passes understanding" comes to us. (Phil. 4:7)

The man of the world, the man centered in Babylon, knows
no such peace. Indeed the Babylonian is really searching for just
that peace but knows not where to find it. In the Bhagavad Gita,
that ancient of Hindu teachings, we read in Chapter 2:64: "But
the soul that moves in the world of senses and yet keeps the senses
in harmony, free from attraction and aversion, finds rest in quietness." Verse 65, "In this quietness falls down the burden of all
her sorrows, for when the heart has found quietness, wisdom
has also found peace." And 67, "For when the mind become
bound to a passion of the wandering senses, this passion carries

away man's wisdom, even as a wind drives a vessel on the waves."⁴ Flowing in a timeless, spaceless, formless dimension is reality and brings us to the throne of God.

And that brings us to the figure "like unto the son of man" sitting on a cloud with a "golden crown upon his head." (Verse 14) Is this Jesus? Is this Buddha? Is this Confucius? Is this Lao Tsu? Is this Moses? Is this Mohammed? The cloud is a figure used throughout the Bible to denote a high spiritual experience. For instance, in I Kings 8:10,11, we have a description of the cloud filling the whole house of the Lord and is likened to the "glory of the Lord filled the house of the Lord." The pillar of cloud that led the Israelites when they left Egypt is another example. Moses entered the cloud and went up on the mountain where he spoke with God. When Jesus went up on the mountain and met with Moses and Elijah, "a bright cloud overshadowed them, and a voice from the cloud said, 'This is my beloved Son, with whom I am well pleased; listen to him.'" And in Revelation 1:7, we are told that he, Jesus Christ, is coming with the clouds. The word cloud is also used in the general sense of betokening rain and also obscuring the sun. I would suggest that metaphysically speaking the figure on the cloud which had a sickle in his hand and who "swung his sickle on the earth, and the earth was reaped" (Verse 16) is an image of our Christ self which directs our thoughts and they are reaping the Truth.

Our thoughts (the sickle) can forcibly expel the harvest of the earth, the lower elements in our nature. Our thoughts can be good or evil (separation from Good). The sickle can be positive or negative, but when directed by our own Christ the reaping will be for the good. When evil is reduced the positive inflows. We reap what we sow. The reaping can be the beginning of that process which brings food for our soul and strength for our will. As the consciousness grows so does the body change and food for the body, the soul, the mind should be chosen by our inner Christ. Since the figure on the cloud is a high being we would expect that the good that we have produced on earth would meet his sickle while the other angels and their sickles seem to be reaping the negative of the earth. The Son of man is you and me, spiritual man.

Since we are studying angelic messages in this chapter, we are not surprised when more angels appear. One has an eternal gospel to proclaim; one gives the command to the Son of man to reap the harvest on earth; another appears with a sharp sickle, coming out of the temple of heaven; another appears who comes out of the altar and has power over fire and also commands the angel with the sharp sickle to reap and gather the cluster of grapes from the earth for they were ready for harvest.

Elizabeth Turner, in her interpretaion, in her book *Be Ye Transformed,* says this: "By now we have learned many spiritual lessons and understand that the time has come for the outer or conscious self to be further refined (harvested). This task is undertaken by our spiritual thoughts (angels) that forcibly expel the mortal beliefs (use a sharp sickle). Later on in our spiritual ongoing it will be revealed to us that there is an easier and more effective way of disposing of undesirable mental states: that is 'let go and let God.'"[5]

Corinne Heline has this interpretation of the four angels: "Man may sow upon the earth as he will, but his causation is marked for reaping under the guidance of the four Recording Angels, the Lords of Destiny. Aquarius, Lord of Air, flies through heaven proclaiming the everlasting gospel of the new Christ Age to every nation, race, and people upon the earth. Scorpio, Lord of Water, follows saying, Babylon is fallen." Regeneration must supersede generation before the New Age can be ushered in. Taurus, Lord of Earth, proclaims, "The time is come to reap, for the harvest of the earth is ripe." Leo, Lord of fire, comes out from the altar. He has power over fire, and cries with a loud cry, 'Gather the clusters of the vine of the earth, for the grapes are fully ripe.' The mystery of fire is the mystery of life. The mastery of fire is the secret of Illumination."[6] All of this quote fits perfectly the basic assumption upon which this book stands.

Chapter 14 seems very confusing if we try to interpret it from the intellect and read it as do the fundamentalist religionists.

So if it is to be for our teaching, a synthesis must be made of the entire chapter rather than an analysis of each portion. We have done some of that, now let us synthesize.

It is obvious that we are given on the one hand a beautiful picture of the overcoming of the beast, the human consciousness, in order to raise the consciousness to Oneness with Him on the throne. The singing, the playing of harps, the beautiful sounds of many waters, the sound of thunder, are all descriptions of our experiences when we come up to the throne, and God and the Lamb are at One. Or Shakti and Shiva are cojoined and there are no opposites.

The heavenly messengers are warnings from our higher consciousness about our centeredness in the beast or being marked by the beast. The hour has come for the earth to turn away from Babylon and face toward Jerusalem. Not only face but actually progress toward it, for if we don't we will be punished by our own choice. Death can come to us many times on earth. We die and are resurrected many times. It is a fluctuation from the highest to the lowest but each time, with God's Grace, we are lifted up. And up a little higher. Our life on this earth is meant for the overcoming of our base desires and attachments, our letting go of pleasure in suffering, our learning to flow with the Spirit. The time is ripe in each of our lives for the harvest. That which we have cultivated on earth may be reaped by the angel of heaven in order to bring us to a higher state of consciousness.

The sickles of the angels (thoughts) are doing their work in our lives each day. Our limited perspective makes it appear bad, but all is good. We may go through many plagues but in the Ultimate we will be added to the 144,000. The mark of the beast must be erased and we will rise as angels sitting on a cloud with a golden crown. Enlightenment comes if we persevere. That figure on the cloud could be you or me. The great religious leaders are personifications of God awareness which is potential in us. In John 14:12, Jesus said, "Truly, truly, I say to you, he who believes in me will also do the works that I do; and greater works than these will he do, because I go to the Father.''

We will be cleansed. The sickle of the angel will reap the fruits of our living. If not of the kingdom, they will be destroyed and we are purified. The wisdom of God prevails, no matter what the appearance in your life. He is. He is Love! And the time is NOW, for ''I tell you lift up your eyes, and see how the fields are already white for harvest.'' (John 4:35) The New Age is here and now and we all sing a New Song!

CHAPTER 15

Seven Plagues for Our Cleansing

The chapter opens on a positive note, albeit a warning that seven angels will bring the seven plagues. But we are assured they are the last "for with them the wrath of God is ended." Again, we have been taught that the "wrath of God" comes from no unknown agent outside ourselves, but it is from within. And the wrath will be a blessing.

Our ailments, our illnesses, our lacks, our pain and sufferings all seem to come from others or forces outside our own self. However, it has been proven that our own thinking brings on these negative circumstances. Elmer and Alyce Green, in their book *Beyond Biofeedback* have much to say about this. In speaking of "body consciousness" they say, "If all the sections of the body, including the voluntary and involuntary organs and tissues, are represented in the brain, as they seem to be, then the phrase "getting control of the body" really means "getting control of the central nervous system.""[1]

The Divine Mind, in our understanding, is impersonal love and intelligence. Our self or mind is subject to personal love and as we think we inject into the Divine Mind within us what we desire. Now we may not think specifically of the negative result but our thinking separates us from the positive and as it reacts the results may give us pain and suffering and ultimately blessing if we let it. This is, of course, a natural fulfillment of Divine Law, "As you sow so shall you reap," and we are experiencing what we entitle the "wrath of God." The wrath is the law, the natural law, that follows according to our thought, word or action. And it is good for it is for cleansing our consciousness, if we desire that.

Mankind is resilient. We have shown this as we have gone through the evolving process from primitive times until now. He has been strengthened many times by holy saints being incarnated on earth to lead the people to a higher level of expression. He has worked, fought, overcome many physical handicaps that kept him chained to the wheel of negative action and reaction.

Each of us is a microcosm of the macrocosm. We each go through our own trials to overcome the forces that are natural to our human existence. In so doing we make incorrect choices and decisions, bring to ourselves negative conditions. We are, usually, doing the best we can at that stage of development and God's love still flows through even the darkest mind. If we are conscious of our need to evolve in Oneness we will use these mistakes, these negative thoughts and actions, to "boost" us up to higher consciousness. Some or should I say most people get bogged down in their unhappy situation and become paranoid, projecting on God and man the responsibility for the condition. Until we accept the "wrath" as the result of our own earthly endeavors, we will not be able to inherit the kingdom of God. "We have really rejected God or the perfect law which is unalterable and unchangeable, impersonal. The law will react on us and we will reap discord and disharmony."[2]

The law reacts to bring us our good, also. Charles Fillmore says: "The 'Wrath of God' is really the working out of the law of Being for the individual who does not conform to the law but thinks and acts in opposition to it. The development of man is under law. God is the all-providing law.[3] God is Mind; man, the offspring of God, is mind. To know the law of God, man must adjust his mind to God-Mind.

If we can see these negative circumstances as good and a means of turning ourselves around toward a deeper awareness of God, then we are well on our way to healing the problem. Illness is the result of being out of "sync" with the good of our being, according to Mary Baker Eddy, founder of Christian Science. So the "wrath of God" is the separation of our good from us by our own self-will. God is love and all that comes from Him is Good for the individual and for the race of men.

Now we come to another sublime description of the "throne." Verse 2, "And I saw what appeared to be a sea of glass mingled with fire, and those who had conquered the beast and its image and the number of its name, standing beside the sea of glass with harps of God in their hands. And they sing the song of Moses." We are always blessed with the love and image of the Good being worshipped by those who have conquered the beast, its image, and the number of its name. We are given new hope that we will be able to reach this high state of consciousness, for what we focus on will eventually come to pass. This is why we are continually given beautiful, love-filled experiences either in our conscious mind or from the unconscious in dreams, visions, and active imagination. They are "out of this world" experiences and call us on to find a means of having those experiences eternally.

They sing the song of Moses, the servant of God, and the song of the Lamb. After the people of Israel were saved from the Egyptians and the Pharaoh at the Red Sea, due to the intercession of God through Moses, they sang a song of praise and thanksgiving to the Lord. Thus we will sing when we reach our goal and should sing all along the way. Singing lifts the vibration of our body and spirit and has always been important in all religions. It is a chanting in many groups as the primitives and the Hindus chant their praise. A mantra chanted by the individual has much the same result. Verses 3 and 4 read:

> "Great and wonderful are thy deeds,
> O Lord God Almighty!
> Just and true are thy ways,
> O King of the ages and of the nations!
> Who shall not fear and glorify thy name, O Lord?
> For those alone art holy.
> All nations shall come and worship thee,
> For thy judgments have been revealed."

It is very necessary for us to continue to worship the Holy Fire, the God of all. Man has demonstrated this by the numbers of different religions that have been founded. Worship is always a part of them. Somehow we Know that we were wondrously made and maintained by a higher energy or love and keeping our mind and words focused on this Higher Good is our rightful worship. Some have made images of precious metals and jewels so that they can look on them and more easily focus the mind in worship. However, the images often get in the way of worship. They are material and given our propensity to become attached to the material we may forget they are images and turn them into idols. Moses was teaching this when he destroyed the golden calf in his rage when he came down from the mountain with the ten commandments given by God. (Exodus 32)

Jesus said, "But the hour is coming and now is when the true worshipper will worship the Father in spirit and truth, for such the Father seeks to worship him. God is spirit and those who worship him must worship in spirit and truth." (John 4:23,24)

So our worship should be with "harps of God" which are in our hands, just as the angels before the throne. Harps are vibratory instruments likened to our vibration of thoughts, feelings or emotions, or the spirit. So we sing our song of praise as we perceive the throne surrounded by peace and fire (the symbol of energy or cleansing agent).

"Out of the inner sanctum, came the seven angels with the seven plagues, robed in pure bright linen, and their breasts girded with golden girdles" (Verse 6). Again, high spiritual thoughts that will be used to cleanse our consciousness, our spirit centers, our body, to prepare us for the final triumph. "The temple was filled with smoke from the glory of God." The temple being the body, the physical body, is filled with the Spirit which like smoke moves at its own will. This could be referring to the ethereal spiritual substance that appeared to the visionary as smoke. And we are assured that we may not enter the temple until the seven plagues are ended. Until we are blessed by God on the throne for our cleansing. We are again given seven steps to our final enlightenment and they come from our greatest Good, God on the throne.

The angels with the plagues, high Spiritual beings, our Spiritual thoughts, were described as "girt" for work with the golden girdles and the plagues are not used against us but for us. The plagues are symptoms of our separation from our Good and will help us to overcome materialism, and we shall be blest. For you see, the "wrath" of God is the "love" of God. Edyth Hoyt says, "In code literature the "wrath of God" is an allusion to the alibi of disobedient man, trying to attribute the effects of his own wrong thinking to his concept of an anthropomorphic Deity, whereas the New Testament teaches that Deity is Love, Truth, Spirit."[4]

Chapter 15 is mainly devoted to preparing us for the time of the seven plagues and although we are assured that they come from the throne of God, we may with mixed emotions approach the next chapter. This is a blessing since it is the unexpected that often throws us off guard. But we are being prepared and are assured that "with them the wrath of God is ended." So we are strengthened and ready.

CHAPTER 16

Misuse of Our Powers

We have come to our day of suffering for our separation from the Good, from the spiritual, from that which we have been taught. Even though we have been shown the beautiful throne, have had a taste of joy and ecstasy, have been given instructions as to how to become One through the raising of our consciousness or kundalini, we are still not pure enough to be accepted into the company of the 144,000. It is a long process; many lives may be spent in reaching our goal, although it need not be. Since seven is the number of completion, we must go through seven more cleansings in order to reap the reward that has been prepared for us from the beginning of time by the One on the throne. So the angels (spiritual thoughts) will cleanse us. A Zen master says, "When you have been spiritually awakened, you should strive even more penetratingly."[1]

Now the seven bowls of the wrath of God, which is the love of God, are to be poured out on the earth. The earth is our negative consciousness, our material concerns, our Mother, for as human beings we are nourished for time and then time again by the materialism of the earth. It is interesting that many of the plagues described in this chapter by the visionary, John, were the same plagues as visited upon the Egyptians by God through Moses in order to gain the release of the chosen people who wanted to go to the Promised Land. Do you see the parallelism?

The Pharaoh is our will, our mind that has control over all of our other faculties and indeed what comes to us. Usually we have to have experiences of suffering and pain to realize our need to turn our will over to the Will of God. The Israelites are our thoughts, our emotions, our body. They are the faculties of our awareness on earth that obey our will until we rise in consciousness and follow the Will of God. Moses, who is like our Holy Spirit or awareness of God, the I AM, is trying to release us from our bondage to the material sense or negative thoughts that keep us from going on our Journey. Moses, our higher sense, was looking only to God for direction and not to the beast or his own ego self. The Israelites, who wanted to leave Egypt but were afraid, distrustful of Moses and unacquainted with the one God and having been in slavery so long to the negative ruler of their destiny and the cruelty of his slavery, were weak and the Holy Spirit, Moses, had to lead them out.

How glorious is the knowledge, the faith, that the Lord of our Being is ever present to lead us to the kingdom of Heaven, even through our trials. The Hindu teaches that suffering is the result of ignorance because we misunderstand our reason for being on earth. When we overcome our enslavement to ignorance we will see with our inner eye that the world is Maya or illusion and Reality is something else.

We, like the chosen people, know there is a better, a happier, a more peaceful home, but it took them many days and nights, many miles of wandering, many losses and gains, many demonstrations of God's love and abundance, and many rejections and acceptances of the power and wisdom of Moses, God's handmaiden, to reach their goal. Thus the Holy Spirit, the power of love and energy within each of us, is ever available.

Jesus, the greatest pattern for us to follow, has given us teachings. Other great religious leaders have done the same for their people. Sometimes it seems that the written word is not the guide, however, as you will remember that the great avatars (those inspired by God to save His people) seldom wrote down their teaching. Their followers did. It was as if they knew that words are often worshipped when coming from the Holiest Ones, and also, the highest in consciousness know that each must eventually look within himself for the directions for reaching Oneness as they portrayed it. As for our teaching, the holy books of various religions are helpful but only when we touch our own sublime Spirit do we find our Truth. So as we interpret the plagues, please be aware that you, yourself, can turn within and gain a superior answer for your own particular Journey. "The Path of the Taoist is individual and pursued alone. It is the way, the road, the truth, it is one, everlasting, unchangeable."[2] (From the *Tao te Ching*.)

The reason for plagues may be coming from without our own conscious awareness. The race consciousness affects us all. We, however, can be protected from this if we raise our thoughts to a higher level. As we gain in our individuation process we will become more immersed in the impersonal love as God loves, and less attached to the surroundings, to the personal.

The first angel pours out his vial upon the earth; and there fell upon men foul and grievous sores "who bore the mark of the beast and worshipped its image." (Verse 2) The beast is evil, the absence of good, as previously discussed. The image is whatever we worship, whatever we concentrate upon and give obeisance to.

Many physical ailments are now known to come from our negative thoughts, our fear, our guilt, our separation from belief in good, our expectation of the worst to befall us. Some day, science may accept this truth, that physical and mental illness is under the control of the individual and how he thinks and feels. However, before that happens, the medical profession will need to reverse its own concentration on curing, to that of prevention, and seeking the cause of the illness. The effect is the illness, and doctors have always tried to treat symptoms, but the real cause is often not ascertained and treated.

Cause and effect, one of the immutable laws, as demonstrated by the Karmic law, must be taken into consideration. Through Holistic Healing we are beginning to turn to that direction. There are many doctors who are turning to the understanding of illness as a result of imbalance in the mind, body, and spirit. Some mentioned in the book *Beyond Biofeedback* are Dr. Norman Shealy, Dr. Carl Simonton, and Dr. Stephanie Simonton.[3] These medical people heal but also teach the patient that the cause of the illness must be sought out in his own thinking and feeling life.

In light of our present age, I would suggest that the noisome and grievous sores would be a symbol for ulcers, the popular disease of this generation, especially of Western man and woman. In years past it was boils on the outside of the body, but because we are taking into our nervous system so many stresses that we experience in our world, the body reacts with boils in the interior. In ages past man had to contend more with nature, with the bacteria of the outer, with that which could be seen. Now, we take within ourselves through our thinking and worship of the beast of materiality, the stress and strain of our society, the race consciousness.

As I became aware of the Western Man's activities of running from one thing to another, from one stressful situation to another, keeping eternally busy, I realized that he was running from something which was Inward. Now I know it is the Lord of his being who is "knocking at the door," who is pursuing him as the "Hound of Heaven." Many workshops and seminars are being provided now for people to help them deal with stress. Some of these lead them to more stress as the teachers do not take into consideration the spiritual need of the person. Others deal with the whole person.

Stress, according to Dr. Jack Holland, is a conflict between what we believe and what we desire. We believe that to have a good time, go to Las Vegas for modern entertainment, go to sports events, give our children all that money can buy, is making us happy. But we may not be listening to our inner desire and so have great stress, through unconscious fear that we will never get fulfillment. Stress is based on fear, a belief that the individual cannot cope even though running faster and faster. Our belief and our desire are not one. A balance of science (mind and body), art (the emotions), and spirit (religion) is necessary.

So one of the results of worshipping the beast and his image is physical illness. I have talked mainly of ulcers. Other physical manifestations may come too. Cancer could be interpreted as a foul and evil sore. I wonder if our researchers will learn that thoughts are at the basis of that scourge which in the late 1970s is still decimating our loved ones. Catherine Ponder has written a book on *The Healing Secret of the Ages,*[4] and reading this book gives ideas about the cause of illness and methods of mental healing, or spiritual. She teaches how to release the intelligent healing power within each of us. Our ignorance is that we have a separate existence from our Self. Knowing that "God is my health" heals, and the healing lies right within us.

Let us bear in mind that the bowls contained the wrath of God from the creature around the throne of God. So divine energy is being poured out on our consciousness for the purpose of cleansing. Verse 3 reports that it is poured into the sea by the second angel and the sea became like the blood of a dead man and everything living died that was in the sea.

Sea, in mythological terms, is symbolic of the unconscious, not only our individual unconscious but the collective unconscious which surrounds us like the sea surrounds the fish. Beneath the surface of the sea lie unfathomed depths which contain treasures which give life or death. In this case the death of man necessitates the drying up of his blood which is the liquid necessary for life. And the account says that *every* living thing died that was in the sea.

The unconscious of the individual contains not only his own experiences in this life but those of his past lives, if we accept the theory of reincarnation. Now this seems a great burden and some people never are able to remove this burden and their life seems beset by vast problems or, because the unconscious, through past incarnations, carries the good also, he may start life at a higher state of consciousness and continue on his Path coming closer to the Oneness.

The living things that died in the drying up of the water in the sea is that which must die in our unconscious in order for us to progress. The divine energy may come to us as intellect, as feeling, as divine intervention, as insight. In any case, we must come to terms with our own consciousness as well as the race consciousness and the collective unconscious.

Carl Jung is my authority on the collective unconscious. So let me quote from him: "Whereas the contents of the personal unconscious are acquired during the individual's lifetime, the contents of the collective unconscious are invariably archetypes that were present from the beginning."[5] And June Singer, in her book *Boundaries of the Soul,* quotes Jung as saying: "While the contents of the personal unconscious are felt as belonging to one's own psyche, the contents of the collective unconscious seem alien, as if they come to me from outside."[6] Obviously, the collective unconscious contains the positive and the negative.

Our unconscious also contains information from our experiences with family and the society into which we were born. Psychology has for years been engaged in attempting to release that which we have acquired and pushed down into the unconscious that is interfering with our mental health. Much of what we believe about spiritual matters came from our experience in race consciousness. Some of this must decrease while some must increase. That is our task. We are affected by our past and will eventually realize that as an individual we must find our own answers which may require our giving up answers we have learned through our experiences.

So the living things in the sea became dead, since our own consciousness, our divine energy, has cleaned out the influence of those around us. To be a functioning spiritual being in a sea of humanity we must let go of the idea that Truth comes from those near to us and, on an individual level, must build our own "mansion." "Build thee more stately mansions (dimensions), oh my soul." (Oliver Wendel Holmes in "The Chambered Nautilus") It is our individual responsibility with Divine energy. And so we are set free to be.

Verse 4, "The third angel poured his bowl into the rivers and the fountains of water, and they became blood. And I heard the angel of water say, 'Just art thou in these thy judgments, thou who art and wast, O Holy One. For men have shed the blood of saints and prophets, and thou has given them blood to drink. It is their due!'"

This angel is saying, it seems to me, that mankind has waged war on the positive forces in the world and is now getting its just due. Not only on the positive forces, the saints and prophets, but on the innocent, the weak, the pure. Through his wars man has shed much blood and now he will have to drink it or suffer the consequences.

I could write at great length on my feelings about war. It has been a scourge since mankind found an instrument to kill when he picked up the first dried up hip bone of an animal and struck his enemy over the head. War never settles anything and through our most recent war in Vietnam we wasted enough precious fuel and energy to supply our nation and many others for generations, to say nothing of the lives of young men. We are still primitive. Whichever nation has the largest instrument of destruction uses it to gain power, food, money, and continued life on earth. But we may have outdone ourselves. The Bomb is too big to use, as it will rebound on us, on all of us, and the water will be changed to blood. And the Law is fulfilled, "It is their due!"

From another point of view we could interpret this passage thusly: Blood, through the ages of religions, has been used as a cleansing agent. In some rituals the blood of the sacrificed animal was allowed to spray over those who needed cleansing. Sometimes the blood was spilled on the altar. In one culture the sacrificial animal was split and planted with seeds. When they grew to maturity the worshippers ate of the fruit of the plant and believed that they had partaken of divinity and they felt cleansed and forgiven of their wrong-doings. The mind is a wonderful agent!

Of course, the greatest example of the shedding of blood of the saints was the shedding of Jesus' blood. "If we walk in the light, as he is in the light, we have fellowship with one another, and Jesus, his Son, cleanses us of all sin" I John 1:7. In the communion or mass as practiced in some Christian churches, transubstantiation is believed, i.e., the actual body and blood of Jesus is contained in the wine and the bread. So blood has been a cleansing agent and is.

Since blood then, through the ages, has been a symbol of cleansing from sin and guilt, this verse indicates that if we go through the cleansing power of the blood or life on this earth we will be able to take our place with the saints. But those who kill the saints and prophets must live out their own Karma and a like event will happen to them.

Verse 8, reports that the fourth angel poured his bowl on the sun. Again the physical is the focus of cleansing. According to Jung, the sun is the image of God, the heart is the sun's image in man, gold is the sun's image in the earth, and God is known as gold. The Alchemists were seeking gold in the material sense and God in the spiritual. The sphere, the image of the sun, is also the image of the soul, the very life itself of man.[7]

The sun is the necessary agent for life on earth and so is the soul. If our soul brilliance is misused, if the kundalini power is misused, we will be scorched.

In so much of our modern life human beings in our Western culture are misusing the soul energy. As a result, heart attacks are on the increase. The medical world has been making great strides in the healing of the problem for a period of years, but many are losing their lives, many are maimed beyond repair. Why is the heart being so damaged?

In our discussion of the chakras we discussed the fourth chakra in terms of love and the need to love the Lord our God and our neighbor as ourself. It is beginning to dawn on many that the reason for heart attack is the lack of expressing love in its most spiritual way. It has been demonstrated by Yogis that they can slow the pace of the beating of the heart as well as stop it by their thoughts. In the book, *Beyond Biofeedback* there are reports of this. So the heart is under our control and our emotions and our thoughts affect it. Through love, we can be healthy.

As we allow the heat of the sun, or the emotions which we place in the heart, to become so intense in our life the heart falters. Or the heat of the sun is worshipped for its material results, and we forget that God is love and the energy from Him is to be used for loving giving, not for getting. And when the sun is worshipped for its material qualities we are scorched. And the scripture says that man curses God and did not repent and give him glory. Cursing God of course is just the opposite of healing. Reverse and worship God. Repent and give him all the glory.

The fifth bowl was poured on the throne of the beast, and its kingdom was in darkness. The beast, being absence of good, is the carnal mind as some would name it. It is the mind centered on things of the flesh, on the sensual, on that which is not spiritual. This is a personality type that lives by the senses. This is one of the functional types of personality, according to Jung. It is necessary to balance the senses with other personality characteristics such as thinking, feeling, intuition. For more on this read Jung's *Psychological Types.*[8] When out of balance, the personality seems to "blaspheme the good," or God.

Using our energy for the comfort of the body, for the thrill of sex, for the satisfaction of the five physical senses, gets many people off the spiritual path and their development seems to be stopped at the lower three chakras. It is believed by many on this earth that we are here to eat, drink, and be merry. This taken in balance with the spiritual will give us a good life, but when the spiritual energy in our bowl, the body and the soul, is poured out on the sense thought, we are building our own downfall for our consciousness. Carnal thoughts use the kundalini power for the satisfaction of the body. What a short life it has. Basically, we all want to live forever, but not in the physical body. Building soul consciousness of God is the better route to our goal, the eternal spiritual body.

We are moving now from the plagues of the body, through the mind sense, to the outer materiality. We are coming close to the end of the plagues and learning through our experiences on earth.

Verse 12, "The sixth angel poured his bowl on the great river Euphrates, and its water was dried up, to prepare the way for the kings from the east." The energy poured from the sixth bowl dried up the great river Euphrates, which was the life line for Babylon, the counterpart of the heavenly Jerusalem, the city of God. So we are preparing for the advent of the kings from the East by using our energy in that direction. God comes from the East.

Spiritual thoughts, understanding, and strength come from the East. The wise men came from the East to visit the baby Jesus. Fillmore says that in Scriptual symbology East represents the within, that from the regions of interior wisdom come thoughts of reverence and rich gifts. So we are turning from our materialism, our blasphemy, and getting ready to receive the spiritual love and gifts from the kings of the East. Our material thinking is drying up and we are preparing for the spiritual.

In Chapter Nine we discussed the river Euphrates as symbolic of the spine and the Holy Spirit using it as a highway to reach all cells, nerves, energy centers of the body and mind in an effort to transform the body into a body of light. In that case the drying up of the river left us open to the enemies of our desire to become One. However, in this instance, the drying up of the river seems to be a turning point in our consciousness development. Let us see how this could be.

We have come a great distance toward our goal since Chapter Nine. Instead of fearing the kings of the East (our spiritual thoughts) we are open and receptive to them albeit troubled by some fear. And so drying up of the river of the Holy Spirit is seen as a blessing for the Holy Spirit finds its Oneness with God in the end and the physical body is lost in the spiritual. The spine, as such, disappears in the Oneness of the Spirit. This "drying up of the Euphrates" then, seems to portend perfection and the admission of spiritual thoughts, words, and actions.

But just as sure as we start to turn to our Spirit, our good, we will be challenged by thoughts, negativity, loved ones who are afraid to free us, the church, the law, our own conscience, our self-centeredness, our ego, our fear of letting God have control of our lives. Verse 13, "And I saw, issuing from the mouth of the dragon and from the mouth of the beast and from the mouth of the false prophet, three foul spirits like frogs; (14) for they are demonic spirits, performing signs, who go abroad to the kings of the whole world, to assemble them for battle on the great day of God the Almighty."

All of these are gathering like frogs coming forth "from the mouth of the dragon and from the mouth of the beast and from the mouth of the false prophet.'' These are demonic spirits. They perform signs to entice the kings of the whole world to assemble for battle against the Lord on the great day of Judgment. So our negative thoughts, our social conscience, our personal consciousness, the race consciousness, our family and friends, our previous beliefs about God, our personal characteristics that separate us from our spiritual destiny, the Kingdom of Heaven, are gathering to do battle with our new consciousness and awareness of our goal.

All the enemies of our desire for Oneness with God may come very stealthily without our being aware of what is happening to us. Or they may come all at once. And we may succomb. Jesus warns of this when he says in John 15:19, "If you were of the world, the world would love its own; but because you are not of the world, but I chose you out of the world, therefore the world hates you."

What we are attempting to do is impossible according to our contemporaries in the field of religion. Western man cannot live in the world and reach this high state of consciousness, they say. The Zen monks withdraw from the world and live in isolation. The Catholic priests are separated from many of the snares of the world as are the nuns and the Hindu pilgrim goes his way. All are reaching for the Divine.

It is true, that Western man has found it much easier to leave religion up to the church's men and women and come to the fount once a week and imbibe of a little spirituality and pay the preacher or the priest to continue to pray for him through the week while he goes out and works in his world. That is where we have been, the huge majority of us since time began. But our religion can be taken with us every moment and should be. The Eastern person takes his religion much more seriously and it becomes or is a vital part of his home, his work, his everyday life. Of course, his worship center is within him and thus is with him always. The Hindu, the Buddhist, the Moslem believe this although they may not always practice it. As a result of Western man's not recognizing this Truth he has his battle at Armageddon many times. But it must be fought if we are to go on.

And verse 15, ("Lo, I am coming like a thief! Blessed is he who is awake, keeping his garments that he may not go naked and be seen exposed!") reminds us of Jesus' words as recorded in Matthew 24:42, "Watch therefore, for you do not know on what day your Lord is coming," and Verse 44, "Therefore you do not expect." It seems to me that this Truth will fortify us for the battle of Armageddon, for His Love shines through as we prepare for our own Armageddon.

"And they assembled them at the place which is called in Hebrew, Armageddon." (Verse 16) Armageddon is a part of the life of the aspirant reaching for the kingdom of Heaven. It can take place here and now, for as Jesus said, "The kingdom of Heaven is at hand," (Matt. 3:2) The Sermon on the Mount gives us the keys to the kingdom of Heaven and helps us in our battle with the kings of the world, the material, the *maya* of our life. (Study Emmet Fox's *The Sermon on the Mount*) The kingdom of Heaven, our goal, is defined by Fillmore as the unlimited spiritual consciousness when mind, body, emotions, and spirit, are equal in all activities.[9] It is the land which is free from fear according to the Bhagavad Gita. It is Nirvana. Let us not forget our goal! Armageddon will try us.

And now let us look at the place of the battle, Armageddon. It is a geographical place which anthropologists claim has been the place of decisive battles since 3000 B.C. Armageddon . . . the word that raises fear and terror in the minds of many people who have been exposed to the Christian translation of Revelation. Interestingly enough, Armageddon is mentioned only once in the entire Bible. Armageddon has been depicted by them as the place of the Day of Judgment, the great and final conflict between good and evil. At that time all will be determined about the eternal future of each soul.

Would it surprise you, having read thus far, that I have taken the position that Armageddon is a battle fought in each of us, not once but many times? For Armageddon is, in my understanding, that eternal battle between our inner ego and our inner Self, or the inner Spirit and the outer world. The battle between *maya* and Reality. The battle between the finite and the Infinite. In the teachings of Buddha, it is the battle between our desires and our release from Karma; the overcoming of the personal for the impersonal. For as we go higher on the scale of consciousness we will be barraged with more and more of the physical, the earthly. As Underhill says in *Mysticism,* "The desolation of that dark night of the soul in which it seems abandoned by the Divine; the painful death of the self; its resurrection to the glorified existence and absorption in its Source is a part of the journey."[10] The Bhagavad Gita says, "In the dark night of my soul I feel desolation. In my self pity I see not the way of righteousness." (Chapter 2:7)

It seems to me, I would much rather face myself and my God in a battle within my own consciousness than to believe that all of mankind will be destroyed by a judgmental God. Jesus Christ came to teach us about Love, and to believe that God will destroy us without our having anything to do about it seems to not be in "sync" with God, which is Love. Even Jesus, the divine example of God the Father and Love, said "If anyone hears my sayings and does not keep them, I do not judge him; for I did not come to judge the world but to save the world." (John 12:47)

No, I believe the judgment we experience is brought on by ourselves, and Armageddon is not one last battle for mankind but a battle that goes on as we develop our higher consciousness of "He who is on the throne." The judgment results from our selfish choices, our desires and attachments to our lower self.

Armageddon is a very important concept in this interpretation and is indeed the focus of the position taken.

In Jung's psychological insight he spoke of the battle of the opposites. His teachings are directed toward what he calls a state of individuation . . . Individuation means individual, or "coming to selfhood" or "self-realization." The Self is defined as a super-ordinate to the ego, the persona. And to reach this state of individuation necessitates our neutralizing the opposites. The conflict of the opposites in human personality may lead to neurosis or psychosis and in the least leads to confusion, fear, worry, anxiety, negativity, illness of body and mind, for "if a house is divided against itself, that house will not be able to stand." (Mark 3:25)

There is a continual battle going on within the psyche when we are rudderless and, like a ship on the angry sea are dashed here and there. Then the man or woman is so uncomfortable and unhappy that he or she looks to things of this world to gain peace. He gets it momentarily through drugs, alcohol, entertainment, sports, work, sex, church, and many other escape hatches to avoid crashing in the sea of life. However, the release is momentary and the world of opposites raises its ugly head again, Monday morning. The battle goes on for the "Hound of Heaven" is still knocking, is still pursuing. And man gives up to the victory of earthly pestilence! "It is done," the end of hope. And death will prevail and looks to be the ideal and only means of escape. But death will only bring him full circle, back to life on earth again until the Battle is won for God, until he awakens to the great Truth that "He has showed you, O man, what is good; and what does the Lord require of you but to do justice, and to love kindness, and to walk humbly with your God?" (Micah 6:8)

The battle of Armageddon, the battle between the negative and positive forces, is beautifully described in the first part of the Bhagavad Gita and indeed the entire book relates to it. This battle goes on in all of mankind and each of the great religions deal with it. We all have that in common as well as the assurance that good will prevail if we let it or even if we do not. The end point is God and Good.

Many are not ready for the battle of Armageddon and because of the chaos of their lives cannot find a way out. But in spite of that the seventh angel "poured his bowl into the air, and a loud voice came out of the temple, from the throne, saying, 'It is done.' And there were flashes of lightening, voices, peals of thunder, and a great earthquake such as had never been since men were on the earth, so great was that earthquake." For ready or not, it comes.

There is one translator of the book of Revelation, Corinne Heline, who says that Verses 17 through 21 are a description of the history of Atlantis. She says, "Drunk with worldly power and revelling in material and sensual pleasures, they failed to heed the warnings from initiate teachers. As a consequence, devastation overcame them and they heard a great voice in the heavens saying, 'It is done'—meaning that their time of probation was over." She adds that this was detailed by Plato. An interesting sidelight. However, she adds, "The culmination of Armageddon has not been reached. The real battle is being fought each day within the hearts and lives of every man and woman, for this "place of troops" as the conflict between good and evil, between the higher and the lower natures within ourselves."[11]

The description of the plague of the seventh angel is enough to make us want to turn and flee from any of these ideas of the kingdom of Heaven. It is just not worth the price of the fury of God, the wrath of God. And the "great hailstones, heavy as a hundredweight, dropped on men from heaven, til men cursed God." And, of course, that is what the majority of mankind does when evil or hard times befall them. But we are of the small minority who are trying to unravel the "mystery of God" and we were not promised a "rose garden." This is the reality of living in the earthly consciousness and we want to find the beauty and bliss of the Ultimate. And so we must dust off our Faith and know that "better days are ahead" for we have been promised, we have seen in the vision of John, that there is a better way.

And then our compassionate nature knows that many are not ready for the battle of Armageddon in its ultimate sense. They have chaos in their lives and cannot find a way to turn from the negativeness of the world. They are caught in a trap, a grip of indecision. Through these experiences they may go until they take a chance, take a leap of Faith and begin their transformation. There are those who are looking with anticipation to the Day of Judgment which they feel is imminent. But we must remember that in going from the Piscean Age to the Aquarian Age, the authority of past religions, government, family, education must be relinquished and the authority of the Spirit, in the individual and in all must take over. And chaos results in our earthly consciousness and our earthly institutions and it will not be stopped until we turn to our Inner Guide, all of us. As we observe the tottering of the past in a very sudden cataclysmic way, let us turn within through prayer and meditation and find that Source of Love which is waiting. Emerson said, "For it is only the finite that has wrought and suffered; the infinite lies stretched in smiling repose."[12]

We cannot let "the Dark Night of the Soul" be our end. We have seen the vision. We will go on!

CHAPTER 17

Judgment of Materialism

Again, we are going to be taught about our separation from the Lamb, the Lord of lords and King of kings. And the angel, who speaks, is one of the seven who had the bowls so is from the Spiritual Throne, our unconscious Spiritual awareness.

"And he carried me away in the Spirit into a wilderness, and I saw a woman sitting on a scarlet beast which was full of blasphemous names, and it had seven heads and ten horns. The woman was arrayed in purple and scarlet, and bedecked with gold and jewels and pearls, holding in her hand a golden cup full of abominations and the impurities of her fornication; and on her forehead was written a name of mystery: "Babylon the great, mother of harlots and of earth's abominations." (Verses 3–5)

The word harlot is defined in Webster's dictionary as a prostitute, an unchaste woman who prostitutes her body for hire. The description of her, an inferior vessel in Bible times as for example Eve, is related to the beast. The seven heads and the ten horns we have "seen" before. The visionary explains that he was "in the Spirit," in another dimension of awareness, and went into the wilderness, another word for the earth, temptations of earthly desire. The wilderness is also a place of quiet and separation from the earth but in this case is symbolic of a confused state of mind.

Now is the time for each of us to search our inner mind and life to determine what the harlot represents for us. Her name was "Babylon the great, mother of harlots and of earth's abominations." So the question is: What in your earthly experience has been most responsible for your separation from your inner Self? I should say, influenced your separation. For we cannot ignore the world and our own involvement in it. We are in the world for a purpose. We are influenced by it. The Ignorance of who we really are, a child of God, needs a world to bring us to true Knowledge. Let us look at the larger dimensions of earth life that have affected our lives, our choices, our Being.

There are at least five and maybe more for you: *Government, Church or religious institutions, Educational institutions, Family,* and *Society* in general. Railing against these institutions in a vituperative outburst will not solve our separation, but accepting the possiblity that they have affected our separation from our Self is a truism. Each should be aware of the effect of these five on the engendering of the ignorance of who we really are.

GOVERNMENT

In America today government is very much a part of our day-to-day existence. We probably have more freedom of choice under our form of government than any other people on the earth but we have lost much personal freedom as we lean more and more on governmental agencies to care for us and protect us. Do you see how this might separate you from turning to God, to that Knowledge, that intuitive knowing, of where our security really is? Government keeps society in a dependent role but also is necessary for society to function. How you have allowed it to affect you is the question.

CHURCH

The church, the Christian church, is an enigma to many and since modern Western man is turning from actively believing all it has taught and used to control him, it is losing power. As man becomes more free of physical lacks he is able to be freer of an institution that many times limited free growth toward his own Being. The church has usurped the independent Spirit of the individual being, many times, and required him to lose it in order to be saved. Dependence on the church, the minister, the priests may separate man from direct contact with God, the source of his Being.

Jesus taught us to speak directly to "Our Father" and that we had no need of intercessories for our salvation. He taught us to follow his example for "going to the Father" and his guru-like directions for our Path. The church seems to have been necessary for our evolution and is still necessary for many of our friends and neighbors, and how wonderful that it exists for those who rely on it. Revelation is teaching, however, that it is the individual who is responsible for his gaining Oneness. However, most of us, to one degree or another, have been affected by the teachings of our historic religion and we should investigate the effect on our present spiritual state. The church which frees its members to find out who they really are, from their private inner Center, will be the church of the future, I believe.

EDUCATION

Education, which I know the most about, is an important part of our world and again necessary. It often, however, is the greatest block to our individuation as it deals with the lower chakras of body and intellect and leaves untapped love, wisdom and searching for knowledge of who we are. Intellectually and physically it does a fair job, but it must change, for as we go into the Aquarian Age it is found lacking. No longer do students sit quietly and get the "word" from the teacher or administrator. They want to be involved in the learning process, and the teaching process, at least part of the time, and be respected for the innate knowing that each, unconsciously, has. Education, as it is in our world, does not really answer "Who am I?" And perhaps, at this point in society's evolvement it cannot teach the student that he is Divine. Know Thyself is to know the Self not the self which is what education recognizes.

In some Western countries religion is far more important in the educational system and certainly the values of the culture are more distinct and more easily taught than in America where we have such a diversity. But values are being taught in our schools, and I am not sure they are the values which will guarantee the survival of our country, or at least our form of government. Democracy was based on religious principles in the beginning and if our young are not getting training in values or understandings based on spiritual laws, one wonders about the future. The emotions and the spirit are also part of the human being and somewhere the young need some help in the development of this side of their nature. Hopefully, the family is doing this, but with the problems of our families in this era the job may be left undone. In any case, you and your relationship to your Self has been affected by the educational system in America whether you know it or not.

FAMILY

Family, in terms of love, we have referred to elsewhere. It can be our greatest strength or our greatest stumbling block but can be very helpful in our search for our goal. The reincarnationists believe that each of us chooses the family into which we are born in order to learn the lessons that are necessary for our evolvement. The astrologist also teaches this. If we accept this idea, it can be a real strength to our growth and development instead of using our energy in decrying our hard luck in having the family we grew up in. Also, the influence of the family goes on and on in our lives. We are not really mature until we get rid of our mother and father complexes, both good and bad, and become that person we were meant to be. So for some of us, this may be our greatest overcoming. (Jung deals extensively with complexes.)

The Piscean Age of authority vested in the family, the church, and the government may be passing, and as it does we are aware that our youth are more resistant to the dictates of any of these. This can be good if it brings them closer to their individual spiritual Self, but if it is for the selfish expression of the small self-desires, we have some real challenges for our societies. Each experience that we as individuals go through, and that a country, church or society goes through, is for the advancement of mankind. It is His-story, history.

SOCIETY

Society has been an enigma to mankind since the first organized effort was made. Society defined is an organization of persons associated together for the promotion of common purposes or objects, whether religious, benevolent, literary, scientific, political or patriotic. It is necessary to our health, well being, our relatedness in Love. Society was one of the greatest creations of God. For all was created by Him. We, in our ego state, think we did it. But He knew our needs long before we did. To be in a society and not of it is the trick. Paul said: "Do not be conformed to this world, but be transformed by the renewal of your mind . . . prove the will of God, what is good, and acceptable and perfect." (Romans 12:2)

Society is the race consciousness that we discussed before. We are social beings realizing, unconsciously, that we are all connected even though we may not know how. We may erroneously believe that it is because of our worldly connections that the society is founded. Basically, however, it is a deeper connection. Emerson in his essay on Society and Solitude says, "A man must be clothed with a society, or he shall feel a certain bareness and poverty, as of a displaced and independent member" and "Solitude is impractical and society fatal. We must keep our head in the one and our hands in the other. The conditions are met, if we keep our independence, yet do not lose our sympathy."[1]

The trouble we have with society in our Journey is that we allow it to usurp our individual consciousness and direct our life according to its dictates. We give up our own soul to society and when we do we will never know who we are. Somehow we need to separate ourself and at the same time be a part of our society, loving and serving our fellowman within it. The mystic decides to become a unique individual and although he still has a few people around him, the important decisions of his life are based on the Will of God which speaks from his Center. The introvert, in a smaller sense, pulls in on himself, not knowing why. The psychotic is an abnormal (according to psychologists) individual separating his awareness of society for a totally selfish reason, a fear of losing himself in his society. All of us to one degree or another are swept up into the race consciousness, and if we are serious about our Journey, we need to learn to think independently in spite of what the mass media is thinking and speaking. Society is a blessing but a hindrance if we are too dependent on it.

Perhaps you have been swept up into the "laws" of science which have added so much to our intellectual understanding and to our physical comfort. Science has been the religion of many, but with the explosion of the atom, the god was taken away for many. "Blessed are the meek for theirs is the kingdom of Heaven" was Einstein's motto, with meek being interpreted as "I don't know everything." Science is a wide open door to the Truths of the Universe and the true scientist knows that. We should also.

The "truths" that psychology has captured have been a great blessing to many, but the acceptance of these "truths" as Truth has limited mankind in taking the next step of including the Spirit as a part of man's psyche. When psychology balances the body, mind, and spirit of the individual, then great progress will be made. Jung started this journey but his teachings are not accepted or even known by many, since Freud still holds full sway in most educational institutions. The better informed know and study Jung's teaching and the New Age psychology will make a great step for mankind when his teaching displaces the teaching of Freud. Freudian teaching does not take into consideration the Spirit and if you are stuck at Freud's level of understanding of mankind, then you may find this your stumbling block to fulfillment.

Perhaps the world holds other hindrances to your spiritual development. Only you can know. Search and find. It is a life or death matter! And know that He is waiting to help you.

The harlot is, of course, our material mind, which centers on things and institutions of the earth believing that they are the answer to our quest. Whore, harlot, is a synonym for the principle of evil, sunk in darkness, wandering in darkness, unconscious and unredeemed.[2] The conscious mind is arrayed in beautiful colors contributing to our pride in the beauty of appearance; gold, jewels and pearls appeal to our desire for wealth of the world; and the golden cup could be the unconscious that is filled with the thoughts of the world. It is beautiful on the outside but as a whited sepulchre on the inner. The King James translation of the Bible reports that Jesus said, "Woe unto you, scribes and Pharisees, hypocrites! for ye are like unto whited sepulchres, which indeed appear beautiful outward, but are within dead men's bones, and of all uncleanness. Even so ye also outwardly appear righteous unto men, but within ye are full of hypocrisy and iniquity." (Matt. 23-27,28) What an indictment! and for our teaching.

"When I saw her I marveled greatly. But the angel said to me 'Why marvel? I will tell you the mystery of the woman, and of the beast with seven heads and ten horns that carries her. The beast that you saw was and is not and is to ascend from the bottomless pit and go to perdition; and the dwellers on earth whose names have not been written in the book of life from the foundation of the world, will marvel to behold the beast, because it was and is not and is to come. This calls for a mind with wisdom. The seven heads are seven mountains on which the woman is seated; they are also seven kings, five of whom have fallen, one is, the other has not yet come, and when he comes he must remain only a little while. As for the beast that was and is not, it is an eighth but it belongs to the seven, and it goes to perdition.'" (verses 6-11)

Again the beast rears its ugly head and the angel explains that the beast will be apparent to mankind, if the name of each is not in the book of life, forever.

The beast (evil, the absence of good) has much power and carries with him seven heads which are called "kings" and also mountains. Continuing our analogy of the opening of the chakra centers, the mountains are the seven chakra centers and our thoughts or concentration on them can be good or ill, for spiritual growth or regression. So our kingly occupancy of them is related to the earthly ways and not spiritual for five have fallen and "one is and another to come." The opening of the chakra centers or consciousness centers are fallen. "Only a purified body may be joined to the wine of the spirit."[3]

Kings, of course, refer to earthly governments and symbolically to our thoughts, feelings and physical being for man is king of the earth. In Genesis 1:28 we read: "And God blessed them, and God said to them, 'Be fruitful and multiply, and fill the earth and subdue it; and have dominion over the fish of the sea and over the birds of the air and over every living thing that moves upon the earth.'" Kings are related to the ten horns which are symbols of power and ten is, by numerology, one. Ten is a symbol for perfection as is one. So our thoughts, feelings, and body have the perfection through our power within which we exert over earthly thoughts, feelings, and actions. So if our thoughts, feelings, and physical being are given over to the power and authority of the negative we will certainly be against the Lamb, the Holy Spirit, or Self, our inner Christ. They are not of the earth. Our Self shall conquer. For "He is Lord of lords and King of kings, and those with him are called and chosen and faithful." (Verse 14)

That verse is so important that we often overlook it. If we are to believe the sages and those who know who they are, we will know that our Self will eventually conquer our self. Notice, "King of kings." For the Self has the power within the king. The King is the power of God within and no matter how powerful the king believes himself to be, the King will win. And then the king or our small self will join the chosen as we are all one in the Spirit. To be true for you, however, experience is the best teacher. Only through our life's journey do we really know who we are, for what our physical and psychological self tells us is not who we are.

Verse 15: "And he said to me 'The waters that you saw, where the harlot is seated, are peoples and multitudes and nations and tongues.'" So everyone on the face of the earth is affected by the harlot, the material conscious and unconscious, as the harlot is sitting on the water, the unconscious. These are opposites and must become one to bring us to unity. It is suggested in verse 16 that eventually the beast will come to hate the harlot. The ten horns (the power of the beast) and the beast will turn on material consciousness and even that which she worships will become the destroyer of her flesh. This is true, if you have observed with wisdom, the experiences of people. That which we worship often turns on us and rends us to pieces; that to which we are attached that interferes with our awareness and acceptance of the Good. For we allow our conscious mind to turn from God, and since God has put into "his people one mind" the words of God shall be fulfilled. For did the scriptures not say to "Requite her (Babylon) according to her deeds, do to her according to all that she has done; for she has proudly defied the Lord, the Holy one of Israel." (Jeremiah 50:29) "Their Redeemer is strong: the Lord of hosts is his name. He will surely plead their cause, that he may give rest to the earth, but unrest to the inhabitants of Babylon." (Jeremiah 50:34) Our Christ spirit is always there waiting to free us from our misconceptions, our illusions, our *Maya*.

Verse 18, "And the woman that you saw is the great city which has dominion over the kings of the earth."

So the harlot is our material consciousness which has dominion over us and we must and will fight the battle with our spiritual consciousness. She is strong, and has greed, lust, power, physical desires, hate and all negative qualities and thoughts in her arsenal. But because we know that God is in control, we are sure that the final outcome will be our spiritual advancement. We know, intuitively, that Love is the stronger.

Other interpreters of Chapter 17 have seen the scarlet woman as symbolic of the misuse of the sexual energy that we have discussed previously. Babylon is a state of confusion in the minds of men and women as to the place that sex should play in their lives, either uncontrolled for sensual pleasure or controlled for the development of their character and spiritual growth. The beast then would be selfishness, they say, and the scarlet woman makes the misuse of sexual energy very attractive for she presents a beautiful appearance that appeals to the senses. Perhaps this is a better interpretation and perhaps each of us should search ourselves to gain insight into our own values in the use of sexual energy. Celibacy may be needed if we are to pursue our Journey. Go to your Center for direction.

The "harlot" could also be an adulterated state of mind which leans to the negative and the negative thoughts, words, and deeds which Jesus mentioned in Mark 7:20-23: "What comes out of a man is what defiles a man. For from within, out of the heart of man, come evil thoughts, fornication, theft, murder, adultery, coveting, wickedness, deceit, licentiousness, envy, slander, pride, foolishness. All these evil things come from within, and they defile a man."

Again, each of us must search and realize through deep insight what is clouding our consciousness of the Most High. And Insight, the Truth about ourself, will solve the problem for when Truth becomes a part of our consciousness we will act from that Center. It IS an Inside Job!!!

CHAPTER 18

Babylon Falls

We have passed the climax. The battle has been fought. For some it will be the last time they will need to experience the contest between the material life and the spiritual. For others there may be recurring battles until the dross of the material consciousness has been burned out and the Philosophers Stone, the new name, the center of gold is all that is left. But each battle makes our spiritual awareness stronger, if that is our goal, and our courage and commitment has grown. The time for rejoicing is near.

An angel with great authority describes what has happened, "and the earth was made bright with his splendor." "Fallen, fallen is Babylon the great!" the angel says, an announcement of great import. Then a description of material consciousness follows which describes what besets us as men and women who are in that place, Babylon. Isaiah 21:9 has a similar quote.

Another voice then addresses us as "my people," spiritual men and women, for that we truly are. We are not material, physical but spiritual. We are Spirit. "I Am that I Am" (Exodus 3:14) Our illusion has been that we are physical beings. Until you, yourself, learn this, that you are Spirit, from experience and inner knowing, you will not know who you really are. Listen to your Inner Voice. Its theme is "You are my own." Verses 4–6:

> Come out of her, my people,
> lest you take part in her sins,
> lest you share in her plagues;
> for her sins are heaped high as heaven,
> and God has remembered her iniquities.
> Render to her as she herself has rendered,
> and repay her double for her deeds;
> mix a double draught for her in the cup she mixed.

The result of a materialistic consciousness being in charge of our lives is given in verses 4-8. She, the whore or the material, shall "be burned with fire for mighty is the Lord God who judges her." (Verse 8) "There is only one Power in the Universe, God the Good Omnipotent," is a wonderful affirmation that will change our thinking and our focus of attention. For we are assured, in Love, that God is All and is caring for us and helping us in our battle.

Then we are given a picture of the mourning by those who are on the material plane as they see mankind turning away from materialism. I feel this is written directly about America at this time. When we realize the control that the industrial/military complex has over our lives we realize how easy it is to get swept into it. If one travels to "lesser developed," more spiritual countries we can compare our culture with others and see how our lives are run by materialism. Our standard of living in this society necessitates our buying every little gadget that comes along, so the hucksters say. We are brain-washed through TV and the news media and unconsciously we believe we must have all those things.

Verses 11-13: "And the merchants of the earth weep and mourn for her, since no one buys their cargo any more, cargo of gold, silver, jewels and pearls, fine linen, purple silk and scarlet, all kinds of scented wood, all articles of ivory, all articles of costly wood, bronze, iron and marble, cinnamon, spice, incense, myrrh, frankincense, wine, oil, fine flour and wheat, cattle and sheep, horses and chariots, and slaves, that is human souls." The rich merchants, our industrialists, get disturbed if their profits do not continue to rise each year and the media pours fear into our minds that a depression is in the offing. "O ye of little faith," Jesus is reported to have cried when talking about anxiety or fear. (Matt. 6:30)

Because the public is materially oriented it decides to buy more and more and to do so must work longer hours and earn more money, so wages go up, cost of living goes up, the merchants smile. And we are further separated from our spiritual goal. Of course, a certain level of comfort is necessary, but too much wealth may separate us from the kingdom. "Truly, I say to you it will be hard for a rich man to enter the kingdom of heaven. Again I tell you, it is easier for a camel to go through the eye of a needle that for a rich man to enter the kingdom of God." Lamsa's translation interprets this passage as: It will be harder for a rope to pass through the eye of the needle than for a rich man to enter the kingdom of God.[1] (Matt. 19:24) And from I Tim. 6:9,10, "But those who desire to be rich fall into temptation, into a snare, into many senseless and hurtful desires that plunge men into ruin and destruction. For the *love* of money is the root of all evils; it is through this craving that some have wandered away from the faith and pierced their hearts with many pangs."

The sailors and seamen were very important to the life in the mid-East at the time the Bible was written. They are still important, but more important to our twentieth century, in the late 1970s, is the military. The military would indeed weep and mourn if we defeated materialism for their livelihood is based on it and although some are sincere in their belief that we must be strong militarily to protect ourselves from aggression, the truth of the matter is that in America the military complex is very necessary for our materialism. In a book written by W. H. Bowart, "Operation Mind Control," he points out that an industrial/military organization is controlling much of our life.[2] I do not necessarily agree with him on everything, but it has a great deal of truth in it, I am convinced.

So the merchants and the sailors will mourn, for selfishly they want to have their own livelihood and wealth.

Taken from the inner view of the person, the merchants could represent our desire for all the things of the world, the beauty of our possessions which we may sell our entire life to accumulate and then pass on leaving them to "rust and turn to dust." The seafaring men, being connected with water, could be our unconscious thoughts which at first mourn but later exult as in verse 20: "Rejoice over her, O heaven, O Saints and apostles and prophets, for God has given judgment for you against her!"

"Then a mighty angel took up a stone like a great millstone

and threw it into the sea, saying, 'So shall Babylon the great city be thrown down with violence and shall be found no more;'" and then continues on the description of the loss of those who had rejoiced in her existence. This is, of course, a demonstration of the loss of life of the materialistic consciousness to make way for the spiritual. The last verse of the chapter reads: "And in her (Babylon) was found the blood of prophets and of saints, and of all who have been slain of earth." Indeed we are slain in Babylon for our spiritual thoughts, feelings and actions often lose their life in confusion of materialistic worship. But this will happen no more, for Babylon is thrown like a great millstone into the sea. And we are free from the confusion that has attended our Journey. However, this experience is necessary to our "salvation" for we learn from each experience.

And thus the eighteenth chapter depicts the fall of Babylon, our earthly consciousness, and the results of our choice of being in it. We are being guided to our Ultimate Good but through a worldly path, for that is the way we must go. When Babylon is cast into the sea or water we are reminded of the scripture, "Unless you be born of water (life on earth) and the spirit you shall not inherit eternal life." (John 3:5-8) So again we are reminded that living on this earth plane and having the baptism of the Holy Spirit is necessary for our goal of sharing with the elders around the throne. The throne is our higher consciousness and when our Holy Spirit or kundalini power is freed of all its physical barnacles it shall join the Father of All, the Brahma of the Hindu, the Buddha of the Buddhist, and we shall overcome the earth and inherit eternal life, nirvana, samadhi, and have been born again never to taste the second death again.

From the King James translation of verse 14 we find: "And the fruits that thy soul lusted after are departed from thee, and all things which were dainty and goodly are departed from thee and thou shalt find them no more at all." In other words, with the spiritualization of the mind, the beast will be dissolved and depart. We will have the mind of Christ and there will be no need. All

Is and we Are. All that we need comes to us without mental purchase, without strain or concern. "I am come that they might have life and have it more abundantly" Jesus said. (John 10:10) What a reward and one to remember as we work through our earthly consciousness. "Prove me now herewith. If I will not open the window of heaven and pour you out a blessing."

CHAPTER 19

Rejoicing for Oneness

We have come to a time of great rejoicing that is almost more
than we can bear, for Babylon, material consciousness, has been
overcome and we are being prepared for the marriage of the
Lamb, the Holy Spirit, and the Bride.

To rejoice is natural to our human and divine nature, for we
are made to rejoice and not to cry. Crying is a blessing, for it
relieves us physically and emotionally, but it is short lived and
passes. Rejoicing can be in our heart forever.

To truly rejoice we need to share with others and the common
element between us intensifies our joy. So the visionary experiences rejoicing as he reaches the rim of the great vessel that
overflows. He "hears" the multitude in the kingdom of Heaven
shouting their Hallelujahs. We have heard this before, but somehow this is different as the greatest stumbling blocks to our
Becoming One, our ego-self, our worldly understandings and
desires, have been overcome.

According to Charles Fillmore from the *Metaphysical Bible
Dictionary:* "Praise keeps the soul fresh and pure and beautiful.
It is the power that opens the inner portals of the soul to the full
and free inflow of spiritual light and aspiration."[1] And so the
multitude (our hungry thoughts) give praise to "our God" and
the twenty-four elders and the four living creatures sing praises
and our consciousness is opened afresh to the inflowing of the
freshness, purity, and beauty of the One on the throne.

God, the One, is really worshipped when we are in the sixth
chakra, the wisdom of God. For to Him belong all. "Our God"
is the best judge of our salvation and as we turn to Him we are
assured that the great harlot that corrupted the earth has been

judged. In verse 2 we read, "he has avenged on her the blood of his servants" which is another demonstration of the karmic law, for God is Law and Divine Law and Principle has always been sought by mankind to direct him in his own searching, both material and divine. It was thought that emperors could fulfill the need for Law, based on the material and spiritual and would be the answer. But emperors often disappointed man in this expectation. God, the Law placed within each person, is the answer.

The twenty-four elders (our twelve powers both material and spiritual which have become one) worship God on the throne and the four creatures which symbolize the mind or intellect, the emotions, the body, and the spirit, worship God with great power with "Amen, Hallelujah!" Let us discuss the word Amen, and Hallelujah.

Amen, according to one authority is used in the same sense as the Muslim uses Amin and as the Hindus and Buddhists use Aum. It is a sacred word, and sound has vibratory effect on the worshipper as well as those around him. Yogananda says, "The infinite potencies of sound derive from the Creative Word, Aum, the cosmic vibratory power behind all atomic energy."[2] Also, from the same book, "The Aum vibration that reverberates throughout the universe (the Word or "voice of many waters" of the Bible) has three manifestations or *gunas,* those of creation, preservation and destruction. Each time a man utters a word he puts into operation one of these three qualities of Aum. The scriptures insist that man should speak the truth."[3]

How powerful are the words of our mouth and when the fifth chakra, at the throat, is opened we have the power that Jesus demonstrated through command. As in "Come forth Lazarus," and he did, though he had been dead four days. And in Revelation 3:14, ". . . The words of the Amen, the faithful and true witness, the beginning of God's creation." So the words of the Amen are related to the "Word" that is mentioned in John 1: "In the beginning was the Word, and the Word was with God, and the Word was God. He was in the beginning with God; all things were made through him, and without him was not anything made that was made. In him was life, and the life was the light of men. The light shines in the darkness, and the darkness has not overcome it." How much power there is in the word Amen, and we have usually been totally unaware of the power of the Word. And uttered in silence, in thought, is equally effective.

Yogananda also points out, "The outward manifestation of omnipresent Christ Consciousness, its witness, is Aum, the Word or Holy Ghost, the invisible divine power, the only doer, the causative activating force that upholds all creation through vibration." Aum, he says became the sacred word Hum of Tibetans, Amin of Muslims, Amen of Egyptians and Greeks and Romans and Jews and Christians. It means sure, faithful.[4] How closely related we all are.

Hallelujah from Hebrew is defined as "Praise ye Jehovah," a song of praise unto God. Metaphysically, according to Fillmore, it means: The whole of man's religious and spiritual nature lifted up in thanksgiving and praise to Jehovah, the Christ, the Father within him. So we are to invoke the creative vibration of the Creator as well as praise Him. Words have power. Study the account of Jesus' healings for more. "Let the words of my mouth and the meditations of my heart be acceptable to thee, my Lord and Redeemer."

Verse 6 refers again to the voice of a great multitude, "like the sound of many waters and like the sound of mighty thunder peals." This is the sound that we hear when the sixth chakra is opened, according to Yogananda. He describes it as "the "symphony of all sounds together—the oceanic roar of the Cosmic Om (Aum) Vibration." Since I have not experienced total samadhi, only small ones of ecstasy and love and peace, I depend on one who has, to describe it; the Amen or Om, and the voice of the multitude or many voices, the sound of waters, the peal of thunder, all have been reported as a part of the experience. It is like a great orchestra as it plays at full volume the last of a Wagnerian overture or the ending of the Ninth Symphony of Beethoven. How the drums clash and clang in a facsimile of thunder or great power. How exciting it is as well. Building a feeling of expectation and of an ending. We know that it is not the end but only the beginning.

And the event being celebrated is the marriage of the Lamb and his Bride. Verses 6 and 7: "Hallelujah! For the Lord our God the Almighty reigns. Let us rejoice and exult and give him the glory, for the marriage of the Lamb has come, and his Bride has made herself ready; it was granted her to be clothed with fine linen, bright and pure—for the fine linen is the righteous deeds of the saints."

In Hindu teaching, as you remember, as well as Tantric Buddhism, the marriage of Shiva and Shakti is the event toward which all their meditation and worship has been tending. The Zen Buddhist sits in meditation for weeks and sometimes months to reach this state. He is helped by his Master, the representative of Higher Knowledge, and his fellow monks. But the marriage of the finite and the infinite is his goal. The mystic of Christianity calls this Spiritual Marriage, the marriage of the Soul. Also, the embrace of Perfect Love. Solomon's Song of Songs, they say, is an allegory of the spiritual life and marriage. Other religious groups have their own description but all of mankind knows subconsciously that his Unity with the Divine is to be sought after and celebrated when achieved.

The Lamb, in my interpretation, is the Holy Spirit, and the Bride is Sophia, the female aspect of God. The Hindus see the Holy Spirit as feminine and the Bride or God Awareness as masculine. In any case, it is the marriage of opposites. Carl Jung teaches this in the individuation process. Individuation means a lifelong journey when a person becomes "a single, homogeneous being, and, insofar as individuality embraces our innermost, last and incomparable uniqueness, it also implies becoming one's own self (or Self in my words). We could therefore translate individuation as 'self-realization.'"[5] Therefore, at the marriage we become whole, we become that Self which has been at the center of our being but unrecognized or covered over with our materialistic self.

Then the visionary hears from his guiding angel, or his spirit within, the Self, words from God. "These are the true words of God." We are able to know directly, when we are "in the spirit" directly from the Omniscient, the Omnipotent, the Omnipresent One. Because we have assumed that this Seer, John, was of this high consciousness, we should pay close attention to his report. "Blessed are those who are invited to the marriage supper of the Lamb."

So we are invited to participate in the joyful occasion attended by the multitude around the throne, the twenty-four elders and the four creatures. Being invited is special and when we are risen in our higher consciousness we will hear the invitation. Some are invited and do not hear and do not come. But those who are invited, whether attending or not, are blessed.

How grateful we should be to know that we are chosen. Remember the story of the marriage feast spoken of by Jesus? Matthew 22:2,3: "The kingdom of heaven may be compared to a king who gave a marriage feast for his son, and sent his servants to call those who were invited to the marriage feast; but they would not come." Matthew 25:1-12 gives the story of the foolish and wise maidens who went to meet their bridegroom. The foolish were not prepared, as they did not have enough oil (love) but the wise had their wicks trimmed and waiting and would not lend to the foolish, as attaining the kingdom of Heaven is an individual task and must be done with one's own supply of love and wisdom. In the former passage those who did not come, although invited, went to take care of worldly business. So the servants invited those from the streets and byways. "Many are called but few are chosen." And in Matthew 7:13,14: "Enter by the narrow gate; for the gate is wide and the way easy that leads to destruction. For the gate is narrow and the way is hard, that leads to life, and those who find it are few."

Our visionary is overcome with gratitude and thanksgiving. He falls down at the feet of the angel in worship. This was, of course, a Christian angel for John, as his thoughts and beliefs were centered in the Christian church of that time. The angel would not accept his obeisance and worship, for our spiritual thoughts are the same as our human ones even though we may not recognize it. So we are being told that we are on an equal footing with the angels from the throne of Love. He is told, "You must not do that! I am a fellow servant with you and your brethren who hold the testimony of Jesus. Worship God. For the testimony of Jesus is the spirit of prophecy (revelation direct from the Holy Spirit)." (Verse 10)

Now the "testimony of Jesus" is that which Christians purport to follow. However, it has gotten mixed up with the testimony of St. Paul. And Paul was an organizer of the church and was far more subject to human interpretation than Jesus. His teachings, however, were divine according to many, and the interpretation of Paul's words have divided many otherwise loving followers of Jesus' teaching, and the peace that Jesus taught has been lost. Paul, to whom we owe a debt of gratitude for spreading the gospel, needs to be reinterpreted by us on this particular spiritual journey.

Let us discuss Jesus and his spirit of prophecy. A prophet is one who interprets, or translates, what he hears from the Holy Spirit. He interprets the old law in terms of the present and projects into the future. He may foretell future events or he may speak for God or a deity, or is divinely inspired. In the early Christian church, they were next after the apostles. Whoever uttered special revelations was a prophet.

The Jews have paid much heed to prophets in their history although they often did not follow them. So our speaker is saying, "The testimony of Jesus is the spirit of prophecy." And more importantly, he said "Worship God."

It is felt by many, who are critics of the Christian church, that the worship of Jesus and his mother Mary, has become a doctrine. Worshipping Jesus as God has been their interpretation. Jesus Himself never asked to be worshipped; in fact he said many times, "It is not I who do these wonders, it is He who sent me." "The Father who dwells in me does his works." John 14:10.

I should like to insert here the teaching of Charles Fillmore about Jesus, Christ, and Jesus Christ.

From *Jesus Christ Heals:* "Christ, meaning 'messiah' or 'anointed' designates one who had received a spiritual quickening from God, while Jesus is the name of the personality. Christ is the name of the supermind and Jesus is the name of the personal consciousness. The spiritual man is God's son; the personal man is man's son. Jesus, the Son of man, is in a state of becoming the Son of God; that is, man is being born again. At the time that Jesus told Nicodemus, "Except one be born again, he cannot see the kingdom of God," he, himself, was undergoing that mysterious unfoldment of the soul called the 'new birth.'"[6]

This explanation has helped me a great deal, as we are as Jesus and he tried to teach us that truth. He came to earth to show mankind what power lies within them and all around. The Christ is within each; our conscious awareness makes us more Christlike. That is our conscious awareness of God.

The testimony of Jesus, for me, is that all men are Sons of man, or an expression of divine idea, as he continuously called himself, and that we have within us the Christ, the spirit of God, which can be raised up to make us Sons of God. Jesus referred to Himself as the Son of man numerous times in the New Testament. As he neared the time of the crucifixion he spoke more and more of his Father and that He was the son of his Father. He was very much man among men who had a highly evolved consciousness and knew and knows how to use it in compassion and love for others. He wanted mankind to know that he was man and God just as He taught we are. Jesus, the human form, was crucified, but Christ, the God Spirit, lived; and according to Biblical accounts so energized the physical form that It was resurrected and ascended into another dimension.

A series of books, *Life and Teaching of the Masters of the Far East,* gives accounts of many highly spiritual beings who lived on earth, and coming from another dimension are now Bodhisattvas and saints helping man find his way in "the veil of darkness." Jesus is, of course, the most highly developed one as is Buddha who dwells in that dimension. The author places that dimension in the Himalayas, the Holy Mountains of Nepal and Tibet. This would be, symbolically, in a high state of consciousness. In Spalding's account, Emil, an adept who guided them, says the following: "Tis Christmas Morning; to you I suppose it is the day that Jesus of Nazareth, the Christ, was born; to you the thought must come that He was sent to remit sins; to you He must typify the Great Mediator between you and your God. You seem to appeal to Jesus as a mediator between you and your God, who seems to be stern and, at times, an angry God sitting off somewhere in a place called heaven, located where, I do not know, except it be in man's consciousness. You seem to be able to reach God only through His less austere and more loving Son, the great and noble One whom we all call Blessed, and whose advent into the world this day commemorates. To us this day means more; to us this day not only means the advent into this world of Jesus, the Christ, but also this birth typifies the birth of Christ in every human consciousness. This Christmas Day means the birth of the Great Master and Teacher, the Great Liberator of mankind from material bondage and limitations. To us this great soul came on earth to show more fully the present, Omniscient One; to show that God is all Goodness, all Wisdom, all Truth, All in All. This Great Master, who came to this world this day, was sent to show more fully that God not only dwells without us, but within us, that He never is nor can be separated from us or any of His creations; that He is always a just and loving God; that He is all things; knows all things; knows all and is all Truth. Had I the understanding of all men, it is beyond my power to express to you, even in a humble way, what this Holy Birth means to us."[7]

Jesus Christ, for me, is the risen Jesus who put on the full white robe, the golden crown of the saints described who are around the throne. He is with us always. He lives! He will come to us if we invite him to speak to us from our unconscious.

Carl Jung has this to say about the Christ: "It is possible to say that whoever believes in Christ is not only contained in him, but that Christ then dwells in the believer as the perfect man formed in the image of God, second Adam."[8]

From John 14:10, Jesus is speaking, "Do you not believe that I am in the Father and the Father in me." Again Jung says in his commentary on *The Secret of the Golden Flower,* "The *Imitatio Christi,* (whereby the individual does not pursue his own destined road to wholeness but attempts to imitate the way taken by Christ Jesus), has this disadvantage: in the long run we worship as a divine example a man who embodies the deepest meaning of life, and thus, out of sheer imitation, we forget to make real our own deepest meaning—self realization."[9] The definition of Imitatio Christi, in parentheses, was taken from Jung's book, *Memories, Dreams, Reflections.*[10]

The name Christ is the nearest we as human beings, limited in our way of expressing, can get to the knowledge of God. Christ is God's Son, existed long before Jesus, the man, walked on the earth and expressed the Christ totally.

Jesus Christ is the name that symbolized the marriage of the human and Divine. Adam, in the beginning, was the Christ and fell from grace, but Christ still is a part of man's consciousness, the Second Adam. So Jesus Christ represents the full blown enlightened man or woman who knows his/her Christ as one with his/her Jesus or human consciousness.

For me, Jesus Christ is my brother, is one with me, is my Guru, is my guide for total enlightenment. He came into the world to raise man's consciousness to God as an everloving, concerned Father who wants nothing more for his children than the best, the happiest, the most joyful. God is love. That is Jesus Christ's message and as Jesus he teaches me that I can also be Godlike as he demonstrated. "Truly, truly, I say to you, he who believes in me will also do the works that I do; and greater works than these will he do, because I go to the Father." (John 14:12) He brought to mankind the glory of the knowing that the Holy Spirit within each one is all powerful and we can do much good for our fellowman as we demonstrate Its power. The Comforter, the Paraclete, was given not only to the apostles but to all of mankind.

As we strip away our limited concept of God, the Holy Spirit demonstrates through our life and "My peace I leave with you; my peace I give unto you; not as the world gives do I give to you" (John 14:27) becomes a reality. Thank God for Jesus Christ. He it was who lifted up mankind to a higher state of being on its evolutionary path back to the Father. He taught us how to live on the earth plane in order to overcome death, for his demonstration leads us to Eternal Life. And the speaker told the visionary to "Worship God."

For some incarnated spirits, the worship of God is where they start their Journey during this time around. For others it is the worship of Jesus, the Buddha, Lao Tzu, the guru, the Bodhisattva. To some Christians it is the worship of Mary, the Mother of Jesus. For each religionist the name is different but each starts from where he is. In John 9:34, we have an account of the consciousness of a blind man as perceived by the Pharisees. They said to him "You were born in utter sin" as a reason for his blindness. But our Karma, which is the point where we start this new life on earth, can be overcome and we can rise on wings of song if we follow the example of Jesus, knowing that we too must take up our cross, must be crucified on the cross of materiality, must rise again to newness of life. Jesus healed the blind man. Jesus' example on the cross and coming from the tomb is the example I must follow as I overcome the illusions of this world and find Oneness with Universal Oneness. "For the testimony (his entire life) of Jesus is the spirit of prophecy (divinely inspired teaching)."

So we are to be married to the Christ, as Jesus was. We are to know that our inner Atman, our soul, is to be our final state of mind. We are to be at One with Him on the throne.

Again we are told of a white horse coming from heaven and "He who sat upon it is called Faithful and True." "His eyes are like a flame of fire, and on his head are many diadems; and he has a name inscribed which no one knows but himself."

The rider of the white horse is a description of the Christ, some say Jesus Christ, for "he is clad in a robe dipped in blood" which is to say that he is immortal and Godlike and so is whole, without opposites. The rider could also be each of us as we reach the Unified state of awareness of the Divine. He, Jesus, and we have paid the price of life on this earth and have reached perfection and we each have a name that is known to no one but ourself. So Nirvana has been reached and the aspirant has "inner joy, inner gladness and he has found inner Light . . . he is one with God and goes unto God." (Bhagavad Gita 5:23,24)

This perfected state, the Ultimate, may not be our goal in this life. Each of us will decide how much consciousness of the Good we want to develop, what goal we seek. If it is intellectual development, well and good. If it is physical satisfaction, fine. If it is wisdom, love, then we will have chosen our path. But for those, the mystics, the devout religionist, the goal of Oneness may be reached. For some of us, it will take many lives, but ultimately we shall all be One, the Omega Point of Teilhard de Chardin which he discusses in *The Phenomenon of Man*.[11] We shall overcome our earthly experience.

Still there is a battle to be fought between our spiritual and material selves. This is the Armageddon mentioned earlier. Our armies are white and pure. Our thoughts, our words, our deeds, our aspirations, our consciousness are white and pure. The Christ is leading all of these positive forces and his sword of truth will smite the forces within us that are still human and the power of the Christ will be in control. He is King of kings, Lord of lords. He has made One, the divine and material, and shines over all.

The birds of prey were then called and we are shown that the forces of negativity, of evil, of materialism of the earthly consciousness, the outer world, will be defeated. The beast, our own personal shadow or Achilles Heel and the false prophet will go down in defeat and be thrown into a "lake of fire" which is total destruction according to the translation of Elizabeth Turner.

And our Christ subdues all and we are free and the birds (symbolic of spiritualization) feast upon those negative forces which have been slain by the Christ spirit; the flesh of kings (the will); the flesh of captains and mighty men; (all that is warlike in our consciousness); the flesh of horses and their riders (the instinctive drives that erupt from the unconscious); and the flesh of all men, both free and slave, both small and great (men is here used in the generic sense of all that is of this world). So all is spiritualized. All are loved. The charactieristics which were our nemesis are destroyed or changed to the spirit, for nothing can be stronger than the Christ, our inner spark of the Divine.

Four of the popular translations of the Bible, the King James, the Amplified, the Living New Testament and the Revised Standard Version, translate that he who sat upon the white horse was named Truth and Faith. Faith, as I have indicated, is the characteristic of the first chakra and Truth is the apex, the seventh chakra. So the one rider, the Christ, the Holy Spirit has made One of the first and the last, the first and the seventh, the lowest and the highest. They ride together with all the others included: the creative, love, seeking and worshipping God, intellect and wisdom. All have been opened and gained the ultimate in Truth.

The picture that has been presented in this chapter is one of great beauty of the Truth and the celebration around the throne of the marriage feast. The spirit of Jesus Christ has taken the visionary into the dimension of the completion and he is able to experience the Hallelujahs and Songs of Praise of the multitude around the throne and he is admonished to "Worship God." The negative forces within the personality have been overcome by the Christ of Truth and Faith and the beast and the false prophet, the shadow, have been thrown into a lake of fire that burns with sulphur, which is used for fumigating or bleaching. So our shadow will be cleansed also. Now we are ready for the last step.

CHAPTER 20

The Book of Life

The chapter opens with: "Then I saw an angel coming down from heaven, holding in his hand the key of the bottomless pit and a great chain. And he seized the dragon, that ancient serpent, who is the Devil and Satan, and bound him for a thousand years, and threw him into the pit, and shut it and sealed it over him, that he should deceive the nations no more, til the thousand years were ended. After that he must be loosed for a little while." (Verses 1–2)

In Chapter 12 we dealt at length with the dragon, so I will not repeat that interpretation. Through the ages, through mythology, man has always been intrigued by the dragon. He is powerful, a sign of the neutralizing of opposites, containing the masculine and the feminine. Other mythological interpretations of the dragon are: the serpent and bird in combination, i.e., uniting the opposites; a hermaphrodite; *prima materia* of alchemy; dark unconscious; the shadow; in Japan it symbolizes infinity and sovereignty and human passion. It also represents deified forces in Taoism. On the shield of the Prince of Wales is the red dragon of the Welsh which is a national emblem of courage and fervor for the longevity, the eternality of the Welsh people. But, back to *our* dragon.

In this interpretation the dragon symbol is translated as evil or the absence of good, and for the individual that shadow must be recognized and sealed off for a thousand years in the bottomless pit, the unconscious.

A thousand years, being the multiple of 10, which is the symbol of wholeness and which by numerology reduces to one, is symbolic of eternity, unity, individuality. Now eternity means, for man, a never ending time sequence and is difficult to envision. However, since in God there is no time, our consciousness being centered in the Divine, must see this symbol of eternity as one that is unknown. For we cannot fathom with God's intelligence, nor can we describe the eternal. It is, as the Buddhists and other Eastern religionists believe, the Void. It is no thing, no time, no dimension. So the awareness of our evil will become void for eternity. There is no reality to it. It is Void.

God is also in the bottomless pit, we must not forget. For, even though some Christian teaching dwells a great deal on Hell, the Bible teaches that God is omnipresent. If so, He is in Hell also. Psalms 139:7-10: "Whither shall I go from thy Spirit? Or whither shall I flee from thy presence? If I ascend to heaven, thou art there! If I make my bed in Sheol (Hell), thou art there! If I take the wings of the morning and dwell in the uttermost parts of the sea, even there thy hand shall lead me, and thy right hand shall hold me." We all know this unconsciously, for in our deepest despairing moments we are aware of the "still small voice" which is calling. And we are saved! The final sentence in Verse 3 indicates that even the dragon may be given mercy, for "he must be loosed for a little while."

James Dillet Freeman, the poet Laureate of Unity School of Christianity wrote this poem which was, incidentally, carried to the moon and left there by the astronauts on the Apollo XV voyage.

I AM THERE

Do you need me?
I am there.
You cannot see Me,
   yet I am the light you see by.
You cannot hear Me,
   yet I speak through your voice.
You cannot feel Me,
   yet I am the power at work in your hands.

I am at work,
  though you do not understand My ways.
I am at work,
  though you do not recognize My works.
I am not strange visions.
  I am not mysteries.
Only in absolute stillness, beyond self,
  can you know Me as I am,
    and then but as a feeling and a faith.
Yet I am there.   Yet I hear.   Yet I answer.

When you need Me, I am there.
Even if you deny Me, I am there.
Even when you feel most alone, I am there.
Even in your fears, I am there.
Even in your pain, I am there.
I am there when you pray
  and when you do not pray.
I am in you, and you are in Me.
Only in your mind
    can you feel separate from Me,
  for only in your mind
    are the mists of "yours" and "mine."
Yet only with your mind
  can you know Me and experience Me.

Empty your heart of empty fears.
When you get yourself out of the way,
  I am there.
You can of yourself do nothing,
  but I can do all.
And I am in all.
Though you may not see the good,
  good is there, for I am there.
I am there because I have to be,
  because I am.
Only in Me does the world have meaning;

only out of Me does the world take form;
   only because of Me does the world go forward.
I am the law on which the movement of the stars
   and the growth of living cells are founded.

I am the love that is the law's fulfilling.
   I am assurance,   I am peace.   I am oneness.
   I am the law that you can live by,
   I am the love that you can cling to.
   I am your assurance.
   I am your peace.   I am one with you.   I am.
Though you fail to find Me, I do not fail you.
Though your faith in Me is unsure,
   My faith in you never wavers,
   because I know you, because I love you.
Beloved, I am there.

—JAMES DILLET FREEMAN

The negative, shadow aspect of our consciousness does not give up easily and we can expect to see another battle, for we are very close to the Summit of Mt. Zion, and the higher we go the greater our challenges so that we may prove our worthwhileness. But the outcome is foreordained.

Since Revelation was written, as I have pointed out, in the time of great persecutions of the Christians, we are given a glimpse of the reward meted out to those who were persecuted for their testimony to Jesus and for the word of God, and who had not worshipped the beast. They were resurrected from the earthly consciousness, seated on thrones and reigned with Jesus a thousand years or for eternity. Verse 4: "Then I saw thrones, and seated on them were those to whom judgment was committed. Also I saw the souls of those who had been beheaded for their testimony to Jesus and for the word of God, and who had not worshipped the beast or its image and had not received its mark on their foreheads or their hands. They came to life again and reigned with Christ a thousand years."

For our personal raising of the consciousness to Oneness with

Christ we could suggest that if we do overcome the negative effect of the materialistic world and the opposite of the good, we will have eternal life in the Spirit. This would be the enlightenment we are searching for as the Christ is the Holy Spirit that combines with the "Word of God" the Aum, and we are not individual but inpersonal vibrations with All that is Good. Resurrection is not only referring to the physical body but since this is a spiritual book, it refers to the spiritual one, to our consciousness of our Spirit which rises from the death of materiality, rises to life. The realization of eternal life is the first resurrection.

"Blessed and holy is he who shares in the first resurrection! Over such the second death has no power, but they shall be priests of God and of Christ, and they shall reign with him a thousand years." (Verse 6) According to the philosophy of rebirth there will be no more death when perfection, God, has been reached. Jesus talked of overcoming death. Death to the human is usually interpreted as death to the body, for we have been taught by Western race consciousness that death is to be avoided at all costs. The Eastern consciousness knows that death is good, as it will give another opportunity to be born again and thus overcome Karma. But those of the resurrection are free of the power of death and are priests of God and Christ for the opposites have been lost in the Oneness of total Enlightenment.

The unconscious, which some interpret as the bottomless pit, is not quiescent. There is still something, some shadow, some emotion, some thought that is negative and rises up to fight against the white-robed figures of the conscious, spiritual mind. They too must be exterminated. They are very deceptive, for if not "washed in the blood" or if not taken into our awareness and consciousness, they rise up to overwhelm us. And when we think we have "got it made" they come back with fuller force. You see, at this stage, we are subject to spiritual pride, for the ego can shift around from the material to the spiritual and when the ego is inflated in our spiritual development it is very subtle. But spiritual ego or pride will separate us from our Good. And so the challenge that may come to us physically, mentally, emotionally, or spiritually should be our signal that our consciousness of the Divine is clouded and in all humility ask our inner Self for guidance and insight.

There is a theory or, should I say interpretaion of the Bible, which teaches that what we call life is really death, that life is around the throne and reigning with Christ while what we call life on earth is death.[1] The author, Mr. Kuhn, uses verses four through six of this chapter as an example of this theory.

Verses 4–6: "They came to life, and reigned with Christ a thousand years. The rest of the dead did not come to life until the thousand years were ended. This is the first resurrection. Blessed and holy is he who shares in the first resurrection! Over such the second death has no power, but they shall be priests of God and of Christ, and they shall reign with him a thousand years."

According to Mr. Kuhn, "they came to life" is saying that when on earth we are dead and when with God and Christ on the throne we are living. "They came to life" is referring to a higher state of consciousness as they have overcome death (what we call life on earth). I believe that this idea may have some merit for as human beings we misinterpret so much and until we realize that we are spiritual beings we do not see the Truth.

The first resurrection refers to the resurrection of our material consciousness to the spiritual, or the realization that life is eternal. Resurrection of the body is symbolic of the resurrection of the consciousness. The changing of the material body to the spiritual body is a result not a cause. The cause is the raising of consciousness through the seven energy centers of personal soul development. Bringing faith through the seven centers to Truth is the first resurrection. The second is the resurrection of the body.

Some interpreters suggest that the thousand years refer to a thousand births. If we interpret the thousand years as a thousand births when the dross of materiality is burned out the idea of resurrection comes in. Resurrection has been a theme for hundreds of years in mankind's thought. In the Judaic and Christian accounts we have Joseph in the cistern; Jonah in the whale;

Jesus Christ in the tomb. It seems to be a part of the mythology of the race. Transformation and resurrection, so the alchemists say, comes through self incubating or "a brooding state of meditation."[2]

So the resurrection brings life from the spirit and the first resurrection has come and materiality is to be surmounted. The second death refers to death to our body. The first death is the passing away of the dross of materiality while the Precious is saved. When enlightenment is reached, this happens. Then death of the body is no more for we have eternal life. We do not need to be alive on earth in the material sense, Fillmore says in *Atom Smashing Power of Mind*. We do not need to be born again into the earth consciousness. Verses 7–10 gives us another view of Armageddon—victory has not been won.

The final battle is being fought. Satan, the negative in our unconscious, will try again to defeat our intuitive knowing and experiencing of the Divine. Gog and Magog, in Ezekiel 38, is Gog *in* Magog. Gog was the chief prince of Meshech and Tubal and God says "Behold, I am against you and I will turn you about." (Verse 3.) Chapter 38 of Ezekiel tells of the Lord God's overcoming the forces of Gog. The Lord God assures him, the "Son of man," that the Forces of Gog will be overcome. Fillmore explains Gog as "the satanic or selfish thought force in human consciousness warring against the true thought force that is based upon the ideas taught and demonstrated by Jesus Christ."[3] Jung says, that this is a symbol for the featureless, hostile masses. "The self threatened at birth by envious collective forces . . . and is only too likely to collapse under the impact of the collective forces of the psyche."[4]

All of these authorities are suggesting that Gog is representative of the negative forces of the material world that will be overcome. The forces of the evil that is in the unconscious are strong and they can even surround our higher consciousness on the throne within and all seems to be lost. This is also referred to as the "night sea journey" when we seem to be going through our special hell or hades. Hell and hades may be experienced many times in many lives before we are fully enlightened and all the forces of the "not Good" seem ready to take over. But wait, for in verse 9 we read, "but the fire of heaven came down and consumed them" just as the Lord God promised in Ezekiel 38.

Fire, as said before, is a symbol of cleansing and is a blessing from heaven. It burns eternally. The fire is eternal but the dross is not, and when error is stopped the burning stops. Mark 9:49–50: "For everyone will be salted with fire. Have salt in yourselves, and be at peace with one another." And Luke 12:49: "I came to cast fire upon the earth and would that it were already kindled." Jesus is speaking in this quote. And John the Baptist in Matthew 3:11: "I baptize you with water for repentance but he who is coming after me is mightier than I, he will baptize with the Holy Spirit and with fire." So, this last scripture indicates that it was Jesus Christ who brought the fire of Lord God to earth in order to overcome Gog, the forces of evil in our consciousness.

And Verse 10: ". . . the devil who had deceived them was thrown into a lake of fire and sulphur where the beast and the false prophet were and they will be tormented day and night." This reminds us of verse 20 of Chapter 19, so along with the beast and the false prophets we have the devil also in the lake of fire. But remember fire is for purification so there is hope for them, as I pointed out previously. This picture is not a pleasant one and if taken allegorically rather than realistically, it simply means that our battle with the material in our life is over, and we are ready for the ascension to the throne. But we still have to wade through the Day of Judgment which is such a bug-a -boo for those reared in the Christian dispensation, for we are told over and over that our deeds, both good and bad, with emphasis on the bad, are being recorded in God's book and we will be judged at the Final Judgment with much fear and trembling. Many of our brothers and sisters who are Christian thus carry much fear in their unconscious about death.

Well, indeed we are judged but we judge ourselves according to the law. Jesus speaks to this in John 12:31, "*Now* is the judgment of this world, *now* shall the ruler of the world be cast out; and

I, when I am lifted up from the earth, will draw all men to myself." And John 8:15,16: "You judge according to the flesh. I judge no one. Yet even if I do judge, my judgment is true, for it is not I alone that judge, but I and he who sent me."

The church fathers have used a great deal of fear techniques to keep us in shape, tying our guilt feelings to the church and loyalty to it. This has been used by officials of the religious movements of the West since the Christian dispensation began. The Buddhist monks, the Hindu priests, the Taoist master all have had those among their number who were unscrupulous enough to tie the people to their religion by strings of guilt feelings. Of all the psychological ills, guilt probably adds more to the ranks than any other personality fault. To feel guilty is to be divided from our inner Self, from God the Good Omnipotent. Guilt does not control our adverse actions always either. Sometimes the most dastardly deeds are done because of a feeling of subconscious guilt.

Now I am not saying that all feelings of guilt are bad. Guilt felt by the individual is a nudging from his inner Self that he has not lived up to his best. Thus nervousness, stress, physical and psychological ills arise because we are not listening. When we feel a dis-ease, as we are on the Path, we should immediately meditate, find the source of the guilt feeling and do something about it. Jesus said, "So if you are offering your gift at the altar (your inner Center), and there remember that your brother has something against you, leave your gift there before the altar and go; first be reconciled to your brother, and then come and offer your gift." (Matt. 5:23,24)

Guilt feelings are an important emotion for a human being as, if given attention, helps us grow toward wholeness. For some, guilt is very important. The criminal who admits no guilt feelings has lost touch with his/her inner conscience, the inner Self that guides us to our destiny. A positive act can come from feelings of guilt if handled rightly. Jesus also said, "Forgive us our debts, as we forgive our debtors." (Matt. 6:12) and "You may know that the Son of man has authority on earth to forgive sins." (Mark

2:10.) So our forgiveness is asked of God and of man and thus our guilt is alleviated. But we must remember that guilt feelings, as with all negative feelings, are a result of our own thinking and cannot be blamed on any one else. Guilt feelings are coming from our false self or the ego. Guilt feelings or negativity do not come from our larger Self. Observe yourself and determine if you really have something to feel guilty about. If so, do something, but if the feelings are unreal then let them go and go to God. More on this is included in a book by Vernon Howard, *The Mystic Path to Cosmic Power.*[5]

Verses 11–12: "Then I saw a great white throne and him who sat upon it; from his presence earth and sky fled away, and no place was found for them. And I saw the dead, great and small, standing before the throne, and *books* were opened. Also another book was opened, which is the *book of life.* And the dead were judged by what was written in the books, *by what they had done.*"[6]

Now we come to the "book of life." The book of life is real and it is our own life and our own conscious awareness of it. And if we have not forgiven or been forgiven (and this includes forgiving our own self) we will add to our Karma and be thrown into the lake of life which is again life on the material plane. This does not happen once only, but many times in our lifetime and for many lifetimes. Perhaps this life is really Death and Hades, as some claim.

In Philippians 4:3 we read, "And I ask you also help these women for they have labored side by side with me in the gospel together with Clement and the rest of my fellow workers, whose names are in the book of life." Paul was speaking. This I believe to be a reference to the book we each keep in our subconscious memory of our positive and negative thoughts, words, actions. Annalee Skarin, in her book, *Ye Are Gods,* has this to say about the Book of Life: "Man himself is the Book of Life, for within him is engraved the complete record of all his thinking and actions and he is the record and he is also the recorder."[6] "Each and every man must open the Book of Life for himself. Those who fail to open it will have to die—they refused to live by what was in the

Books that were opened."[7] Unseal yourself for you are the Book of Life. You are the glory of God.

Isn't His Love wonderful! How we scurry around in our every day world looking for His Love and there it is, right within the temple of our body, the temple of our consciousness, the temple not made with hands. His great Love is nowhere better illustrated than in verse 12, which deals with "the books" and the "Book of Life." This has created many horrendous interpretations which reflect anything but His Love. Let us interpret this verse in terms of the core teachings of this book.

The Book of Life is contained in our own knowing. Knowing the contents of which lead us to Life. Each of us bring judgment upon ourselves, for in our knowing is the Book of Life and what we do with It will be recorded on each page, for "man is the record as well as the recorder." God has given us freedom to do what we will with our life and at the same time has written on our heart what needs to be done. We must read our own book!

It seems to me that the Book of Life has much in common with the scroll mentioned in Chapter 5 that must be opened by the individual for his advancement on the Path. Directions were given for his attainment of his goal, while the Book of Life has recorded on it the progress that has been made. The Rosicrucians recommend that at the end of each day we should review our thoughts, words, and deeds for that day and learn from them how far we are on the path and what needs to be cleared out. They say then, that at the end of life on the earthly plane, each of us does the same thing for his entire life. Thus, he learns and records on his soul these learnings so he will not repeat the same mistakes in a future life. Such may be the Book of Life for some. For others, the record is clear and they are invited to come to the marriage feast.

Let us always keep in mind that we are talking about consciousness raising within ourself in the here and now. It is not in a far off time and place. As we grow and become at One with Him, this record is being cleared, and at the end of our earthly life our record will have been made and then the next life will give us a new chance. The marriage feast is inevitable for each of us.

Not only is our record one of this life, but of the lives we have lived previously, and unless we have overcome some of that Karma written in our own Book, then we may die again or not inherit eternal life. Remember that direction for overcoming our Karma can come from ourselves and from reading and practicing the scriptures that apply to our need. We do have a day of reckoning. It may be today as we go about our duties or tomorrow, for we bring on ourselves judgment many times in our life on earth. Our death to the earthly *maya* will be life with the One on the Throne. Our own Book of Life is our greatest guide and our own record, for He writes upon our heart. His love beats with our love. He will not condemn you to Hell forever—for Light and Life are His Essence and you are His.

Since you are reading this book, I assume that it is not the first one you have read along spiritual and metaphysical lines. Most of us, in our searching, have read many books. Most of us, however, pass up the books that would be of most value to us since we either do not know about them or have been "turned off" by the interpretation given by our theologians, ministers, and priests on whom we have depended. I am, of course, speaking of the scriptures of the world religions, for they are our greatest source and direction. But you may think, "I don't understand them." If you can understand this book you can understand them, maybe not as fully as an oriental mind trained in that way of thinking, but if you read with a prayerful attitude and seek in all humility to be guided you will understand, for the Spirit of Truth abides in each of us and in those books.

These books are given to people at different times throughout the history of mankind. Each religious group that centers around these books has usually had the interpretation made by their religious leaders for man could not always read and had to depend on someone who was educated or gifted with intuition or other-world understanding to tell him what it meant and what he should do. Besides, the common working man of that time had no time to meditate on such matters. But we are in a New Age now! A large percent of the world population is literate, but is still living in the dark ages in their belief that someone else must read for them, interpret and pray for them. But you and I now know that the creative spirit is within each to interpret, direct, and inspire. Jesus taught this. So we are held responsible to know "what was written in the books."

The many scriptures of the world are now available through libraries or bookstores. Let me list some of them: The Bhagavad-Gita; the Upanishads: The Ramayana and the Mahabharata; The Diamond Sutra; The Analects of Confucius; The Tao Te Ching; The Koran; The Old Testament and the New Testament of our Bible; The Ayaranya Sutra (Book of Jainism); The Yasna of Zorasterism; The Vinaya Pitaka, The Sutta Pitaka, and the Abhidhamma Pitaka of the Buddhists; and the Apocrapha, writings which were not included in the Old Testament for various reasons. Read them and follow as your Guide directs. You will be surprised to find how many similarities exist between teachings of various religions. Or why should surprise be our reaction! For Truth comes from One Consistent Source!

Let me return now to discussing the "second death." It is death of the material body, and is called the "lake of fire," for when our soul is reincarnated, we are again "tried by fire" to burn the dross from our conscious awareness of our Good, our Self, God. Our universe is alive with energy that consumes the dross of materiality and sense consciousness, but energy cannot be destroyed. This energy burns eternally and is His Love. God gives us many chances to come to eternal life when purified.

Verses 13-15: "And the sea gave up the dead in it. Death and Hades gave up the dead in them, and all were judged by what they had done." The Death and Hades were thrown into the lake of fire. This is the second death, the lake of fire; and if anyone's name was not found written in the book of perfection then he was also thrown into the lake of fire (life on earth). Death, the dark spectre of the human condition, is to be also purified as is Hades, a symbol of the imperfect state. Hades, you see, is not a real place but is an invention of the mind of man and is, for some a dwelling place in this incarnation. It is the realm of sense rather than spirit, but since both dwell in us, we can through our devotion to our Goal, overcome the negative. It can be burned away.

Let us not forget, "To him who conquers I will give some of the hidden manna (the Word of God), and I will give him a white stone (Christ identity), with a new name written on the stone (identified with God) which no one knows except him who receives it." (Rev. 2:17) Only God knows Who we really are!

So we are ready for our new Life. We have overcome and we are going to be shown what to expect when our Ultimate Goal is reached. Let us prepare ourselves for this moment by "being in the spirit on the Lord's Day" for *this* is the Lord's Day!!!!!

CHAPTER 21

Enlightenment

The opening verse gives us the setting of the scene. "Then I saw a new heaven and a new earth; for the first heaven and the first earth had passed away, and the sea was no more."

These are not merely words to be passed over lightly, for coming into the view of the revelator is the Reality of what IS and SHALL BE forever. He has reported before the description of the goal as a small samadhi or enlightenment. Now he is being prepared for the Final Step, for now Eternity is in view. It is indeed a new heaven and a new earth.

The aspirant "sees" a new heaven and a new earth and gives us the feeling that this will be our abode forever. The negative scenes of the past are gone. A whole new vista is opening for us. All the suffering of the past has wiped out the old; the new has come.

We have come a long way. From the time of our beginning when the world was formed and our spark of the Divine began taking on new bodies and new lives to begin or continue the climb back to the Holy of Holies, back to Oneness with Him on the throne, back to realization of our true Self, back to the I AM of Moses, back to who we really are. And it is a new concept of relatedness to God. It is new, fresh, new born, and the old or the first earth and heaven have passed away.

In the individual this new concept of Reality will bring great joy, light, enlightenment. It will bring new works, more creative activity. Our desires and attachments to worldly considerations are gone for the "old has passed away." All is new.

Just imagine for a moment the difference between the old heaven and the new heaven, the old earth and the new earth. Let your fancy range. How would earth and heaven appear?

Symbolically the earth is materialism, mother, opposites, conscious mind. Heaven is spirit, consciousness of the divine, perfection, completion, lack of opposites, happiness, joy, above us, kingdom of God, creative and transformative qualities, the Spiritual substance.

Since we know that the old heaven has been depicted as above us, away from our conscious experience, we can expect the new heaven to be right here and now. In verse 3 we have, "Behold, the dwelling of God is with men," so heaven, the Kingdom of God is with us. The new heaven is within us and not a place, a far off place, to reach when we die. The new heaven is to be enjoyed right here and now. Our eyes have been opened, visions of truth are before us. The new heaven is not a "place" but a condition of mind that gives us peace, joy, and Oneness. "The kingdom of Heaven is in the midst of you," so Jesus is reported to have said. (Luke 17:21)

Earth, our mother, our human life, is also new, for earth is also a state of consciousness. We have always said "down here" as opposed to "up there" when speaking of heaven and earth. But this earth is new. And how new?

"He will wipe away every tear from their eyes and death shall be no more, neither shall there be mourning or crying nor pain anymore, for the former things have passed away." (Verse 4) Now does this mean that everyone on this earth will be free from pain and suffering? Of course, as every soul finds its way back to its creator. For the individual let us look at the earth as a state of consciousness.

The earth is good. It gives us so much, not the least of which is the opportunity to grow in consciousness. The conscious mind is not to be denigrated. It is our tool for growth and development as is materialism. The new earth will give more opportunities to grow as the whole race of mankind grows.

Our world is changing, a truism! We are on the beginning cusp of the Aquarian Age. The Aquarian sign in the Zodiac, according to John Jocelyn in *Meditations on the Signs of the Zodiac* is bound up with the human and the humane; it embraces all humanity. Its characteristic feature is its love of human beings, a feeling of cosmic kinship with all mankind. Intense sensitivity is a pronounced trait of the Aquarian Age; a sensitivity that is mental, psychical, spiritual (and physical). The two wavy lines symbolizing Aquarius indicate that we have equal and harmonizing vibrations between the earthly ego and the higher "I."[1] So when this age is completed that is where mankind will be. The new earth and the new heaven will be in total vibration and we will know. We will be there too, all one in God. A few of us will reach that goal easily and will help others come to that level of consciousness. Each of us can make the decision of what our focus will be. But a new earth is coming and a new heaven and it will be in the midst of us, you and me and the earthly ego and the higher "I" will vibrate in harmony.

> Oh, Father, I am floating
> Far above the earth
> Filled with joy and laughter
> Filled with Cosmic Mirth.
> Who am I to seek Thee
> Who am I to Know
> That thy Love unfolding
> Means my way to go?
> Father in thy kindness
> In thy Holy Mein
> Go before me ever
> As to Thee I cling.
> Then I become only
> Thee and all thou art
> For myself is lost forever
> There within Thy Heart!

Let us now look at the phrase "and the sea was no more." (Verse 1) The sea is deep and mysterious and although our marine experts have learned a lot about it, there is much to be learned. It is the chthonic (dark) side of our knowledge. It holds dark, deep secrets. As the sea, the unconscious, also. The sea is a symbol for the unconscious both personal and collective. In the New Age the sea will be no more, for in order to reach wholeness the conscious and unconscious are one, the unconscious becomes conscious, One with God.

Thomas Troward, who wrote in the early 1900s and who has had great influence on New Thought men and women, says, "Our relation to the sub-conscious, whether on the scale of the individual or the universal, is the key to all that we are or ever can be. . . . On the universal scale it is the silent power of evolution gradually working onwards to that 'divine event, to which the whole creation moves.' The closer our rapport with it becomes . . . we shall control our whole individual world."[2]

The goal for this process, however, must be a Divine one, else we will run onto the shoals of ego and self inflation. Only through humility, through centeredness on the Divine Self as the Alpha and Omega can the Journey, the Tao, be completed and the new Jerusalem come into existence in our consciousness.

Verse 2: "And I saw the holy city, new Jerusalem, coming down out of heaven." Jerusalem, the holy city on Mt. Zion, was always a goal for the Jewish people. It was the center of their awareness of God. Jesus mourned over Jerusalem and it has become the symbol of the consciousness of God.

New Jerusalem is a very important concept for it is the symbol chosen by John to denote the new consciousness, the enlightenment, the totality of awareness of who man really is. For a fuller description of the New Jerusalem I refer you to Chapter 2,3.

New Jerusalem is called "a bride coming down out of heaven adorned for her husband." (Verse 2) The consciousness of man is Wisdom, the female aspect, and as we gain in Wisdom we come closer and closer to the Ultimate, the throne of God. The aim of most religions is this final state of being when the bride, the individual consciousness, the Holy Spirit, the kundalini power becomes married to God Himself. Let me give some descriptions of this state of being from various religions:

Hindu: "Nirvana is highest happiness. The devotee, whose happiness is within himself, and whose light (knowledge) also is within himself, becoming One with the Brahma, obtains the Brahmic Bliss." From Bhagavad Gita 5:22-24: "He who, in this earth, can endure the storms of desire and wrath, this man is a yogi, this man has joy." And "He has inner joy, he has inner gladness, and he has found inner Light. This Yogi attains the Nirvana of Brahman; he is one with God and goes into God."

Buddhist: There is no suffering for him who has finished his Journey, and abandoned grief, who has freed himself on all sides, and thrown off all fetters . . . His thought is quiet, quiet are his words and deeds when he has obtained freedom by true knowledge.

Sufis: Light upon Light.

Taoist: He who knows does not speak.
　　　　He who speaks does not know.

> The eightfold yoga
> The six regions of the body
> The five states
> They all have left and gone
> Totally erased
> And in the open
> Void
> I am left
> Amazed
> There is but a red rounded moon
> A fountain of pure milk
> The Unobtainable Bliss
> Has engulfed me
> A Precipice
> Of Light.[3]

Light, Happiness, Joy, Oneness with God, no suffering, Freedom, all speak through the Great Religions as state of Being in the Enlightenment.

Verse 2,3: ". . . prepared as a bride adorned for her husband; and I heard a loud voice from the throne saying, "Behold, the dwelling of God is with men. He will dwell with them, and they shall be his people, and God himself will be with them.

The Bride in white, the holy city, is pure. The marriage is being arranged and the heaven from God will be ours. John the Baptist, in discussing Jesus, said: "He who has the bride is the bridegroom." John 3:29 which means, I believe that the Bride, the heaven of God, is One with the bridegroom, the Christ, the Holy Spirit. In II Cor 11:2 "I betrothed you to Christ to present you as a pure bride to her one husband. But I am afraid that as the serpent deceived Eve by his cunning (a reference to the misuse of the kundalini or Holy Spirit) your thoughts will be led astray from a sincere and pure devotion to Christ." Paul is speaking.

So our consciousness of the Holy Spirit must be pure and undefiled as the marriage occurs. The Song of Solomon, in the Old Testament, has many beautiful descriptions of the Bride, symbolic of the essence of the Divine. Chapter 1:15,16 is one:

> Behold, you are beautiful, my love;
> Behold, you are beautiful;
> your eyes are doves.
> Behold, you are beautiful, my beloved,
> Truly lovely.

"God himself will be with them"—what great knowledge. We all know this unconsciously for the Self, or Christ, dwells in our conscious and unconscious mind. And the kingdom of Heaven is within us.

In the Old Testament we find a great description of man's consciousness before he KNOWS God. This is in the book of Lamentations. Our state of earthly consciousness and being is aptly described there. Listen to some of it. Chapter 1:20: "Behold, O Lord, for I am in distress, my soul is in tumult, my heart is wrung within me, because I have been rebellious. In the street the sword bereaves; in the house it is like death." Chapter 4:1: "How the gold has grown dim, how the pure gold is changed." Chapter 5:15: "The joy of our hearts has ceased; our dancing has been turned to mourning." This, the book of Lamentations, is a description of the fall of Jerusalem which symbolizes the fall of our spiritual consciousness.

By contrast then, let us enjoy the description of our new state of awareness. No sorrow, no tears, no pain because "God himself will be with them."

Now you may say logically that this is impossible, for man's lot is to suffer. Thus did Guatama the Buddha teach. But he also taught how to get out of this suffering and reach Nirvana. Jesus spent his three teaching years trying to demonstrate the result of man and God being One in consciousness in order to lift man above the human lot. It was such a majestic truth that men and women of that time persecuted Him because of His demonstrations. But now is different, for now man has had a viable example of tremendous power that he can unleash that can destroy the planet—the Bomb. At the same time man cannot be blind to the teaching of the religionists, and God is still active in the unconscious in the race and individual minds. So now more than ever, God is expressing through us and the time is ripe for an ushering in of the New Age and the New Age will be God-centered and God or Good directed. It seems a long time off but enlightenment comes in a split second, as the explosion of the Bomb. Do not underestimate God! Get ready. "For as the lightening comes from the east and shines as far as the west, so will be the coming of the Son of man (our super-consciousness). (Matt. 24:27.)

So John is told that we have reached our heavenly home. "The former things have passed away." No more dragon, no more beasts. No more war. No more hate. All is light within our Being.

And he who sat upon the throne said, "Behold I make all things new." Our life will be filled with new thoughts, new actions, new experiences. It will be a whole new world. We will not be limited by our past. We will not be limited by our intellect. We will release love, wisdom, and all the good qualities that are God-like. No more Karma, for the old has passed away. We have overcome. "He who conquers shall have his heritage, and I will be his God and he shall be my son." Truly the Son of God! Can't you feel the excitement of this? Jesus promised that this time would come but we didn't really believe it.

"And death shall be no more," will catch the deep attention of anyone who reads Revelation while deeply centered in Spirit. For death is that which we all must deal with, either through the resurrection or through dying to be born on earth again or death to our earthly consciousness.

Death, in the earthly sense, has come to all of us either in the death of a loved one or of our fellow beings. Will Durant, in *Our Oriental Heritage,* has said: "Death is the origin of all religions and perhaps if there had been no death there would be no gods."[4] I would paraphrase this: The fear of death may be the origin of all religions and perhaps if there had been no death, man would not have allowed spirit to break through. Another quote from Elmer Green in *Beyond Bio-Feedback:* "As a Tibetan teacher put it about 1880, life in the West became a 'struggle for life' because of a belief in hell, and religions through their 'hell and damnation inculcated the greatest dread of death.'" Green quotes Elizabeth Kubler-Ross as having found from counseling eleven hundred dying persons, that fear and guilt plague many dying Westerners. In India death is different. The essence of India was realness, for life and death are very present and very obvious.[5]

Charles Fillmore wrote a great deal on death. It was his belief that we did not need to die, that death would be overcome when we had raised our consciousness high enough to be at One with God. A paragraph from *The Twelve Powers of Man* illustrates this: "This theory of continuous progressive life after death contradicts the teachings of the Bible. God did not create man to die; death is the result of a transgression of law. Christianity teaches that man was created to live in his body, refining it as high thoughts unfold, and that the world of the Christ—the super-mind in man—is to restore this state; that is, unite spirit, soul, and body here on earth. This must be fulfilled in the whole race, and every thought of death, or the possibility of leaving the body, must be put out of mind." And "We must proclaim this great truth taught by Jesus Christ: 'Whosoever liveth and believeth in me (spiritual I AM) shall never die.' " (John 11:25,26)[6]

Thus death in Revelation refers to the fear that most of Western humankind carry about death. For as man grows and becomes conscious of race consciousness he picks up this fear, especially in our Christian community, for the judgment day has been *writ large* in our conscious and unconcious mind.

Fear of death has "worked" for a long time to keep us in line but as we grow in consciousness of our Inner Spirit we lose this fear and are free. The *Tao Te Ching* has this to say: "When the people are not afraid of Death, what is gained by frightening them with Death?"[7] And the Bhagavad Gita "The Eternal in man cannot kill; the Eternal in man cannot die."[8]

When we develop our Faith and Trust in God we know that all is well at death, for we know we are loved by the greater Being of our way. If I am loved now I know I will be loved then. If I love the Lord my God now and am aware of His Love, I lose all fear. Yogananda expresses it thusly: "Life by life, each man progresses toward the goal of his own apotheosis. Death, no interruption in this onward sweep, simply offers man the more congenial environment of an astral world in which to purify his dross.[9] But I want to live forever, don't you? And Revelation is the map, "for there shall be no death."

All religions of the world have had their answers to the fear of death. And perhaps what we call life *is* really death. Jesus words: "Truly, truly I say to you, he who hears my word and believes him (God) who sent me, has eternal life; he does not come into judgment, but has passed from death to life." (John 5:24) Eternal life has always been man's goal and not necessarily life on this earth plane.

I have lost loved ones through death many times. I can never be too grief-stricken, although the death of my twenty-year-old son in the Vietnam War was devastating, but that was before I understood reincarnation. Death can be accepted as a glorious resurrection because the physical is dropped like the hull of the cicada and the Spirit or soul goes on.

So in our beautiful verse, we find assurance that there will be no more death, which to a person this high in consciousness is known already. For death presupposes life on earth again and life on earth, the dross of materiality, has been separated and is no more. When the perishable puts on the imperishable, and the mortal puts on immortality, then shall come to pass the saying that is written:

> Death is swallowed up in victory.
> O death, where is thy victory?
> O death, where is thy sting?
>
> (I Cor. 15:54,55)

And Verse 5, "He who sat upon the throne said, 'Behold, I make all things new,'" is replete with meaning. Behold could be translated as an imperative. Be Whole! and all will be new in your life.

It is done! Verse 6, "And he said to me, 'It is done. I am the Alpha and the Omega, the beginning and the end. To the thirsty I will give from the fountain of the water of life without payment. He who conquers shall have this heritage, and I will be his God and he shall be my son.'" The ultimate grace has been visited upon the revelator and mankind. And God says "It is done!" We feel as though He should also say "It is good!" "And God saw that it was good!" (Genesis 1:10) For He says "I am the Alpha and the Omega, the beginning and the end."

It is interesting that John has God speaking in this chapter for "he who sat upon the throne" has been silent. But those who have reached this high consciousness listen to the Voice of God, their inner Guide and follow in the way. By "listen" I mean, pay attention to, have conversations with this inner guide. Those of us who are on the Way can also have this experience. There are numerous accounts in the Bible and other religious books, of man talking with God and God talking with man. The Bhagavad Gita is a fine demonstration of this as well as our Old Testament.

In the teachings of Carl Jung we find this inner conversation called "active imagination." Imagination and meditation are sometimes parallel, but he teaches that to listen to our inner Guide will bring us on the path to individuation and help us uncover the contents of the unconscious. "Active Imagination is an inner dialogue with someone unseen."[10]

"It is an undeniable psychological fact that the more one concentrates on one's unconscious content, the more they become charged with energy; they become vitalized, as if illuminated from within. I have called this method active imagination."[11] This active imagination, to me, is a Spiritual experience with my Inner Being.

After one has meditated enough to go into the silence he/she may be aware of figures appearing in the imagination with whom conversations can be carried on or a thought will come to one that is not from the conscious mind, it is from another level. Jesus talked to God. Moses talked to and was answered by God. The stories of the prophets carry many experiences of this kind. We have been taught that they were superior beings and thus capable of direct access to God direction, but so are we. Sometimes it is a still small voice; sometimes it thunders. Direction from our inner Spirit is available to anyone who is serious about developing a close relationship with the Self, the Spirit within. When we learn to discriminate between a conscious and unconscious thought, between the heart and the head, between the outer forces and the inner, then we will know that our Guide, our friend, our companion, our Self is the I AM and our eternal guide. Listen!

God, He on the throne, calls Himself the Alpha and Omega, the beginning and the end, the first and last letters of the Aramaic alphabet and the Greek. If he is the beginning and end He is also all that lies between or He is All. He is Genesis and Revelation. He is the coming together of the opposites. He is the Whole, the Holy, the One without divisions or dichotomies. He is thought of as All. He is man reconciled with God in Paradise. In Genesis, we have the symbology of man and God becoming separated. In Revelation we have man and God, One. Alpha and Omega is man's poor attempt to name the ineffable. So we use words that approach the Reality. The conscious and unconscious are together and One. A powerful statement!

I should like to quote from the classic book *The Phenomenon of Man* by Teilhard de Chardin: "The higher pole of evolution is in Omega in its flower and integrity—the hoard of consciousness liberated little by little on earth by noogenesis and is itself together and concentrated. This will be done by love or the affinity of being for Being. Love alone is capable of uniting living beings in such a way as to complete and fulfill them for it alone takes them and joins them by what is deepest in themselves."[12] Teilhard was a Jesuit father and a distinguished paleontologist. He brought together in this book the material and spiritual worlds, the world of mind and spirit; of the past with the future; and of variety with unity; the many with the One. Human evolution was his thesis.

And the last of verse 6, "To the thirsty I will give from the fountain of water of life without payment" is a beautiful analogy, for water to quench the thirst was so scarce in the desert setting that almost anything would be given for it. And here man is promised a fountain of *living* water without payment.

Water is symbolic of many conditions and powers. Water has within it the power to take life or to give life. Water is erosive or a builder. Water is power. Water is what a large percent of earthly forms are made of. Water is an absolute necessity for life on earth. Foregoing food for days will not cause death, but water is a necessity. So what symbolic allusion does the "Fountain of living water" have for us?

Living water is spoken of often in the Old and New Testaments. It is used as a metaphor for life, for eternal life. Solomon 4:15: ". . . a garden fountain, a well of living water." Jeremiah 17:13: "They have forsaken the Lord, the fountain of living water." Jesus told the Samaritan woman at the well, "If you knew this gift of God . . . he would give you living water."

The fountain of living water may also refer to the spine and the Holy Spirit flowing up and down which activates the chakras mentioned before. The spine with its branches of nerves is very similar to a tree or a fountain and as the Shakti moves it is living water flowing through the fountain. And when this happens we will thirst no more for we have all.

The water of life, according to Corinne Heline, has reference to Initiation, of a deeper understanding and use of spiritual power than is possessed by the masses.[13]

Remember that all the way through our ascent of Mt. Zion we made one step forward and then seemed to slip back two steps? We were paying a price through suffering, either physically or psychologically. We were on the Path but allowing our focus of attention to be diverted from the pinnacle. (Concentration is important for any achievement.) But now, now . . . there is no payment, no suffering, no negative, no loss of our identity for our Identity has been found. It is God! It is Self! It is All!

And "He who conquers shall have this heritage, and I will be his God and he shall be my son." (Verse 7) There it is! There is the Truth! For we are all sons of God. If we haven't arrived at the Peak we are still sons, albeit Sons of man, but we are sons of God when we conquer. Moses, Jesus, Buddha and other great religious leaders have been called sons of God and we have been taught in various religions, especially the Christian, that only *they* are sons of God. But here "he who sat upon the throne" says: "I will be his God and he shall be my son." You and I, we, are sons of God always, but until we accept his gift of divine water we don't KNOW this. With our new heaven and new earth we will KNOW!

He then defines again those who will not make it, who will burn in the lake of fire and sulphur, who will experience the second death. For you see, even though we have reached the pinnacle, we can slide down so easily if it snows or rains and our footing becomes unsteady.

Those who are mentioned are those who are centered on the material world and their own ego, their own "I did this" and not on their "I Am." All of these have a common characteristic of fear which is basically a lack of faith! "But as for the cowardly, the faithless, the polluted, as for murderers, fornicators, sorcerers, idolators, and all liars, their lot shall be in the lake that burns with fire and sulphur, which is the second death." These will reincarnate again and again until the dross has been burnt out by the purifying action of sulphur and fire, until through suffering they turn to "He who waits for you ever and ever." For to be One with Him we must start with faith.

Then our revealer says that one of the seven angels comes who had one of the bowls of the seven plagues and invited him to "Come, I will show you the Bride, the wife of the Lamb."

For the Christian, this is interpreted as the church (bride) and Jesus Christ (Lamb). This is well enough if we are still focused on the outer, but let us see what it means if we focus on our own consciousness, on our personal consciousness.

I have already discussed at some length the Hindu teaching of the marriage of Shakti and Siva. The Bride could in that sense be Siva and the Lamb would be the kundalini power, the Holy Spirit, the source of love and light. The Bride is a beautiful choice to help us understand the New Jerusalem, for that is what John is going to be shown. Jerusalem is called the bride as the traditional picture of a bride, the wife of the Lamb or Jesus Christ would be one of purity, beauty, love, grace, bedecked with a white robe and jewels. So the bride is the ultimate state of being of the aspirant when all the materiality, the dross, of the world is washed away and the pure consciousness is at one with the Lamb.

There may be some confusions, however, as the Bride is considered female while the Lamb is the male. In my examples from Hinduism, the reverse was true. However, in some Eastern religions it is believed that the initial action toward enlightenment comes from the Godhead which is above, or in the brain area and is the Bride, Sophia, seeking the masculine which is the kundalini at the base of the spine. Whatever the position on this, we know that it means that the aspirant will now experience the great moment of fusion of the personal consciousness of God (the Christ) and God himself. And now we come to the most beautiful symbolic description of which we have had a glimpse formerly. And we are reminded of I Corinthans 13:12, "For now we see in a mirror dimly, but then face to face. Now I know in part; then I shall understand fully, even as I have been fully understood."

Verse 11, ". . . the holy City Jerusalem. . . . having the glory of God, its radiance like a most rare jewel, like a jasper, clear as crystal." (Jasper, according to some Bible interpreters, is pure light. Jasper is also considered by some to be the diamond.)

First we are told about the wall. Verse 12, "It had a great high wall, with twelve gates, and at the gates twelve angels, and on the gates the names of the twelve tribes of the sons of Israel were inscribed." It is important that the number twelve be included in the vision, in the mandala of the Holy City, as it is divisible by 3 and 4 and has symbolized perfection in very ancient writings, as metaphysical and spiritual perfection. "It denotes the full spiritual realization that comes when permanent union is made with the Christ."[14] So writes Elizabeth Turner about twelve.

Twelve has been an important number throughout the Bible and in other ancient religions. Twelve tribes of Israel, twelve apostles, twelve months in a year, twelve signs of the zodiac and in this description, the twelve gates to the Holy of Holies. We also find in Ezekiel 48:30–34, the twelve gates are names with the twelve tribes of Israel. In Exodus 28:15–21, we have twelve stones with the names of the sons of Israel.

Twelve is, of course, a significant number in astrology. Astrology was once considered the science of the Universe but through the years as Western science became a religion, astrology has been deprecated. However, Western man should not forget that astrology has for thousands of years been accepted by man as having some validity. In the Eastern sector it is still seriously considered. The Hindus still use the astrological natal chart of a man and woman when marriages are arranged by the parents. The tribes of the sons of Israel were arranged in deference to their astrological sign. In spite of our nonacceptance of it, there are those who believe that we each go through each sign of the zodiac in one or more lives until we have made full circle and reach completion.

Studying astrology with an open mind is a study of psychology and the spiritual journey of each person, they say. Whether this knowledge and influence comes from the stars or from our Gods or gods, makes no difference. If there is Truth within that astrological chart we should pay attention. By experiencing this ancient "science" we may learn much. But this is only one way; there are many others which may be more attractive to you. Carl Jung experimented with astrology and at one time cast charts for his analysands but gave it up as he could gain the same knowledge from his own, and their, intuitive faculties. In any case, it is agreed that the scribes of the Bible were influenced by astrology. It was very much alive in those times.

The twelve tribes of Israel are an important concept for John as they represent various personality characteristics which the aspirant has been reaching for. Edyth Hoyt names them as follows: Judah, dominion; Reuben, strength; Gad, justice; Asher, happiness; Naphtali, blessing of the Lord; Manasseh, blessing and fruitage; Simeon, obedience and hearing; Levi, holiness and purity of associations; Issachar, recompense and reward; Zebulun, spiritual activity; Joseph, fruitage; Benjamin, protection.[15] And these are the gates to the Holy City.

Now Christian writers, preachers, interpreters have always associated this description of heaven as a physical place with streets of gold and with pearl gates. This has given the devout Christian much surcease from pain and suffering as he, in his imagination, lifted his thoughts, his concentration to this heavenly place to which he would go when he was saved. Of course, he would go there after death, he believed. I have never understood why he feared dying since this heavenly Jerusalem awaited him and was materially and spiritually just what he had longed for all of his life, that is, gold and jewels. How wonderful that the revelator gave us this description. For as the Christian lifted his thoughts to this Holy City he inadvertently concentrated on a mandala, the center of the Self, the representative of perfection and his consciousness was raised. What a blessing!

Verse 14: "And the wall of the city had twelve foundations, and on them the twelve names of the twelve apostles of the Lamb."

According to Charles Fillmore, the twelve foundations are the "Twelve Powers of Man" as the twelve apostles of Jesus. This is a viable interpretation, I believe, and I should like to discuss this theory here.

In his book by the same name, he makes the point that in order to reach superconsciousness, we must develop twelve centers in our soul and body. These he calls centers of action with twelve presiding egos or identities. These twelve powers are located in the body at "ganglionic centers" with the I AM on His throne in or on top of the head. As we grow in consciousness these twelve powers are developed and are in perfect balance when we reach our goal of Oneness. He also gives the name of an Apostle of Jesus to each one. They are faith, Peter; strength, Andrew; Judgment, James; love, John; power, Philip; imagination, Bartholomew; understanding, Thomas; will, Matthew; order, James, son of Alphaeus; zeal, Simon the Canaanite; renunciation, Thaddaeus; generative or life conserver, Judas.[16] These "ganglionic centers" could be likened to chakra centers. The above explanation may be of value to you in your upward climb to perfection, for the teachings of the twelve Apostles are the foundation. Twelve steps on pyramids that are found throughout the world give us another symbolic representation of the wall around the Holy City.

Let us continue. The mediator was shown a rod of gold which the angel used to measure the city and its gates and walls. The rod of gold may symbolize the mastery of Christ dominion when we have gained the Christ consciousness. It may symbolize the power of God as indicated in the use of the rod by Aaron and Moses when freeing the children of Israel from Egypt. The golden rod might also refer to the kundalini serpent. Some say the rod symbolizes Mercurius, or the *caduceus* of Mercurius which unites the opposites, in mythological terms.

You will note that all the measurements are divisible by four, our symbol of totality. Four is divine. Four is equal. Four is in balance. The Christian Church and the Bible have also made much of the Trinity as being the divine number. I should like to refer the reader to Carl Jung for more on this. In *Psychology and Religion,* the section on "A Psychological Approach to the Dogma of the Trinity" is excellent.[17]

Verse 16 indicates that the "city lies foursquare, its length the same as its breadth." In Ezekiel 40 we have a description of the temple with some of the same characteristics, i.e., the court was foursquare, etc. He was given the measurements of a city that he saw in a vision. In our scripture from Revelation the city was foursquare. Foursquare is a symbol of absolute truth. The cube is the Holy of Holies in the temple of the Jews; the Ka'ba Stone of the Muslims; the perfected life of Jesus for the Christian. All are symbols of perfection, of God present.

As I have pointed out in discussing the mandala, the symbol that is in the center of the mandala is important to the religious belief of the individual who has drawn the mandala or worships by concentrating on it. In this mandala or the Holy City we have no temple in the center, no representation of our Source, our God, or a material symbol. For the temple is God and the Lamb and God and the Holy Spirit cannot be depicted by material means. Verse 22, "And I saw no temple in the city, for its temple is the Lord God and the Almighty and the Lamb." They are ineffable, non-formed, beyond our ability to see in the body sense. The Zen Buddhist indicates The Void as being God. Many Westerners misunderstand that as "nothing." The Void, however, is All. It is like space, It is like the ethers. Let me give a few references. Jung quotes from the *Tibetan Book of the Great Liberation* and then says: "The One Mind being verily of the Voidness and without any foundation, one's mind is likewise as vacuous as the sky. And then Jung adds, "only the collective and the personal unconscious can be meant by this statement."[18]

Phillip Kapleau speaks from the framework of Zen Buddhism:

"Zen tells us that the *is* is holy and the Void is home and Zen is a method for attaining to the direct experience of the truth of these affirmations. When the bottom of heart or consciousness is broken open, not the slightest doubt will remain that your own Mind is itself Buddha, the Void-universe."[19] From this we get an idea of the Godhead which is on the throne.

Verse 19: "The foundations of the wall of the city were adorned with every jewel; the first was jasper, the second sapphire, the third, agate, the fourth emerald, the fifth onyx, the sixth carnelian, the seventh chrysolite, the eighth beryl, the ninth topaz, the tenth chrysoprase, the eleventh jacinth, the twelfth amethyst.

Let us discuss the jewels that are displayed. Jewels bring to our mind great beauty, perfection, light, color, precious qualities, indestructibility, something to be desired, and a thing of highest quality. All of these jewels named have a metaphysical meaning. They form the foundation of the wall that surrounds the New Jerusalem and indicate characteristics that have been perfected in the consciousness of the aspirant. The Funk and Wagnall Standard Bible Dictionary has given them these interpretations: Jasper, courage; Sapphire, constancy and truth; Chalcedony, truth about eternal life; Emerald, immortality; Sardonyx or onyx, unity of the bride and groom; Sardius, wisdom; Chrysolite, gladness; Beryl, joy and agelessness; Topaz, love and spirituality, Chrysoprasus, eternal life; Jacinth, might; Amethyst, love and perfection. If you will study each of these carefully as well as the Ideas behind the twelve tribes of Israel and the twelve Apostles, you will find a complete map of the way to the Holy City, for these characteristics will develop as we meditate, live an exemplary life, and express through the opening of the seven chakras.

Jewels are a part of God's glory and all of mankind has responded to them with joy and bliss. In the Persian architecture they were often embedded in buildings to make it shine and glow as a facsimile of the God Light that was intuitively known. The Taj Mahal is an example of such beauty and was built as a dedication to love. The jewels may be lost but the essence of what they symbolize remains. So jewels, another of man's attempt to express beauty, is a part of the foundations of the kingdom of God.

Gold, like jewels, has been much sought after by man. It too, is a pure, clear, shining symbol for that which we cannot describe. The alchemists used gold as a symbol of pure spiritual essence. When the Philosophers Stone is found, they said, it would turn all into gold. A beautiful analogy to total enlightenment.

Pearls, likewise, are symbols of Truth, and Truth which grows in the dark recesses of the ocean, the unconscious and are sought by man from other living organisms. They contain the spectrum of colors which flow from the pure light of Creative force.

Again all of this description is a mandala to be focused upon to gain the Treasure or to be used as a symbol of the Perfection that we all seek. Streets of gold, gates of pearls, foundations glowing with jewels, crystaline purity of the Holy City are our inheritance as we reach our goal. Having once "seen" this we know that all that our lives have held has been worth the effort. For all led to the City of God!

We should not, of course, get bogged down in analyzing the beauty of the kingdom of God for it is not a place, it is not physical, it is not made of precious metals and jewels. It is a state of mind, a different dimension of knowing, an ineffable effulgence which escapes man's ability to describe. We should remember that John, in his high state of ecstasy, "saw" this palace, this temple, this kingdom as a vision as did Lahiri Mahasaya "saw" the beautiful palace of gold and precious stones as he was initiated into the Mysteries.[20] (Lahiri Mahasaya is one of the line of gurus leading to Yogananda and the teaching of Kriya Yoga to the Western world.) But because we like to see or know in terms of our own experience, this description captures our attention and we can understand better. We "see" in our mind's eye and our experiences on earth and studying the religious scriptures helps us understand it.

Now we come to the Essences, for Light is the Essence. We usually pass over the word Light as we read the Bible, with no real understanding. If we knew it, Light is the essence of all being for Light is that which vibrates and makes all that Is, the glory of His Presence. Light, the wisdom of His way. Light, our real energizer and Life. For Light, Life, Love, Energy are the same.

Let us look at several scriptural passages with a new view, a new *enlightenment*. Read these with the new consciousness that total Light is our goal. For the description of the kingdom of Heaven in Revelation 21:23-25 reads: "And the city has no need of sun or moon to shine upon it, for the glory of God is its light, and its lamp is the Lamb. By its light shall the nations walk; and the kings of the earth shall bring their glory into it, and its gates shall never be shut by day—and there shall be no night there." This indicates that we will all be Light, for the glory of God is the light which we are since we have changed our physical consciousness to robes of white. Matt. 17:2 reads, "And he (Jesus) was transfigured before them, and his face shone like the sun, and his garments became white as light." And Isaiah 60:1, "Arise, shine, for your light has come, and the glory of the Lord has risen upon you." And I John 1:5, "This is the message we have heard from him and proclaim to you, that God is light and in him is no darkness at all." And Exodus 40:34, "Then the cloud covered the tent of the meeting, and the glory of the lord filled the tabernacle." And lastly, Jesus is reported to have said in John 8:12, "I am the light of the world; he who follows me will not walk in darkness, but will have the light of life."

In the beginning God said, "Let there be light" and there was light. That is from whence we came and that is to which we are going. The scriptures of all religions refer to this truth. From the Upanishad, Chandogya: "The light that shines above the heavens and above the world, beyond which there are no others . . . that is the light that shines in the heart of men." The Bhagavad Gita 8:26: "There are two paths that are forever: the path of light and the path of darkness. The one leads to the land of never-returning; the other returns to sorrow." Also, from the Gita 11:17, "I see the splendour of an infinite beauty which illumines the whole universe." The *Tao Te Ching,* 58: "Therefore the sage (the enlightened one) is as bright as light but does not dazzle." And from the book *The Sufis* by Idries Shah, page 431: "Allah is the Light of the heavens and earth."[21]

In the series of books, *The Life and Teaching of the Masters of the Far East,* we are given graphic descriptions of the light body. You see, our body is light but overcovered with Maya, the Shadow, the Humanness of our belief. We come out of darkness into Light when we are born. Our consciousness, likewise, comes from the Shadow of our human understanding to that of Light of the Eternal. But how wonderfully we are made as we are both light and shadow. When the shadow is demolished or raised up in Light then we become pure light, not only our body but our consciousness; or should I say they rise together? In our modern study of psychic phenomena, so called, we are learning about auras. And the auras are being photographed, which proves that a light shines around all living matter and science can accept that. Also, there is an aura of light around what we designate "dead" matter. This is *the* Light.

Now our scripture says "there is no need of sun or moon to shine upon it, for the glory of God is its light and its lamp is the Lamb." The sun symbolizes the masculine, the moon the feminine and they have become one in the Impersonal of the glory of the Lord. How much plainer could it be. The Glory and the Lamb are the Light. The ineffable Brightness of all there Is.

Since the Lamb is a symbol of the Holy Spirit I should like to suggest that we are again having described what happens as the human person raises the Power through the spine and opens all the psychic chakra centers. The body eventually is filled with Light. Thus, the body is transfigured as a pulsating light-filled entity. It is that which we have in potential and as they become open and vibrating, our physical body is joined by an etheric body or subtle body, a body of light. The Rosicrucians go into great detail on this.[22] As we are wedded to the Divine Source of life we become that Light and all around us is Light.

Let me now give some illustrations of descriptions from the

mystics (Christian) who have reached this glory of God. From an account about Jacob Boehme in *Cosmic Consciousness,* by Richard Bucke: "Earthly language is entirely insufficient to describe what there is of joy, happiness, the loveliness contained in the inner wonders of God." From the same book, Walt Whitman's enlightenment was described as "I am satisfied. I see, dance, laugh, sing. Oh the joy of my spirit, it is uncaged . . . it darts like lightning. The ocean filled with joy . . . the atmosphere all joy." (From "The Mystic Trumpeter" in Whitman's book, *Leaves of Grass*) From *Mysticism,* by Evelyn Underhill, is taken a quote from the mystic Ruysbroeck: "We behold that which we are, and we are that which we behold; because our thought, life and being are uplifted in simplicity and made one with the Truth which is God." And the Buddha is reported to have said: "Enlightenment will bestow on man the ecstasy of contemplation; cause him to become an inheritor of the highest heaven; make him become one to become multiple, being multiple to become one."

"And the glory of the Lord shone all around him." Glory is understood as Light, as the realization of Divine Unity. In Isaiah 24:23 we read: "Then the moon will be confounded, and the sun ashamed, for the Lord of hosts will reign on Mt. Zion and in Jerusalem and before his elders he will manifest *glory*." And Isaiah 60:19,20: "The sun shall be no more your light by day, nor for brightness shall the moon give light unto thee but the Lord will be your everlasting light and glory." And II Corinthians 3:18: "And we all with unveiled face, beholding the glory of the Lord, are being changed into his likeness from one degree of glory to another; for this came from the Lord (Christ) who is the Spirit." Psalms 24:7–10:

> Lift up your heads, O Gates
> and be lifted up, O ancient doors
> that the King of Glory may come in.
> Who is the King of glory?
> The Lord strong and Mighty,
> the Lord mighty in battle!
> Lift up your heads, O gates!

and be lifted up, O ancient doors!
that the King of glory may come in.
Who is this King of glory?
The Lord of hosts,
he is the King of glory!

Also: "And behold, the glory of the God of Israel came from the east; and the sound of his coming was like the sound of many waters; and the earth shone with his glory." (Ezek. 43:2)

Revelation 21:24: "By its light shall the nations walk; and the kings of the earth shall bring their glory into it." Not only the individual consciousness is described here but the glory of the rulers of nations and the honor of nations. However, metaphysically, nations could symbolize aggregations of thoughts which will be enlightened with spiritual essence.

Obviously, as each of us reaches a higher state of consciousness the nations will be affected. For as each rises, the whole world consciousness is raised. All people of whatever conviction are One as we think of them in spiritual terms and we are all connected through the Love of God. And so we are affected by each other through the great mind of God. Our responsibility is great and we live for divine love, not personal. In Divine Love, All are raised.

So it is the Father of Light and Love that we have been seeking in our lives. He has always been near at hand, within us, but mankind through the ages has looked elsewhere. Now we KNOW! He is closer than seeing, hearing, breathing. His glory shines through the face of the mystic and through his caring for others. Jesus, our Divine example, shown with the glory of God, was misunderstood by the ruling class. He spent most of his ministry in the mid-East where violence of emotion in terms of hate was rampant. He brought the message of Love. The mystics of all ages and religious persuasion have talked about the indwelling spirit—the Father of Light. Jesus referred to his Father many, many times. Our light, our God is shining albeit in darkness. When we let it glow with effervescence and are in the unity with Spirit then our New Jerusalem will come. We will be the Kingdom of God, we will be in the majestic Glory and Presence of God.

We will then be free from uncleanness, falsehood, negativity for we are in the Lamb's Book of Life, of eternal life which the Holy Spirit IS. We are not dual but One. We are the Holy Spirit! Hallelujah! Let us rejoice for "Many are called, but few are chosen." (Matt. 22:14) Let us accept the calling and be among the chosen!

CHAPTER 22

Love, Freedom, Joy Forever!!

We come at last to possibly the most important chapter in the Book of Revelation for in it is the summing up of all that is taught from Genesis through Revelation. I realize that is a shocking statement, but when we have finished studying it I think you will agree. If you can bring to this chapter an open mind, a centeredness in your higher Self, a desire to know—then you will *know*. For Revelation was recorded for you and for me. So far we have let Light shine on the esoteric teaching contained in this great Book. Now let us see what it says in summation.

The first seven verses of Chapter 22 seem to belong to the description of the kingdom of Heaven and should be in the 21st chapter. I shall, however, discuss them as a part of this chapter.

Since I have introduced into this interpretation the idea of the raising of the kundalini power, I shall approach the first two verses from that direction. Then I will take it to the metaphysical interpretations.

The first verse reads: "Then *he* showed me the river of the water of life, bright as crystal, flowing from the throne of God and of the Lamb through the middle of the city; also, in either side of the river, the tree of life with its twelve kinds of fruit, yielding its fruit each month; and the leaves of the tree were for the healing of the nations." "He," you will note, refers to "one of the seven angels who had the seven bowls of the seven last plagues." (Revelation 21:9)

That verse has mystified the common reader, theologians of intellectual greatness, preachers and ministers for centuries. The church has given it interpretation and most religionists, rather than go to their own Center to interpret it, lean on the authority of the church. I believe *this* interpretation will strike a chord in your consciousness and it will vibrate with Truth as I am able to write it.

The "river of the water of life" is the river of energy, the power that flows through the spine, the Holy Spirit, Love that flows always through our body. The water of life is energy or God. The spine is the central part of our anatomy, and if we are to live, the spine must be intact. Very few operations on the back are successful, for the medical person is tampering with the river of life, an etheric substance that they do not know about or are blind to. This river flows through our spine and feeds the nerves and nerve centers in our body.

Fillmore defines "river of water of life" as "the pure life of God flowing into man's consciousness through the spiritual body and is sensed by the physical at the point in the loins. This is the "river of water of life, bright as crystal, proceeding out of the throne of God and of the Lamb" referred to in the 22nd chapter of Revelation. Only those who have come into consciousness of the spiritual body can feel this holy stream of life . . . It cannot be described, because all the sensations of the mortal consciousness are coarse, compared with its transcendent sweetness and purity. Many feel its thrills in part in silent meditation or in religious enthusiasm, and are temporarily stimulated by its exquisite vibrations."[1] This supports my position.

It is bright as crystal for it is not water but a spiritual substance that the physical eye cannot perceive. It is clear and pure and builds not only the physical body but also the spiritual body, the etheric or subtle body.

It flows from the throne of God and of the Lamb when they are united. Again a reference to the marriage of the Siva and Shakti of Hindu teaching. As we grow in consciousness in our Divinity this marriage will occur and we are blessed with Oneness with God, for we are not separate then as our Holy Spirit and the Source of our Good are One. So the essence flows from the throne.

The middle of the street of the city refers to the central tube of the spinal chord up which flows the kundalini and on either side the Ida and Pingala, the masculine and feminine aspect, but more feminine, and thus kundalini is referred to as "she." I have discussed this in a previous chapter.

Then we have "on either side of the river, the tree of life." We have referred to Ida and Pingala and their connection with the nerve centers or nerves of the body and with the energy centers in the spiritual body. Through Ida and Pingala flows the prana, the energy, brought into the body through the breath that enters the body through the nostrils. This feeds the body and is why breathing is an important concept in all yoga practice. Since this part of Revelation is describing the state of Enlightenment the spiritual and the physical bodies are One, as was Jesus' body after the Resurrection.

Now, the tree of life, both feminine and masculine, is the spine and the nerve centers on each side as well as the chakra centers attached to the spine. According to Jung in "Psychology and Religion," the tree stands for the development and phases of transformative process, and its fruits or flowers signify the consummation of the work. The alchemists saw the union of opposites in the symbol of the tree. The tree symbolizes the Paradise of God which is a major theme in Genesis. So the "tree of life" is the spine that has coursing within it the energy of the Divine with which man may become One.

The flowers or fruits are, as Jung suggests, the open centers that spiritualize the physical body, and when these are all opened or producing, the ultimate for man's seeking has been reached. Again we have the number 12, as "on either side of the river, the tree of life with its twelve kinds of fruit, yielding its fruit each month" is stated. It is understood by those mystics who discuss the kundalini power raising that these are twelve centers which vibrate with high energy when opened. Nine and seven centers are mentioned by others. However, since we are at the stage of completion, the twelve fruits may refer to the perfection completed in the seven chakra centers and the five senses or the twelve fruits may refer to the six chakras and the two aspects of each, the positive and the negative.

Some have suggested that the reference to "yielding its fruit each month" refers to the signs of the astrological chart which have been completed, full circle has been made, and completion of the individual's growth toward Oneness is finished. Astrology did figure in the writings of the prophets, as we have pointed out, and this may be a viable suggestion. I would suggest that the 12 months refer to the completion and coming to Oneness as we think of 12 months as a year. A full circle of time. The 12 astral signs have been depicted as the aspects of the 6 spinal centers, the symbolic cosmic man. So all of our signs are included and no matter what our astral sign, we can become divine in this lifetime and not have to continue through all the rest of the signs. We must always remember, God is the center of our life and our astral chart and sign do not control what He does.

"And the leaves of the tree were for the healing of the nations" could refer to the process of healing that has come about through our own efforts and the Grace of God. "For there shall be no more death, nor pain." We are healed through the divine essence flowing through our spine, from faith to truth or enlightenment.

In the beginning of the second chapter of Genesis we are given a description of the Garden of Eden and God's admonition to Adam that he eat not of the tree of the knowledge of good and evil. In Chapter 3, after Adam and Eve had eaten from the tree, they are banished from the Garden, for God said, "Behold, the man has become like one of us, knowing good and evil; and now lest he put forth his hand and take also of the tree of life, and eat and live forever" and they were sent forth from the Garden and cherubim and flaming sword which turned every way, to guard the way to the tree of life, stood at the east of the Garden. The flaming sword and cherubim is said to symbolize man-spirit and the spine inflamed with the Holy Spirit which guards Paradise. East symbolizes our inner Spirit consciousness.

From this we can assume that if one eats from the tree of life he will have eternal life so that God in his love does not want us to carry for eternity the dichotomy, the duality of good and evil, but wants us to find our way back to All, God and then eat of the tree of life, eternal life. Revelation shows us how.

So we are shown the tree of life, accessible to all who are around the throne, and whose fruits and leaves are for them and their healing. And all the negative, the evil, shall not be near the throne and all of God, or Good, will be revealed. And there shall be no more dark, no more evil or negative, for Good or God is the light and the servants shall worship Him for ever and ever.

It takes mankind, each man/woman, many, many lives to come full circle back to the source, back to God, who created him in the first place and who disobeyed the admonitions of God. We have been up and down in the account of the Judeo/Christian history. But now as Isaiah says, "The way of the righteous is level, thou dost make smooth the path of the righteous." (Chapter 26, verse 7)

If we will look back into the history of the Old Testament we will see that various giants of Spirit, chosen by God, helped us to evolve to our present level of understanding. I should also add that the New Testament teachers, beginning with Jesus, have helped that evolution. The great spiritual leaders relate to the seven churches with which we dealt in chapters 2 and 3. A diagram will appear on page 270 which will make this clearer.

In the beginning we have God, Genesis 1:1. Adam was his representative on earth, so the Spirit of God was in Adam, as in each of us.

The first great patriarch was *Abraham* who symbolizes *faith* and father of a multitude. Faith is the first chakra. Then *Isaac,* his son, became a great leader. He symbolizes *creative force.* He was born of the spirit or the creative force which may be used either for physical or spiritual reasons. This is the second chakra. He, Isaac, used it spiritually.

Jacob and Esau, children of Isaac, symbolize the spiritual and animal-like nature of man. Esau was born first so should have received Isaac's blessing. Instead Jacob received his blessing, so the spiritual side of man continued to grow and connect the creative force with the intellect. Jacob represents an idea of the I AM identity, through which the faculties of the mind receive their original inspiration.

The third chakra symbolizes the *intellect* and Jacob, spiritual intelligence, is the go-between for the creative force and the intelligence. The third chakra is symbolized by Moses. Moses gave the law to the people so that they could continue their growth, their spirit-led evolution back to the Promised Land. So Moses is the intellect, the characteristic which makes rules, which directs our lives, which helps us make choices, in Moses' case the right choices, for he was enlightened.

Saul, or personal will, is the door I spoke of, or the gate through which we must go if we are to enter into higher consciousness. Saul vascilated a great deal between the head and heart, the intellect and the emotions. He allowed one and then the other to rule his life. He was not always wholly dedicated to the Lord. The will functions in the limitation of personality and should be inspired but often asserts its own initiative. The will is natural and needed to go through the door or gate.

Saul's life is very much like our own as we choose the better and then fall back into our negative thinking and acting but finally or at some time will make the correct choice and go forward. Saul forgot to listen to the direction of the Lord and offered sacrifices which Samuel told him was not right. Samuel said, "Behold, to obey is better than sacrifice, and to harken than the fat of rams." (I Samuel 15:22) Saul was inclined to follow the old religious customs and not listen to his inner voice of God.

David, the anointed, represents personal love, divine love personalized. His place is at the heart center. (It is said that he had a ruddy complexion signifying blood.) David had his ups and downs, but his great work was done in love for the people. He called the Lord "my shepherd." And so the rulership is withdrawn from the will or intellect and gradually transformed to the heart or love. (King David) But David strayed from listening to the Lord, too, and had his challenges.

This brought man to a high state of loving and serving. But something called him to perfection. Man knew there was a higher state and so he chose to seek God, to worship God, to return to the Garden of Eden where the tree of life, eternity, could be experienced. So the fifth chakra of seeking God is symbolized.

Whoever has a desire for completion, for religion, is developed because of man's feeling of incompleteness, will move to this level. As man seeks he finds through the great love of God. He finds wisdom. He contacts God through meditation, through worship, and goes to higher states of consciousness. Man is both spiritual and human and our conscious thoughts will not bring us to the spiritual unless love, David, wills it. So man seeks God, or Unconditional Love, Impersonal Love, and wisdom is the result. Worship and building the temple, the spiritual temple, then will be his or our task.

Solomon, it will be agreed, is associated with wisdom as we remember the account of his life. He it was to whom God offered anything, and Solomon chose wisdom. Solomon symbolizes wholeness, peace, integrity, soundness, rectitude, completeness, prosperity. Solomon, a representative of mankind, unified love and wisdom. However, Solomon fell from sound mind at times and then it was that David, Love, restored his balance. Coming so close to the Infinite Goal may cause us to waver in our mental balance at times. But Solomon is still an example for our higher growth. Wisdom must be tempered with love and man is the connecting link, for as the Holy Spirit is pure love and God is wisdom then we, mankind, bring them into unity. Solomon depended upon God's direction for wisdom and intuition which is the same. This is the sixth chakra, the Third Eye of the Hindus. And then we come finally to Jesus at the seventh chakra.

Jesus, our pattern of perfection; Jesus, who taught us how to overcome our earthly consciousness; Jesus, who showed us eternal life that is inanimate in our consciousness; Jesus, who lived as man, who was tempted as man with materialism, power, ambition, and who controlled and overcame them all; Jesus, who became pure life and light, whose physical body did not decay, who lives on a plane of existence which is possible for all. Did he not say, "Ye are gods"? (John 10:34)

Jesus, the second Adam, is a personification of each of us. In I Corinthians 15:45-47 we read: "Thus it is written, 'The first man Adam became a living being.; the last Adam became a life-giving spirit.' But it is not the spiritual which is first but the physical, and then the spiritual. The first man was from the earth, a man of dust; the second man is from heaven." So Jesus, represented by the seventh chakra, is the second Adam of the spirit, is Enlightenment, is Nirvana, is Samadhi, is One with our Creator, is the I AM. And our journey through Revelation has taken us from "In the beginning" to this state of Being. For Jesus is the Son of God and so are we. He brought to earth the Being and Promise and taught us how to reach the second Adam state.

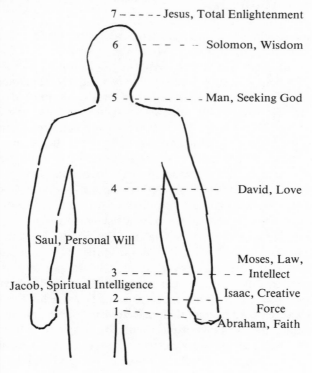

7 – – – – – Jesus, Total Enlightenment

6 – – – – – – Solomon, Wisdom

5 – – – – – – – Man, Seeking God

4 – – – – – – – – David, Love

Saul, Personal Will

3 – – – – – – – – Moses, Law, Intellect

Jacob, Spiritual Intelligence

2 – – – – – – – Isaac, Creative Force

1 – – – – – – Abraham, Faith

The Chakra Centers symbolized by great leaders of the
Israelites and
Jesus Christ

And as it is written in Psalms 82:7, "You are gods, sons of the Most High, all of you; nevertheless you shall die like men, and fall like any prince." The latter is our human state, the former our spiritual.

Verse 6 brings us back to the angel of Jesus Christ spoken of in the first chapter to give us some final messages. He reiterates that "The Lord, the God of the spirits of the prophets, has sent his angel to show his servants what must soon take place." And verse 7, "And behold, I am coming soon." This I interpret as Jesus Christ's assurance that his spirit will be in all and through all as we grow in consciousness of God. Verse 6 begins an epilogue of the seven last statements of John which Edyth Hoyt lists as follows:

1. Blessed is he who keeps the words, verse 7
2. Worship God only, verses 8 and 9
3. Study and use the words of this book, verse 10
4. Realize the Oneness of the One, verse 13
5. Be alert to claim your inheritance, verse 14
6. Be aware of the spiritual source of life, verse 16
7. This Revelation is a free gift to all, verse 17[2]

Seven, our symbol of completion. And the source of all of this is God through his servant Jesus Christ, and we are the recipients.

In verse 8, John identifies himself and says he saw and heard all the foregoing, the vision, that has been described. And so he fell down at the feet of the angel to worship him because he showed him the New Jerusalem but the angel would have none of it and said "You must not do that! I am a fellow servant with you and your brethren the prophets, and with those who keep the words of this book. "Worship God," (Verse 9) So we are to worship God, not Jesus Christ.

In verse 10 John is told not "to seal up the words of the prophecy of this book, for the time is near." It is interesting, isn't it, that the words of the prophecy of this book have been sealed up for 2000 years. Each one of the religionists has tried from his own frame of reference to understand it, but the world did not really get the message. The time is Now for the hope that it will be unsealed and each of us will be able to follow the admonitions and directions for obtaining the New Jerusalem.

Verse 11 also gives us the insight that we all have the freedom to be who we are, as the evil may continue to be evil, or our negative nature may continue to act and our holy nature may continue to act for those who are not of the thronely multitude are still in a state of duality.

Verse 12 reads: "Behold, I am coming soon, bringing my recompense to repay every one for what he has done." The Spirit is coming soon and will recompense everyone for what he has done. The Law of Karma is fair and when we accept responsibility for our own behavior and its outcome this will make sense to us. But when we are in God we will be free and there is no karma in God. It is when we have loaded our "sins" on others, in some cases Jesus Christ, in others our parents, in others the government, that we do not see the fairness of recompense. For our recompense will come from our Good, as well as our lack of Good in our thoughts, words, and actions.

In verse 13, the speaker, the spirit of Jesus, repeats, "I am the Alpha and the Omega, the first and the last, the beginning and the end." God created us in the beginning, He will be there at the end. Alpha and Omega have been discussed elsewhere. From Rev. 21:6, he who is on the throne says: "I am the Alpha and Omega, the beginning and the end . . . He who conquers shall have this heritage, and I will be his God and he shall be my son." So Christ, our inner knowing, and God are the same. We have come full circle from our Creator to our Creator.

Washing the robes as mentioned in Verse 14, I believe, refers allegorically to purifying our consciousness and becoming pillars of light for as pointed out previously we enlighten our bodies and the spiritual interpenetrates the physical with high energy which makes us appear as robed in white, or pure consciousness. And those who are clothed in white will have the right to eternal life, "and they may enter the city by the gates." Remember the high wall around the city? Wall is symbolic of our intellect or any obstruction which prevents us from experiencing life in the Holy City. To scale that wall is possible but very difficult. We are being told that as we reach this point in consciousness we will be allowed to enter by the gates. How much easier to go through the gates as they are opened by our awareness of our Maker, our God.

In verse 15, he reminds us that those who take the path of the animal, the sensual, the psychic, the dishonest, the destroyer, will be outside the wall, for all of these who practice the earth consciousness are those who are not of the Truth and the Truth is our goal as well as our Path. So this warning does not apply to us.

As a crossover to the last verses of the Book of Revelation I should like to encourage you to read Isaiah 11:1-10 which gives a prophecy that has always been read as a prophecy of the advent of the Messiah. And so it is but it can be read as the advent of the Messiah in our own Being. It is a beautiful passage. And the promise: verse 9, "They shall not hurt or destroy in all my holy mountain; for the earth shall be full of the knowledge of the Lord as the waters cover the sea." *All* shall be covered by the Lord or Jehovah as some translations read. Read the entire passage and read it as though you, yourself, are being prophesied for the potential, for the beauty described by this passage. This beauty lies within each of us. We are the peace makers, we are full of wisdom, the Spirit of the Lord rests upon you and me. The passage says, "There shall come forth a shoot from the stump of Jesse" and the root meaning of Jesse is Jah, Jehovah, or I AM, representing eternal existence. So the I AM is the root and the offspring is Love, Divine Love, that for which we search.

The last verses of this magnificent book have contained within them the entire teaching of the Book of Revelation. I would remind you of the great mystery that was revealed to John and to us in chapter 12. You see, John, the disciple, who is purported to have written Revelation, is interpreted metaphysically as "the spiritual faculty of love." So love, our divine goal, our inner Holy Spirit, has given us this teaching. This should be easily understood for Love is our action and Love is our goal in all of our "coming out and our going in."

Because verse 16 starts with "I Jesus" I would draw your

attention to the lack of commas which are normally placed around the name of one who is speaking. "Jesus" is not set off by commas. In the Amplified New Testament and the Living New Testament it is written, "I, Jesus," which would indicate that Jesus is speaking. However, in the red letter edition of the R.S.V. the verses are not printed in red which designates the words directly spoken by Jesus. For these reasons I suggest the following interpretation:

"I Jesus" refers to the I AM presence within each of us. You will note that "I Jesus Christ" is not used but I Jesus. The *Metaphysical Bible Dictionary* says that power, raised to divine understanding—the I AM identity—is the meaning of the name Jesus.[3] Therefore, "I Jesus" is the Christ within you and me raised to Oneness (divine understanding and power) with God, the Good Omnipotent, our own inner Spirit, for we are raised to the highest of Oneness, of Illumination, of Enlightenment and the Inner Soul is speaking. The "I" is speaking, the "I AM." It is a very important message, a summation. LISTEN! He who has an ear, an inner ear. LISTEN!

"I Jesus (the I AM within) have sent my angel (the Holy Spirit) with this testimony (truth or proof of truth) for the churches (the divine centers of life, the chakras, the energy centers which transfer the physical from death to life eternal). I am (the I AM of each of us, God Likeness) the root (the Alpha) and the offspring (Omega) of David (the love faculty, the life of the physical and the Divine) the bright morning star (evidence of total immersion in God)." The testimony is coming from within John as from within us. This is Truth and we are engendered to listen. So now that we know "who" is speaking, let us see what the message is.

Verse 17, "The Spirit and the Bride say, "Come." God and our Holy Spirit (the Bride) are inviting us to "Come." Do not pass over this quickly. Realize that the invitation is to every one who understands, to everyone who reads this Book of Revelation. Not only to us of the Judeo/Christian background but the invitation is to the unlimited multitude to "Come." Come to the Fountainhead of all desire and knowledge. Come to God the

Supreme essence of our own Holy Spirit. But *you* must hear, *we* must hear, for the next sentence says as much, "And let him who hears come." Remember it is your own inner I AM that is extending the invitation. We must listen to our Inner Knowing, Knocking, if we are to "Come." And to those who are thirsty for understanding and completion and peace, who cannot survive without the water of life, the imperative is offered, "Come." And if you desire to take the water of life without price, "Come." It is free! It is there for our taking. All we need to do is listen to our inner Knowing and act, to "Come."

And then a warning in verse 18, to those who do hear the words of the prophecy of the book: "if anyone added to them, God will add to him the plagues described in this book." If you remember the plagues were horrible and devastating experiences that resulted from negative, separated ideas and thoughts that caused duality and separation from God. But we know that the plagues were really blessings for the cleansing of our consiousness as they came from the throne of God. So if we once "hear" these prophecies in the reality of Truth we must not add on our own ideas but follow closely the meaning and once having gained that meaning must stay within the parameter of what we have heard. It is said by Bible scholars that Revelation has been tampered with, and added to, less than any Book of the Bible, because of this warning. Praise God! for the purity that has abided in the translation of this Book, the account of the great mystery of God!!

And verse 19, "and if anyone takes away from the words of the book of this prophecy, God will take away his share in the tree of life (eternal life) and in the holy city (a state of enlightenment), which are described in this book." A warning not to be taken lightly and is indicative of a personal ego on the part of the one who adds to or takes away from the Book. And we all know that our personal ego is the aspect of our personality which may keep us from LISTENING. This, of course, is the same as the copyright that our present books carry and with the same meaning.

As I come to the end of this interpretation I am beginning to realize the effrontery of one who has attempted to discern the hidden meaning, and with all humility and meekness of spirit I come to the close, hoping that I have neither added meanings not intended or taken away from the clear message from all men of all races. Only through the instance of the Holy Spirit have I undertaken the task, and my prayer was always for guidance in discernment and understanding. So be it! It is done and the glory is all for the Father of all nations and climes. My prayer is that I be only the instrument that he intended and inspired.

The final two verses are from John, "He who testifies to these things says, 'surely I am coming soon.' Amen. Come Lord Jesus!"

And so we are coming soon, for soon in the mind of God is Now, is eternal, is unlimited, and He, through Universal Love, gives us eternity to "Come." To listen and "Come." Listening with our inner Knowing, our Inner Conviction, will happen soon (and with some soon is later) for we all are being gathered one by one into the New Jerusalem, and when we are transfigured our only response will be one of great Joy, and we will say with John, "Come Lord Jesus."

It is Done! We have come on a long Journey from the "In the Beginning" to "Come Lord Jesus." What a Journey! Through Divine Visions; through earthquake, fire and hail; through ups and downs of divine and material; through uncertainty and sureness; through conscious and unconscious; through our will and His; through life and death; through masculine and feminine; through Karma and reincarnation; through land, sea, ether; through glory and pain; through our own self will to our own Self Will. How could this Journey be described in any other way than symbolically? It is for all nations, all peoples, all races. All ages. All!! For He is All and we are All One in Him. We are one world in the New Age and our captain is One Force, God, Energy, Love, Wisdom, Brahm, Heaven, Ultimate Reality. He is Vibration, Void, Nothingness, Spirit, Allah and our brothers on other planets are Our Brothers activated by the same Force.

Yes, our "God is Too Small," as J. B. Phillips writes,[4] but that is because our thinking is too small. Bring your thoughts to Love, meditation, wisdom and experience the Vastness of the Universe. Having arrived, let us now serve and teach so others may learn of the Glory of God, the Holy City. Let us be on our Way! And, "Lo, I am with you always, to the close of the age." (Matt. 28:20) and "Blessed are the poor in spirit for theirs is the Kingdom of Heaven." (Matt. 5:3)

And the strains of Beethoven's Ninth Symphony dedicated to the Joy of Being are heard:

> Praise to Joy, the God-descended
> Daughter of Elysium!
> Ray of mirth and rapture blended
> Goddess, to thy shrine we come!
> By thy magic is united
> What stern custom parted wide,
> All mankind are brothers plighted
> Where thy gentle wings abide.
> O ye millions, I embrace ye,
> With a kiss for all the world!
> Brothers, o'er yon starry sphere
> Surely dwells a loving Father.
> O ye millions, kneel before Him
> World, dost feel thy Maker near?
> Seek Him o'er yon starry sphere,
> O'er the stars enthroned, adore Him!
> Joy, thou daughter of Elysium,
> By thy magic is united
> What stern custom parted wide.
> All mankind are brothers plighted
> Where thy gentle wings abide.[5]

—From *Ode to Joy* by Friedrich von Schiller

And John, the Revelator, wrote: "The grace of the Lord Jesus be with all the saints" (and that is all of us).

Amen   Aum   Amin

References

Chapter 1

1. Turner, Elizabeth: *Be Ye Transformed,* page 202. Lee's Summit, Missouri: Unity School of Christianity (1931).
2. Fillmore, Charles: *Metaphysical Bible Dictionary,* page 629. Unity Village, Missouri: Unity School of Christianity (1931).
3. Hoyt, Edyth: *Studies in the Apocalypse of John of Patmos,* page 110. Ann Arbor, Michigan; Edwards Brothers (1978).
4. Paramahansa Yogananda: *Autobiography of a Yogi,* page 243. Los Angeles, California: Self Realization Fellowship (1969).
5. Spalding, Baird T.: *Life and Teaching of the Masters of the Far East,* Los Angeles, California: DeVorss and Company (1964).
6. Yogananda, op. cit., page 166n
7. Green, Elmer and Alyce: *Beyond Biofeedback,* page 209. New York: Delta Publishing Company, (1977).
8. Edyth Hoyt, op. cit., page 122
9. Yogananda, op. cit., page 166n
10. Ibid., page 21
11. von Franz, M. L.: *Interpretation of Fairy Tales,* Zurich: Spring Publication, (1975).
12. Jung, Carl: *Psychology and Religion; West and East,* page 237, Princeton: Princeton University Press, (1969) Bollingen Series XX.

Chapter 2-3

1. Jung, Carl: *Psychology and Alchemy,* page 63. Princeton: University Press, (1974) Bollingen Series XX
2. Fillmore, *Metaphysical Bible Dictionary,* page 585
3. Ram Das; *Be Here Now,* New York: Crown Publishing (1974)
4. Fillmore, *Twelve Powers of Man,* page 28. Kansas City: Unity School of Christianity, (1934)
5. Ibid., page 30
6. Bhagavad Gita translated by Juan Mascaro. Chapt. 4: Verses 39,40. London: C. Nicholis and Company Ltd., (1978)

7. *Metaphysical Bible Dictionary,* page 178
8. Fillmore, *Twelve Powers of Man,* op. cit., page 162f
9. Heline, Corinne: *New Age Bible Interpretation,* Vol. IV, Part III, page 71. Los Angeles: New Age Press, (1952)
10. Jung: *Two Essays on Analytical Psychology,* Princeton: Princeton University Press, (1972) Bollingen Series XX.
11. Suzuki: *Introduction to Zen Buddhism,* New York: Causeway Books, (1974)
12. Upanishads: Swami Prabhavananda and Frederick Manchester, Mundaka, page 48. New York: Signet Classic, The New American Library, Inc. (1957)
13. Jung: *A Study of Dreams,* Princeton: Princeton University Press, (1974) Bollingen Series XX
14. Jung: *Psychology and Religion,* op. cit., page 331
15. The Way of Lao Tzu (Tao-te-ching): translated by Wing-Tsit Chan, Chapter 67. Indianapolis: The Bobbs-Merrill Company, (1963)
16. *The Wisdom of Confucius* edited and translated by Lin Yutang, New York: The Modern Library, (1938)
17. Upanishads, Mundaka, op. cit., page 54
18. Bhagavad Gita, op. cit., Chapter 18: Verses 55,57
19. Fillmore, *Meta. Bible Dict,* op. cit., page 303 under Israel
20. Ibid., page 406
21. Bhagavad Gita, Chapter 12:8
22. Upanishads, page 120
23. Smith, Huston: *The Religions of Man,* page 186. New York: Harper and Brothers, (1960)
24. Idries Shah: *The Sufis,* page 223. Garden City: Doubleday and Company, (1971)
25. Kapleau, Philip: *The Three Pillars of Zen,* page 9. Boston: Bacon Press, (1967)
26. Jung: *Psychology and Alchemy,* op. cit., page 8f
27. Charles Fillmore, *The Revealing Word,* page 167. Unity Village, Missouri: Unity School of Christianity, (1931)
28. Bhagavad Gita, Chapter 4:35
29. *The Apocrypha:* Translated by Edgar J. Goodspeed. The Wisdom of Solomon, Chapter 7:25,26,28. New York: Vintage Books, Random House. (1959)
30. Fillmore, *The Revealing Word,* op. cit., page 108f
31. Fillmore, *Meta Bible Dict.,* page 638 (under Tabernacle)

32. Wilhelm, Richard (translator), *The Secret of the Golden Flower,* page 61. New York: Harcourt, Brace and World, Inc. (1962)
33. Ibid, page 76
34. Smith, *The Religions of Man,* page 42f op. cit.
35. Jung: *Psychology and Alchemy,* op. cit.
36. Teilhard de Chardin: *The Phenomenon of Man,* New York: Harper and Row, (1965)
37. Quoted in Evelyn Underhill, *Mysticism,* page 426. "The Festival of Spring" by Jalalu 'd Din. Cleveland and New York: The World Publishing Co. (1967)

Chapter 4

1. Hoyt, op. cit., page 44
2. Jung, op. cit., *Psychology and Religion,* page 104
3. Wilhelm, op. cit., *Secret of the Golden Flower*
4. Hoyt, op. cit., page 8f
5. Churchward, James: *The Children of Mu,* New York: Paperback Library, (1971)
6. Turner, op. cit., *Be Ye Transformed*
7. Fox, Emmet: *The Four Horsemen of the Apocalypse,* page 22f, New York: Harper and Row, (1942)
8. Heline, op. cit., page 215
9. Fillmore: op. cit., *Twelve Powers of Man*

Chapter 5

1. Fillmore, *Metaphysical Bible Dictionary,* page 372f under Judah.
2. Ibid., page 394 under Lamb of God
3. Jung, op. cit., *Psychology and Religion,* page 157
4. Pandit Usharbudh Arya: *Superconscious Meditation,* page 55, Honesdale, Penn: Himalayan International Institute, (1978)
5. Turner, op. cit., page 224
6. Skarin, Annalee: *Yer Are Gods,* page 300, New York: Philosophical Library, (1952)
7. Ibid., Frontispiece

Chapter 6

1. Jung, op. cit., *Two Essays on Analytical Psychology*
2. Fox, op. cit.
3. Shealy, Norman: *90 Days to Self-Health,* New York: Bantam Books, (1979)

4. Faus, Grace: *The Eternal Truth in a Changing World,* page 58, Self published by Grace Faus, Bailey, Colorado, (1979)
5. Underhill, op. cit., 382f

Chapter 7

1. Fox, op. cit., page 38
2. Yogananda, op. cit., page 370n
3. Ibid, page 161n
4. Fillmore, op. cit., *Twelve Powers of Man*
5. Heline, op. cit., page 222
6. Fillmore, *Metaphysical Bible Dictionary,* page 303 under Israel
7. Translated by A. J. Arberry, from the *Mystical Poems of Rumi,* by Jalal Al-din Rumi, page 86. Chicago: The University of Chicago Press, (1974)

Chapter 8

1. Underhill, op. cit., page 83
2. Ibid, page 308
3. Bhagavad Gita, op. cit., page 62
4. Tao te Ching, op. cit., page 128
5. Jung, op. cit., *Psychology and Religion,* page 36
6. Jung, op. cit., *Psychology and Alchemy,* page 354
7. Singer, June: *Boundaries of the Soul,* page 95. New York: Double-day-Anchor Press, New York, (1973)
8. Hoyt, op. cit., page 59f
9. Jung, op. cit., *Psychology and Alchemy,* page 201
10. Ibid., page 134
11. Ibid., page 437

Chapter 9

1. Jung, op. cit., *Psychology and Alchemy,* page 371f
2. Jung, op. cit., *Psychology and Religion,* page 237n
3. Noss, John: *Man's Religions,* page 101f. New York: Macmillan Publishing Co., Inc., (1969)
4. Ibid., page 129f
5. Ibid., page 110f
6. Ibid., page 230
7. Yogananda, op. cit., page 266n
8. Ibid., 179n

9. Jung, Carl, Editor: *Man and His Symbols,* page 214, an article by M. L. von Franz, London: Aldus Books Limited, (1964)
10. von Franz, op. cit., *Fairytales*
11. Jung, op. cit., *Man and His Symbols,* page 171f

Chapter 10

1. Jung, op. cit., *Man and His Symbols,* page 211f

Chapter 11

1. Leadbeater, C.W.: *The Chakras,* page 32. A quote from Madame Blavatsky. Adyar: Theosophical Publishing House (1972)
2. Ibid., page 32
3. White, John, Editor: *Evolution and Enlightenment,* page 27f, an article by Swami Rama entitled "The Awakening of the Kundalini." New York: Anchor Books, (1979)
4. Ibid., page 32
5. Fillmore, op. cit., *The Twelve Powers of Man,* page 163
6. Gopi Krishna: *Kundalini the Evolutionary Energy* in Man, page 49, Boulder: Shambhala, (1971)
7. White, op. cit., Article by Alice Bailey, page 447f
8. Heline, op. cit., page 228
9. Underhill, op. cit., page 178
10. Ibid., page 179

Chapter 12

1. Jung, op. cit., *Psychology and Religion,* page 161f
2. Ibid., page 114n
3. Ibid., page 387
4. Ibid., page 439
5. Ibid., page 388
6. Ibid., page 467
7. Singer, op. cit., page 284f
8. Chaney, Robert: *Unfolding the Third Eye,* page 48. Los Angeles: Astara, (1970)
9. Goldsmith, Joel: *The Mystical I,* page 73. New York: Harper and Row, (1971)
10. Jung, Carl: *Aion,* page 41, Princeton, N.J; Princeton University Press. Bollington Series XX, (1978)
11. Jung, op. cit., *Psychology and Religion,* page 168

12. Yogananda, op. cit., page 44
13. Fillmore, op. cit., *The Revealing Word,* page 88
14. Jung, op. cit., *Psychology and Religion,* page 55
15. Ibid., page 462
16. Brunton, Paul: *A Search in Secret Egypt.* New York: Samuel Weiser, Inc., (1970)
17. Churchward, op. cit.
18. Goodavage, Joseph: *Astrology: the Space Age Science,* page 182. New York: New American Library Inc., (1966)
19. Jung, Carl: article in *Spring Magazine,* 1975. New York: Spring Publications, (1975)

Chapter 13

1. Jung, op. cit., *Psychology and Alchemy,* page 187
2. Fillmore, *Metaphysical Bible Dictionary,* page 149 under "Chosen people"
3. James, William: *Varieties of Religious Experience,* page 105. New York: Modern Library (1929)
4. Ibid., page 87
5. White, op. cit., page 418, article by J. M. Pryse entitled "From the Restored New Testament."
6. Turner, op. cit., page 248
7. James, op. cit., page 96 (a quote from Horace Fletcher)
8. Shelley, Violet: *Symbols and the Self,* page 17. Virginia Beach, Virginia: Edgar Cayce Foundation, A.R.E. Press (1976)
9. Jung, op. cit., *Psychology and Archemy,* page 366
10. *The Book of Changes,* "I Ching", translated by Richard Wilhelm

Chapter 14

1. Swami Nikhilananda: *Vivekanda: A Biography,* page 63. Calcutta: Advaita Ashrama, Distributed by Vedanta Press, Hollywood. (1971)
2. Ferguson, Marilyn: *The Aquarian Conspiracy,* page 23. Los Angeles: J. P. Tarcher, Inc. (1980)
3. Tao te Ching, op. cit., Chapter 2
4. Bhagavad Gita, op. cit., Chapter 2: verses 64,65,67
5. Turner, op. cit., page 249f
6. Heline, op. cit., page 235

Chapter 15

1. Green, op. cit., page 155
2. Fillmore, op. cit., *Revealing Word,* page 117f
3. Ibid., page 215
4. Hoyt, op. cit., page 78

Chapter 16

1. Ando, Shoei: *Zen and American Transcendentalism,* page 193. Tokyo: The Hokuseido Press, (1970)
2. Tao te Ching, page 6
3. Green, op. cit.
4. Ponder, Catherine: *Healing Secrets of the Ages.* West Nyack, New York: Parker Publishing Company, (1969)
5. Jung, op. cit., *Aion,* page 8
6. Singer, op. cit., page 81
7. Jung, op. cit., *Psychology and Alchemy,* page 343f
8. Jung, op. cit., *Psychological Types.* Princeton: Princeton University Press, (1969) Bollingen Series XX
9. Fillmore, Charles: *Atom Smashing Power of the Mind,* page 169 Lee's Summit, Missouri: Unity School of Christianity, (1949)
10. Underhill, op. cit., page 121
11. Heline, op. cit., page 239f
12. Atkinson, Brooks, Editor: *The Writings of Ralph Waldo Emerson,* from "An Essay on Spiritual Laws" by Ralph Waldo Emerson, page 190. New York: The Modern Library, (1940)

Chapter 17

1. Atkinson, op. cit., Emerson, Essay on Society and Solitude, page 745
2. Jung, op. cit., *Psychology and Religion,* page 209
3. Ibid., page 209

Chapter 18

1. Lamsa, George: *Idioms in the Bible Explained,* page 66. Philadelphia: A. J. Holman Company
2. Bowart, W. H.: *Operation Mind Control.* New York: Dell Publishing, (1978)

Chapter 19

1. Fillmore, op. cit., *Metaphysical Bible Dictionary,* page 374, *Judah*
2. Yogananda, op. cit., page 13n

3. Ibid., page 21n
4. Ibid., page 245n
5. Jung, op. cit., *Two Essays on Analytical Psychology,* page 173f
6. Fillmore, Charles: *Jesus Christ Heals,* page 10
7. Spalding, op. cit., page 15f, Vol. I
8. Jung, op. cit., *Psychology and Religion,* page 441
9. Wilhelm, op. cit., *Secret of the Golden Flower,* page 133
10. Jung, Carl: *Memories, Dreams, Reflections,* page 280. New York: Vintage Books, (1963)
11. Teilhard de Chardin, op. cit.

Chapter 20

1. Kuhn, A.B.: *The Lost Key to the Scriptures,* page 48. Wheaton, Illinois: The Theosophical Press, (1966)
2. Jung, op. cit., *Psychology and Alchemy,* page 339
3. Turner, op. cit., page 267
4. Jung, Carl: *Four Archetypes,* page 80. Princeton: Princeton University Press (1959) Bollingen Series XX
5. Howard, Vernon: *The Mystic Path to Cosmic Power,* West Nyack, New York: Parker Publishing Co., Inc. (1979)
6. Skarin, op. cit., page 146
7. Ibid., page 272
8. Ibid., page 274

Chapter 21

1. Jocelyn, John: *Meditations on the Signs of the Zodiac,* page 216f Blauvelt, New York: Rudolph Steiner Publishers, (1970)
2. Troward, Thomas: *The Edinburgh Lectures,* New York: Dodd and Mead Co., (1909)
3. Zvelebil, Kamil V.: *The Poets of Power,* page 101–102
4. Durant, Will: *Our Oriental Heritage,* page 425. New York: Simon and Schuster (1935)
5. Green, op. cit., page 274f
6. Fillmore, op. cit., *Twelve Powers of Man,* page 169f
7. Tao te Ching, verse 74
8. Bhagavad Gita. Chapter 2:19
9. Yogananda, op. cit., page 491
10. Jung, op. cit., *Psychology and Alchemy,* page 274
11. Jung, op. cit., *Psychology and Religion,* page 496
12. Teilhard de Chardin, op. cit., page 260f

13. Heline, op. cit., page 149
14. Turner, op. cit., page 274
15. Hoyt, op. cit., page 207
16. Fillmore, op. cit., *Twelve Powers of Man,* page 16
17. Jung, op. cit., *Psychology and Religion,* page 107
18. Ibid., page 505
19. Kapleau, op. cit., page xiii
20. Yogananda, op. cit., page 317
21. Idries Shah, op. cit., page 431
22. Max Heindel: *The Rosicrucian Cosmo-Conception.* California: The Rosicrucian Fellowship, (1937)

Chapter 22

1. Fillmore, op. cit., *Twelve Powers of Man,* page 162
2. Hoyt, op. cit., page 94
3. Fillmore, op. cit., *Metaphysical Bible Dictionary,* page 345 under Jesus
4. Phillips, J.B.: *Your God is Too Small.* New York: The Macmillan Co., (1968)
5. Translated from the German and quoted from *Beethoven's Nine Symphonies* by Corinne Heline, page 67: For certain political reasons, Schiller does not use the word "Freedom," and so substituted for it the word JOY. Beethoven understood this. For him the poem was an expression of spiritual freedom. It meant the emancipation of the soul; the freedom of the spirit from all physical and material limitations. It meant freedom to roam at will through the higher spiritual realms, to contact celestial beings who inhabit those realms and to listen to the glorious music of the spheres. Los Angeles: New Age Press, Inc., (1971)

Appendices

The Kundalini Power

Dear Ones, I come to you with a deep and important message that has remained a secret for aeons because the ignorant have not known how to receive it, have misused the information. So I directed my servants to receive the knowledge only for those who were seriously on the Path. For what I am about to reveal can either demolish society and the individual lives or give them eternal life. Each one of you will make the choice, but the Time is Now when this secret should be revealed.

In the beginning of man's life on earth I put within him the Essence of my Presence. And ever since then he has been looking outside of himself for It. But this is good, for as he looked for It, he knew not what, he has developed and civilized his world which made a better environment for the progress, the evolution of man. For all on earth are evolving—plants, minerals, animals, man. In the beginning I gave man everything for his physical and spiritual needs. His physical needs were simple—food was the only need to maintain his physical body. But through that appetite he lost his Oneness with me and I banished him from the Garden. Ever since he has been trying to become One with Me and the time is bringing him closer to that Supreme Moment of Total Immersion in my Being.

And now, since history is recorded in books, I will not review his progress but know that it is progress. And to help in his Spiritual search I have revealed to him through my Prophets, Masters, Teachers, Saviors, Writers, Preachers, gods and goddesses, the secrets that will assist him in reaching Oneness which was lost in the Garden. Most of what I have revealed has been misunderstood and misused, but since more and more of my people, my human expression, are reaching for me, within themselves, the ultimate secret will be revealed.

I placed within each of you a mind, an instrument of consciousness. This mind was only a computer to record the past, to live in the now, and to project the future. How it has been misunderstood! The consciousness of man and woman is My Consciousness operating through each one's mind, for I dwell in that mind. I AM that Mind and the use of it will ultimately be centered in my Purpose.

As I have said, I placed within each of you a spark of the Essence of my Being which is activated at birth and gives the vitality, the energy, the love, the knowledge of all the past, and the prediction of the future. This Essence has been called by various names through the ages. The occultist, the soothsayer have called it the Intellect. The religionists have called it Kundalini, Holy Spirit, Christ, Lord of my Being, Serpent Power, the Dragon, the Devil, the glory of His Presence, the Soul. Each man or woman sees it in light of his/her own perception of Reality.

This Essence courses through the body and gives life. It is active as long as breath comes into the body. At the death of the physical body it leaves and the long story of its existence will have to be told elsewhere.

Now this Power is so strong, so intense, for it is my Spark, that is has been used and misused for selfish and unselfish purposes unconsciously. Most of Western man is ignorant of it and its power and in ignorance are wasting it. If they only knew that it could bring them back to Me in total Oneness and full Glory!! But then most of mankind does not know consciously that this is what they seek.

At the base of the spine of the human body, (we will not be discussing the animal, plant and mineral worlds although they have the same Energy) I have placed this great Fire Power. Perhaps that was a mistake, as it is at the lower extremity of the body which man has tended to designate as dirty, gross, not to be handled or recognized. But because this power is necessary for the activation of the spine and all the nerves attached to it, the location seemed best.

Many of the religions of the world have described this Essence with various terms. At the present level of evolution the Hindu description seems best. (See the second part of this chapter.) The Buddhists also, as well as the Sufis, the Egyptians, the American Indians, the Jews and the Christians. You see, it is there in all religions and has been known by those who have devoted their lives to Me and the expression of my Will. In so doing they lovingly protected the majority of the adherents of their religion from the knowledge. This was right and good, for mankind needed to evolve to a closer walk with Me before they could handle this Essence of my Power, Wisdom and Love.

The mystic, the sheikh, the Zen master, the temple priest, the sorcerer, the soothsayer have known about and activated this Force. Some were centered in Me and were doing their work for my Glory. Others, sad to say, were selfish and used the great Essence of Joy for selfish purposes. As they did this, the results, the karma brought destruction and Death, for the Life Force is for the upliftment of mankind, not for the degeneracy of man.

This Force gives intense, however, brief, bliss to the sexual act of man and woman. As a result the Energy is wasted on bodily pleasure, on material gain. The sexual aspect of man is to be used for propagating humankind and for many as a means of expressing love. Unfortunately this is confused with Love when in many cases it is lust. If you, my child, are interested and vitally devoted to becoming the Light (enlightenment) then you will learn the right use of this Essence in the expression of your Spiritual Desire and not your physical ones.

In the body there are special centers that collect energy from the kundalini and thus raise the vibration of the physical body so that its essence becomes high vibration and changes the flesh to Light. These centers have been called chakras by the Hindu. There are many centers in the body but the major ones are spoken of by other religionists. The chakras are in the location of what medical men have called glands of the body. As the Essence flows into the nadis or nerves, the chakras receive the energy and change the body. These chakras have not been found by material scanning instruments, but are being investigated due to the surge of inquiry about the kundalini and the knowledge of acupuncture which the Orientals have known for centuries.

Now why do I want you to know about this? Because I want you to be in the Garden again walking in simplicity, love and light, for that is your destiny, the destiny of all mankind on earth. And through the raising of the physical vibrations of the body, and the growth in consciousness of Me you will become beings of Light and Life and be One with Me.

The kundalini has been called the "evolutionary energy" and thus it is, for through its activation mankind has evolved, has reached a higher state of awareness and expression of my Divine Plan. The Energy has been poured out in physical labor, in replenishing the earth with incarnated souls in physical bodies, in discoveries of science, and in the use of the intellect to express my Ideas (for all Ideas come from Me for the good of mankind). Now you are approaching the time when you are given more rest, less activity that drains your Energy Essence, and it will be used for the growth of your awareness and consciousness of Me.

All illness of mind and body is a misuse of the kundalini power. All healing is from the right use of the kundalini power. Through your thoughts you have directed the Energy. It and your thoughts have brought you challenges which ultimately brought you closer to Me through these challenges.

Right use of this Power will bring you all prosperity in every phase of your life. It will bring you health of body, soul, and mind. It will bring into a balanced whole all of your instruments. And it will ultimately bring Perfect Peace and Bliss. But right use is the key.

Now you may be asking, How can I activate this Power? Well, you already have, but for the purpose of directing it for your use on the Spiritual Path I would refer you to a teacher, a yogi, books, and especially to the activity of prayer and meditation for centeredness on Me, bringing your mind to a quiet state of the Void, being quiet and away from the world, is a must. All of these help the Power to be activated. Meditation over a period of years will start It moving. Prepare your mind and your consciousness by making your Supreme Goal a greater understanding of my Will in order to gain Enlightenment, Nirvana, Samadhi. Misuse will bring pain and suffering, and death. Read Revelation in the New Testament for directions and the results of righteousness (right-use-ness) and the wrong use.

The kundalini Energy, the Holy Spirit, is my greatest gift to you. Mankind is beginning to awaken to this knowledge and will make right use of It. For as you go into the Aquarian Age you will see the blessing I have given you in allowing this to be revealed to you. It contains all you need for the achievement of happines on earth and Joy in the kingdom of Heaven.

World Religions
On the Kundalini Power

The following are some quotes from various books dealing with different world religions. I have understood all the quotes as relating to the activation of the kundalini power, the serpent fire, or the Holy Spirit.

HINDU

Taken from *The Serpent Power, the Secrets of Tantric and Shaktic Yoga,* by Arthur Avalon (Sir John Woodroffe). This is considered a classic.

The two Sanskrit works here translated deal with a particular form of Tantric Yoga named Kundalini-Yoga or, as some works call it, Bhuta-suddhi. These names refer to the Kundalini-Sakti or Supreme Power in the human body by the arousing of which the Yoga is achieved, and to the purification of the Elements of the body which takes place upon that event. This Yoga is effected by a process technically known as piercing of the Six Centres of Chakras or Lotuses of the body by the agency of Kundalini-Sakti, which, in order to give it an English name, I have here called the Serpent Power. Kundala means coiled. The power is the Goddess of Kundalini, or that which is coiled; for Her form is that of a coiled and sleeping serpent in the lowest bodily center, at the base of the spinal column, until by the means described, She is aroused in that Yoga which is named after Her. Kundalini is the Divine Cosmic Energy in bodies. The Saptabhumi, or seven regions, are, as popularly understood, an exoteric presentment of the inner Tantric teaching of the seven centres.

From the Upanishads, Chapter V, Mundaka:

The Effulgent Self is to be realized within the lotus of the heart by continence, by steadfastness in truth, by meditation, and by superconscious vision. Their impurities washed away, the seers realized Him.

Chapter XII:

Control the vital force. Set fire to the Self within by the practice of Meditation. Be drunk with the wine of divine love. Thus shall you reach perfection.

BUDDHISM

Taken from *Sources of Chinese Tradition,* Volume I, compiled by William Theodore de Bary, Editor. Page 268.

Buddhists make a great goal of Nirvana. Nirvana was conceived as a transcendent state, beyond the possibility of full comprehension of the ordinary being enmeshed in the illusion of selfhood, but not fundamentally different from the state of supreme bliss as described in other non-theist Indian systems. The process of rebirth can only be stopped by achieving Nirvana, first by adopting right views about the nature of existence, then by a carefully controlled system of moral conduct, and finally by concentration and meditation.

Three Pillars of Zen by Phillip Kapleau, Editor, Page 11:

Thus breathing becomes a vehicle of spiritual experience, the mediator between body and mind. It is the first step towards the transformation of the body from the state of a more or less passively and unconsciously functioning physical organ into a vehicle or tool of a perfectly developed and enlightened mind, as demonstrated by the radiance and perfection of the Buddha's body.

Page 13:

Zazen that leads to Self-realization is neither idle reverie nor vacant inaction but an intense inner struggle to gain control over the mind and then to use it, like a silent missile, to penetrate the barrier of the five senses and the discursive intellect.

TAOISM

The Secret of the Golden Flower translated by Richard Wilhelm, Page 61:

The way leads from the sacrum upward in a backward-flowing way to the summit of the Creative, and on through the house of the Creative; then it sinks through the two stories in a direct downward-flowing way into the solar plexus, and warms it. . . . The crystallized spirit radiates back to the spirit-fire and, by means of the greatest quiet, fans the 'fire in the midst of the water,' which is in the middle of the empty cave. . . . When the pupil keeps the crystallized spirit fixed within the cave of energy and, at the same time, lets greatest quietness hold sway, then out of the obscure darkness a something develops from the nothingness—that is the Golden Flower of the great One appears.

Page 62:

If the pupil does not understand this principle, and lets the energy flow out directly, then the energy changes into seed; but every man who unites bodily with a woman feels pleasure first and then bitterness; when the seed has flowed out, the body is tired and the spirit weary. It is quite different when the adept lets spirit and energy unite. That brings first purity and then freshness; when the seed is transformed, the body is healthy and free.

Page 63:

The fool wastes the most precious jewel of his body in uncontrolled lust, and does not know how to conserve his seed-energy. When it is finished, the body perishes. The accumlated seed is transformed into energy, and the energy, when there is enough of it, makes the creatively strong body:

Page 64:

A man who holds to the way of conservation all through life may reach the stage of the Golden Flower, which then frees the ego from the conflict of the opposites, and it again becomes part of the Tao, the undivided, great One.

SUFISM

The sufi branch of Islam has taught about this Force and much of their poetry and stories gives information about it to the knowledgeable few. *The Sufis,* by Idries Shah, is my source. Page 332:

Whithin the Orders, when the disciple has been accepted for a training course under a master, it is termed the "activation of the subtleties." This is the opening of the *latifa* or "purity spot," "center of reality." In order to activate this element it is assigned a theoretical physical situation in the body. . . . The disciple has to awaken five *latifa,* receive illumination through five of the seven subtle centers of communication. . . . As each *latifa* is activated through exercises, the consciousness of the disciple changes to accommodate the greater potentialities of his mind. Through breathing exercises, dancing, meditation, these centers are activated. The areas which are involved in the activation of the *latifa* are Self, under the navel; Heart, at the place of the physical heart; Spirit, on the side of the body opposite the heart position. The Secret *latifa* is exactly between the Heart and Spirit positions. Mysterious is in the forehead; Deeply Hidden is in the brain. The seventh subtlety is accessible only to those who have developed the others, and belongs to the real sage. If activation of the centers is not part of comprehensive development, the consequences can be very dangerous, and include, like all one-sided mental phenomena, exaggerated ideas of self-importance, the surfacing of undesirable qualities, or a deterioration of consciousness following an access of ability.

JUDAISM

In the Jewish religion the Secret was given in the directions for the building of the Tabernacle. Edyth Hoyt, in her book, *Study in the Apocalypse of John of Patmos,* relates the building of the Tabernacle in the wilderness as God's attempt to help the Israelites realize that God was in the midst of them. The different stages one had to go through to realize "the presence of God in the midst of them." She lists the seven stages as follows: (Page 8)

1. Narrow entrance—desire
2. Altar for burnt offering—give up material world
3. Laver—purify the thoughts
4. Golden Candlesticks—everpresent spiritual illumination
5. Shew bread—spiritual sustenance—meditation
6. Altar of incenses—recognition of God's allness or Wisdom
7. Holy of Holies—communion with God.

It seems to me these are parallel to the seven churches in Revelation and the chakra centers symbols which are activated to reach Oneness with One God. I would like to call your attention to the same characteristics or stations that one must bring the Holy Spirit through in order to reach enlightenment as outlined in this book, i.e., faith, sacrifice of sex energy to creative energy, intellect, love, meditation, wisdom, and communion with God.

CHRISTIANITY

Even the Christian New Testament has the knowledge hidden. The New Testament was written in symbolic language so that those who had the Key could understand. Corinne Heline, in *New Age Bible Interpretation* suggests: (Page 200)

> The spinal cord plays a leading role in alchemist Mysteries of the body. It connects the generative organ in the lower part of the body with the regenerative located in the head. The precious spinal essence is symbolized by the sacred rivers mentioned in all world religions. When the ascending spinal fire stimulates all twelve chakra centers (which she gives names of the 12 apostles) it finally unites the pineal and pituitary glands. The Tree of Life (the spine) becomes the illumined Christmas Tree in the one who is spiritually awakened.

Page 208:

> The Book of Revelation is an account of the redemptive process as it works in both men and the universe. The first of the seven visions refers to the sevenfold body of man, the true church or temple of the spirit, and to the seven planes on which the spirit manifests during its journey Godward.

Some scriptures to be considered as being esoteric truth about the raising of the kundalini power are: Acts 1 and 2; I Corinthians; the Book of James; I John; Matthew 3:11, "I baptize you with water for repentance, but he who is coming after me is mightier than I, whose sandals I am not worthy to carry; he will baptize you with the Holy Spirit and with fire" (John the Baptist is speaking of Jesus); Hebrews 12:29: "For our God is a consuming fire"; John 4:14: "but whoever drinks of the water that I shall give him will never thirst; the water that I shall give him will become in him a spring of water welling up to eternal life."

The Christian mystics, unaware of the Hindu terms, described the same phenomenon but named the ascending motivating spiritual force at work within them, the Holy Spirit. St. Hildegarde, a Christian mystic, is quoted as saying, "Omnipotent Father, out of thee flows a fountain of fiery heat; lead thy sons by a favorable wind through the mystic waters." And St. John of the Cross: "Oh flame of love so living, How tenderly you force to my soul's inmost core your fiery probe.''

From Charles Fillmore in *The Twelve Powers of Man* we read about the Life Force. On page 58:

When the seminal substance in the organism is conserved and retained, the nerves are charged with a spiritual energy, which runs like lightning through an organism filled with the virgin substance of the soul. In the conservation of this pure substance of life is hidden the secret of body rejuvenation, physical resurrection, and the final perpetuation of the whole organism in its transmuted purity. (John saw Jesus in this state of purity, as described in Revelation 1:12–16.) No man can in his own might attain this exalted estate, but through the love of God, demonstrated by Jesus, it is attainable by every one. . . . The work can be done through individual effort, and there must always be continuous constructive action between the masculine and feminine faculties of soul and body; but the anointing with the precious love of the divine feminine is necessary to the great demonstration.

From the same author in his *Metaphysical Bible Dictionary,* page 347:

Through interior thought concentration the subtle essences of the organism are transmuted to vibratory energies and become important factors in building up that pure body which is to triumph over death.

From page 275:

Generation and regeneration are opposites. Those who live under the law of generation give up their kingdom to their progeny, and die. Those who come out of this Egypt conserve their substance, and transmute it through thought to spiritual energy, which is the foundation of the new body in Christ.

Through this conservation and control of the divine life and substance, they finally attain the kingdom of God, and sit on the right hand of the Father with Christ . . . "To him that overcometh," is the oft repeated promise of the Holy One in Revelation. Strength and power and purity come to the soul through mastery of its passions and appetites, and in no other way.

AMERICAN INDIAN

From *Unfolding the Third Eye* by Robert Chaney, we have a reference to the American Indian headdress and the band which crossed his forehead which symbolize the auric colors of his unfolded spiritual powers. The Third Eye was obvious in the grand array of feathers arranged so that each feather emanated from that area.

EGYPTIAN

From *Unfolding the Third Eye* Mr. Chaney draws attention to the symbol used in paintings, statues, and other art forms of both modern and ancient origins depicting the Third Eye as a serpent head and signifies using the inner psychic faculties for the purpose of becoming wise as the Serpent.

I am sure that further research would reveal other rich information pertaining to the raising of this power through the spine and the various centers of the body in order to reach a high state of Light and is in all religions of an ancient variety. When one accepts this as the Truth of his Being and of his physical body he can then begin his own search. Several books that might be of help in this search are listed below:

1. Arthur Avalon, *The Serpent Power* (New York; Dover Pub. 1974)

2. *Kundalini, Evolution and Enlightenment,* edited by John

White (Garden City, New York; Anchor Books, 1979). Contains a long list of books on the subject of Kundalini.

3. Gopi Krishna, *Kundalini, The Evolutionary Energy in Man* (Boulder and London, Shambala, 1971)

4. Gopi Krishna, *The Awakening of Kundalini* (New York; Dutton and Company, 1975)

5. Lee Sannella, M.D., *Kundalini—Psychosis or Transcendence?* (San Francisco, H. S. Dakin Company, 1976)

6. C. W. Leadbeater, *The Chakras,* (Wheaton, Ill. The Theosophical Publishing Co., 1927)

7. Swami Muktananda, *Kundalini, The Secret of Life* (South Fallsburg, New York; SYDA Foundation 1979)

8. Anna Billion, *Kundalini: Secrets of the Ancient Yogis* (West Nyack, New York; Parker Publishing, 1979) This may be a book that indicates the misuse of the kundalini. However, it is one demonstration of its power.